CLASSIC WOK
COOKING

CLASSIC WOK
COOKING

SENSATIONAL STIR-FRIES FROM EAST AND WEST:
160 SIZZLING RECIPES SHOWN IN 270 BEAUTIFUL PHOTOGRAPHS

Sunil Vijayakar, Becky Johnson
and Jenni Fleetwood

LORENZ BOOKS

This edition is published by Lorenz Books,
an imprint of Anness Publishing Ltd,
Hermes House, 88–89 Blackfriars Road,
London SE1 8HA
tel. 020 7401 2077; fax 020 7633 9499

www.lorenzbooks.com; www.annesspublishing.com

If you like the images in this book and would like
to investigate using them for publishing, promotions
or advertising, please visit our website
www.practicalpictures.com for more information.

UK agent: The Manning Partnership Ltd;
tel. 01225 478444; fax 01225 478440;
sales@manning-partnership.co.uk

UK distributor: Grantham Book Services Ltd;
tel. 01476 541080; fax 01476 541061;
orders@gbs.tbs-ltd.co.uk

North American agent/distributor: National Book
Network; tel. 301 459 3366; fax 301 429 5746;
www.nbnbooks.com

Australian agent/distributor:
Pan Macmillan Australia;
tel. 1300 135 113; fax 1300 135 103;
customer.service@macmillan.com.au

New Zealand agent/distributor: David Bateman Ltd;
tel. (09) 415 7664; fax (09) 415 8892

Publisher: Joanna Lorenz
Editors: Doreen Gillon and Kate Eddison
Designer: Nigel Partridge
Photographers: Nicki Dowey, Gus Filgate and
  Craig Robertson
Additional recipes: Yasuko Fukuoka, Deh-Ta Hsiung
Editorial Reader: Lauren Farnsworth
Production Controller: Stephen Lang

Front cover shows Shredded Duck and Noodle Salad
– for recipe see page 106.

ETHICAL TRADING POLICY

At Anness Publishing we believe that business should be conducted in an ethical and ecologically sustainable way, with respect for the environment and a proper regard to the replacement of the natural resources we employ.

As a publisher, we use a lot of wood pulp to make high-quality paper for printing, and that wood commonly comes from spruce trees. We are therefore currently growing more than 750,000 trees in three Scottish forest plantations: Berrymoss (130 hectares/ 320 acres), West Touxhill (125 hectares/305 acres) and Deveron Forest (75 hectares/185 acres). The forests we manage contain more than 3.5 times the number of trees employed each year in making paper for the books we manufacture.

Because of this ongoing ecological investment programme, you, as our customer, can have the pleasure and reassurance of knowing that a tree is being cultivated on your behalf to naturally replace the materials used to make the book you are holding.

Our forestry programme is run in accordance with the UK Woodland Assurance Scheme (UKWAS) and will be certified by the internationally recognized Forest Stewardship Council (FSC). The FSC is a non-government organization dedicated to promoting responsible management of the world's forests. Certification ensures forests are managed in an environmentally sustainable and socially responsible way. For further information about this scheme, go to www.annesspublishing.com/trees

© Anness Publishing Ltd 2009

Recipes in this book previously appeared in *Wok Works*.

Although the advice and information in this book are believed to be accurate and true at the time of going to press, neither the authors nor the publisher can accept any legal responsibility or liability for any errors or omissions that may be made nor for any inaccuracies nor for any harm or injury that comes about from following instructions or advice in this book.

NOTES

For all recipes, quantities are given in both metric and imperial measures and, where appropriate, measures are also given in standard cups and spoons. Follow one set, but not a mixture, because they are not interchangeable.

Standard spoon and cup measures are level.
1 tsp = 5ml, 1 tbsp = 15ml, 1 cup = 250ml/8fl oz

Australian standard tablespoons are 20ml. Australian readers should use 3 tsp in place of 1 tbsp for measuring small quantities of gelatine, cornflour, salt, etc.

American pints are 16fl oz/2 cups. American readers should use 20fl oz/2.5 cups in place of 1 pint when measuring liquids.

Electric oven temperatures in this book are for conventional ovens. When using a fan oven, the temperature will probably need to be reduced by about 10–20°C/20–40°F. Since ovens vary, you should check with your manufacturer's instruction book for guidance.

Medium (US large) eggs are used unless otherwise stated.

Contents

Introduction

The wok is a wonderful invention, as suited to contemporary cooking as it is to re-creating classic recipes from its country of origin, China. It will prove its worth over and over again, allowing you to stir-fry, deep-fry, sauté, steam and simmer. It makes short work of soups and sauces, and is as handy for poaching pears as it is for braising beef.

When it comes to design, the wok is a hugely effective cooking vessel. Heat radiates up the sides to produce a pan that cooks fast and efficiently. Its depth allows plenty of room for tossing and turning, and the sloping sides ensure that the food always returns to the heat at the narrow base.

Wok sales have rocketed in recent years. In the 1960s and 70s, a wok was something of a novelty, often bought in a burst of enthusiasm after a visit to a Chinese restaurant, then left to rust at the back of a kitchen cupboard. And rust they did, largely because people didn't know how to look after them. Part of the problem was the fact that most of the woks on sale were constructed of carbon steel. This is an excellent material, but it needs an initial treatment to develop a non-stick, rust-resistant surface.

Fortunately, there were enough fans of this excellent pan to spread the word, and the wok gradually gained ground. It was still used mainly for Chinese food only, however, and was sold alongside other specialist equipment such as fondue pots or waffle irons. The arrival of fusion food in the West changed all that. When chefs no longer viewed each nation's cuisine as sacrosanct, and started inventing new dishes that combined ingredients from several sources, they did us all a favour. The wok stopped being used solely for sweet and sour pork, and came to be seen as a practical pan for all sorts of dishes.

Around the same time, the pattern of everyday life was changing. People weren't just eating out more: they were adopting more flexible eating habits. Often there wasn't enough time to cook an elaborate meal, so something that could be whizzed up in a wok was absolutely ideal.

When it became apparent that this utensil was a fixture, rather than a short-lived culinary craze, manufacturers started producing woks in different materials, including non-stick ones that needed little aftercare or special treatment. Flat-based versions were

LEFT: *The wok is a great tool for frying small pieces of meat or balls of mince.*

ABOVE: *The wok is ideal for steaming food, such as fish wrapped in banana leaves.*

ABOVE: *Spectacular dishes are simple and speedy to make in the wok.*

ABOVE: *Tender chicken becomes deliciously crisp when shallow-fried with a spicy coating.*

developed for use on modern electric stoves, the first electric appliances appeared, and more cookbooks catered for the quick and convenient style of cooking the wok promised.

Throughout this, the wok delivered, and is still delivering. Today, its role in promoting healthy eating is catching the public imagination. What the wok does extremely well is to cook a sizeable quantity of vegetables with a small amount of protein and the minimum of fat. When carbohydrate is added, in the form of noodles or rice, you have a well-balanced dish that any nutritionist would approve of. Deep-frying doesn't score a lot of brownie points in the

health stakes, but if the oil is hot enough, the outer surface will be sealed immediately, and the amount of oil absorbed will be limited. Steaming, however, gets a gold star. This is one of the healthiest ways to cook and the wok is an ideal utensil. Since no additional fat is needed, the natural flavour of the food is preserved, and colours remain bright and true.

When you own a wok, you will find yourself discovering new uses for it, whether cooking spaghetti sauce, braising chicken portions, simmering fruit in syrup, making risotto, steaming asparagus or smoking salmon. It may not be the only pot you'll ever need, but it will be the one you use most often.

How to use this book

A collection of fabulous recipes from classic Eastern cuisine to contemporary Western dishes demonstrates the amazing versatility of the wok. You don't have to be experienced with a wok to get the most out of this book. First-time wok-users will benefit from the Wok Basics chapter, which has all the information to get you started. It demonstrates the range of woks and tools available, shows you how to take care of your wok and has detailed tips and techniques for the vast range of cooking methods suited to the wok – from steaming to stir-frying and simmering to deep-frying.

Crispy Snacks and Finger Foods

A wok is a great accessory when it comes to

the little treats that add spice to life.

Spring rolls, samosas and wonton parcels

can be cooked to crisp perfection in

minutes, ready for dipping into scrumptious

sauces. For serving with drinks, try Roasted

Coconut Cashew Nuts – piled in paper

cones to save fingers from getting sticky

– or choose one of the more substantial

snacks that can double as an appetizer.

Roasted coconut cashew nuts

Serve these wok-fried hot and sweet cashew nuts in paper or cellophane cones at parties. Not only do they look enticing and taste terrific, but the cones help to keep clothes and hands clean and can simply be crumpled up and thrown away afterwards.

SERVES 6–8

15ml/1 tbsp groundnut (peanut) oil
30ml/2 tbsp clear honey
250g/9oz/2 cups cashew nuts
115g/4oz/1¹/₃ cups desiccated (dry unsweetened shredded) coconut
2 small fresh red chillies, seeded and finely chopped
salt and ground black pepper

1 Heat the oil in a wok or large frying pan and then stir in the honey. After a few seconds add the cashew nuts and desiccated coconut and stir-fry until both are golden brown.

2 Add the chillies, with salt and pepper to taste. Toss the mixture until all the ingredients are well mixed. Serve the nuts either warm or cooled in paper cones or on small plates or saucers.

Nutritional information per portion: Energy 301Kcal/1247kJ; Protein 7.2g; Carbohydrate 9.7g, of which sugars 5.5g; Fat 26.2g, of which saturates 11.1g; Cholesterol 0mg; Calcium 14mg; Fibre 3g; Sodium 95mg.

Tung tong

Popularly referred to as 'gold bags', these crisp pastry purses have a coriander-flavoured filling based on water chestnuts and corn. They are the perfect vegetarian snack – crunchy on the outside, with a beautifully succulent filling.

MAKES 18

18 spring roll wrappers, about 8cm/3¼in
   square, thawed if frozen
oil, for deep-frying
plum sauce, to serve

FOR THE FILLING
4 baby corn cobs
130g/4½oz can water chestnuts,
   drained and chopped
1 shallot, coarsely chopped
1 egg, separated
30ml/2 tbsp cornflour (cornstarch)
60ml/4 tbsp water
small bunch fresh coriander
   (cilantro), chopped
salt and ground black pepper

1 To make the filling, place the baby corn, water chestnuts, shallot and egg yolk in a food processor or blender. Process to a coarse paste. Place the egg white in a cup and whisk it lightly with a fork.

2 Put the cornflour in a small pan and stir in the water until smooth. Add the corn mixture and chopped coriander and season with salt and pepper to taste. Cook over a low heat, stirring constantly, until thickened.

3 Allow to cool slightly, then place 5ml/1 tsp in the centre of a spring roll wrapper. Brush the edges with the egg white, then gather up the points and press them firmly together to make a pouch or bag. Repeat with the remaining wrappers and filling.

4 Heat the oil in a wok to 190°C/ 375°F or until a cube of bread browns in about 40 seconds. Fry the bags, in batches, for about 5 minutes, until golden. Serve hot, with plum sauce.

Nutritional information per portion: Energy 55Kcal/229kJ; Protein 1.2g; Carbohydrate 6.3g, of which sugars 0.4g; Fat 2.9g, of which saturates 0.4g; Cholesterol 12mg; Calcium 19mg; Fibre 0.5g; Sodium 42mg.

Aubergine and pepper tempura with sweet chilli dip

These crunchy vegetables in a beautifully light batter are quick and easy to make, and taste fantastic when given a Thai twist with this piquant dip.

SERVES 4

2 aubergines (eggplants), sliced into batons
2 red (bell) peppers, thinly sliced
vegetable oil, for deep-frying

FOR THE TEMPURA BATTER
250g/9oz/2¼ cups plain
**   (all-purpose) flour**
2 egg yolks
500ml/17fl oz/2¼ cups iced water
5ml/1 tsp salt

FOR THE DIP
150ml/¼ pint/⅔ cup water
10ml/2 tsp granulated (white) sugar
1 fresh red chilli, seeded and finely chopped
1 garlic clove, crushed
juice of ½ lime
5ml/1 tsp rice vinegar
35ml/2½ tbsp Thai fish sauce
½ small carrot, finely grated

1 Make the dip. Mix together all the ingredients in a bowl and stir until the sugar has dissolved. Set aside.

2 Make the tempura batter. Set aside 30ml/2 tbsp of the flour. Put the egg yolks in a large bowl and beat in the iced water. Add the remaining flour with the salt and stir briefly together – it should resemble thick, lumpy pancake batter. If it is too thick, add more water. Use the batter immediately.

3 Pour the oil into a wok or deep-fryer and heat to 190°C/375°F, until a cube of bread browns in about 40 seconds.

4 Take a small handful of the aubergine batons and pepper slices, dust with the reserved flour, then dip into the batter. Immediately drop them into the hot oil, taking care as the oil will froth up. Repeat with a further two or three handfuls of vegetables, but cook no more than this at once as the oil may overflow.

5 Cook the fritters for 3–4 minutes, until they are golden and crisp, then lift them out with a slotted spoon. Drain thoroughly and keep hot. Repeat until all the vegetables have been coated in batter and cooked. Serve immediately, with the dip.

Nutritional information per portion: Energy 404Kcal/1699kJ; Protein 9.4g; Carbohydrate 61g, of which sugars 12.5g; Fat 15.4g, of which saturates 2.4g; Cholesterol 101mg; Calcium 124mg; Fibre 5.8g; Sodium 15mg.

Potato pakoras with coconut and mint chutney

These delicious golden bites are sold as street food throughout India. They make a wonderful snack drizzled with fragrant coconut and mint chutney.

MAKES 25

600g/1lb 6oz potatoes, peeled, diced
15ml/1 tbsp sunflower oil
20ml/4 tsp cumin seeds
5ml/1 tsp black mustard seeds
1 small onion, finely chopped
10ml/2 tsp grated fresh root ginger
2 fresh green chillies, seeded and chopped
200g/7oz fresh peas
juice of 1 lemon
90ml/6 tbsp chopped fresh coriander
   (cilantro) leaves
115g/4oz/1 cup gram flour
25g/1oz/1/4 cup self-raising
   (self-rising) flour
40g/1 1/2 oz/1/3 cup rice flour
large pinch of ground turmeric
10ml/2 tsp crushed coriander seeds
vegetable oil, for deep-frying
salt and ground black pepper

FOR THE CHUTNEY

105ml/7 tbsp coconut cream
200ml/7fl oz/1 cup natural (plain) yogurt
50g/2oz fresh mint leaves, finely chopped
5ml/1 tsp golden caster (superfine) sugar
juice of 1 lime

1 Boil the potatoes until tender.

2 Heat a wok and add the oil. When hot, add the cumin and mustard seeds and stir-fry for 1–2 minutes. Add the onion, ginger and chillies to the wok and cook for 3–4 minutes. Add the cooked potatoes, stir a few times, then add the peas and stir-fry for 3–4 minutes. Season, then stir in the lemon juice and coriander leaves.

3 Leave the mixture to cool slightly, then divide into 25 portions. Shape each portion into a ball and chill.

4 To make the batter, put the gram flour, self-raising flour and rice flour in a bowl.

5 Season and add the turmeric and coriander seeds. Gradually whisk in 350ml/12fl oz/1 1/2 cups water to make a smooth, thick batter.

6 To make the chutney, place all the ingredients in a blender and process until smooth. Season, then chill.

7 To cook the pakoras, fill a wok one-third full of oil and heat to 180°C/350°F, until a cube of bread browns in about 45 seconds. Working in batches, dip the balls in the batter, then drop into the oil and deep-fry for 1–2 minutes. Drain the pakoras and serve with the chutney.

Nutritional information per portion: Energy 126Kcal/525kJ; Protein 4.1g; Carbohydrate 8.3g, of which sugars 2.6g; Fat 8.8g, of which saturates 5.2g; Cholesterol 0mg; Calcium 35mg; Fibre 1.3g; Sodium 16mg.

Potato, shallot and garlic samosas

Most samosas are deep-fried. These are baked, although their filling is made in a wok. They are perfect for parties, since the pastries need no last-minute attention.

MAKES 25

15ml/1 tbsp groundnut (peanut) oil
2 shallots, finely chopped
1 garlic clove, finely chopped
**1 large potato, about 250g/9oz,
    diced and boiled until tender**
60ml/4 tbsp coconut milk
5ml/1 tsp Thai red or green curry paste
75g/3oz/³/₄ cup peas
juice of ¹/₂ lime
**25 samosa wrappers or 10 x 5cm/
    4 x 2in strips of filo pastry**
oil, for brushing
salt and ground black pepper

1 Preheat the oven to 220°C/425°F/Gas 7. Heat the oil in a wok and cook the shallots and garlic over a medium heat, stirring occasionally, for 4–5 minutes, until softened and golden. Add the cooked potato, coconut milk, curry paste, peas and lime juice to the wok. Mash together coarsely with a wooden spoon. Season to taste and cook over a low heat for 2–3 minutes, then remove the pan from the heat and set aside until the mixture has cooled a little.

2 Lay a samosa wrapper or filo strip flat on the work surface. Brush with a little oil, then place a generous teaspoonful of the mixture in the middle of one end. Turn one corner diagonally over the filling to meet the long edge. Continue folding over the filling, keeping the triangular shape. Brush with a little more oil if necessary and place on a baking sheet. Repeat for the other samosas.

3 Bake for 15 minutes, until golden and crisp. Cool slightly before serving.

Nutritional information per portion: Energy 42Kcal/178kJ; Protein 1.2g; Carbohydrate 8.5g, of which sugars 0.6g; Fat 0.6g, of which saturates 0.1g; Cholesterol 0mg; Calcium 14mg; Fibre 0.5g; Sodium 4mg.

Spiced noodle pancakes

Delicate rice noodles puff up in the hot oil to give a fabulous crunchy bite that melts in the mouth. Serve the pancakes immediately to savour the subtle blend of spices and wonderfully crisp texture.

SERVES 4

150g/5oz dried thin rice noodles
1 fresh red chilli, finely diced
10ml/2 tsp garlic salt
5ml/1 tsp ground ginger
1/4 small red onion, very finely diced
5ml/1 tsp finely chopped lemon grass
5ml/1 tsp ground cumin
5ml/1 tsp ground coriander
large pinch of ground turmeric
vegetable oil, for shallow-frying
salt
sweet chilli sauce, to serve

1 Break the noodles into a large bowl. Pour over boiling water to cover, and soak for 4–5 minutes. Drain and rinse under cold water. Dry on kitchen paper.

2 Transfer the noodles to a bowl and add the chilli, garlic salt, ginger, red onion, lemon grass, cumin, coriander and turmeric. Toss well and season with salt.

3 Heat 5–6cm/2–2¹/₂ in of oil in a wok. Working in batches, drop tablespoons of the noodle mixture into the oil. Flatten using the back of a skimmer and cook for 1–2 minutes on each side until crisp and golden. Drain on kitchen paper.

4 Serve immediately with the chilli sauce for dipping.

COOK'S TIP
For deep-frying, use thin rice noodles. They can also be cooked without soaking.

Nutritional information per portion: Energy 190Kcal/791kJ; Protein 2g; Carbohydrate 31.8g, of which sugars 0.9g; Fat 5.6g, of which saturates 0.7g; Cholesterol 0mg; Calcium 9mg; Fibre 0.2g; Sodium 496mg.

Prawn and sesame toasts

These attractive little toast triangles are ideal for serving with pre-dinner drinks and are always a favourite hot snack at parties. They are surprisingly easy to prepare and can be cooked in a wok for just a few minutes. Serve them with a sweet chilli sauce.

SERVES 4

225g/8oz peeled raw prawns (shrimp)
15ml/1 tbsp sherry
15ml/1 tbsp soy sauce
30ml/2 tbsp cornflour (cornstarch)
2 egg whites
4 slices white bread
115g/4oz/½ cup sesame seeds
oil, for deep-frying
sweet chilli sauce, to serve

1 Process the prawns, sherry, soy sauce and cornflour in a food processor.

2 In a bowl, whisk the egg whites until stiff. Fold them into the prawn and cornflour mixture.

3 Cut each slice of bread into four triangular quarters. Spread out the sesame seeds on a large plate. Spread the prawn paste over one side of each bread triangle, then press the coated sides into the sesame seeds so that they stick and cover the prawn paste.

4 Heat the oil in a wok or deep-fryer, to 190°C/375°F or until a cube of bread, added to the oil, browns in about 40 seconds. Add the toasts, a few at a time, prawn side down, and deep-fry for 2–3 minutes, then turn and fry on the other side until golden. Drain on kitchen paper and serve hot with sweet chilli sauce.

Nutritional information per portion: Energy 392Kcal/1634kJ; Protein 19.1g; Carbohydrate 21.1g, of which sugars 1.2g; Fat 25.8g, of which saturates 3.4g; Cholesterol 110mg; Calcium 270mg; Fibre 2.7g; Sodium 557mg.

Crisp-fried Japanese panko prawns

When butterflied and battered tiger prawns are deep-fried in the wok, they curl up beautifully, and look gorgeous on dark green seaweed topped with white rice. Wasabi, soy sauce, sweet chilli sauce and pickled ginger are traditional accompaniments.

SERVES 4

20 large raw tiger or king prawns
   (jumbo shrimp), heads removed
30ml/2 tbsp cornflour (cornstarch)
3 large (US extra large) eggs,
   lightly beaten
150g/5oz panko (Japanese-style
   breadcrumbs)
sunflower oil, for deep-frying
4 sheets of nori
400g/14oz cooked sushi rice
wasabi, soy sauce, sweet chilli sauce
   and pickled ginger, to serve

1 Peel and devein the prawns, leaving the tails on. Using a small, sharp knife, cut down the back of each prawn, without cutting all the way through, and gently press the prawns out flat to butterfly them.

2 Place the cornflour, beaten eggs and panko in three separate bowls. Dip each prawn first in the cornflour mixture, next in the egg and then in the panko, to coat evenly. Fill a wok one-third full of sunflower oil and heat to 180°C/350°F, or until a cube of bread, added to the oil, browns in about 45 seconds.

3 Working in batches, deep-fry the prawns for 1 minute, or until lightly golden and crisp. Remove with a slotted spoon and drain on kitchen paper.

4 Carefully cut each nori sheet into a 10cm/4in square. Place each square on a serving plate and divide the sushi rice among them, then spread out the rice using the back of a spoon. Top each serving with five deep-fried prawns and serve with wasabi, soy sauce, sweet chilli sauce and pickled ginger.

Nutritional information per portion: Energy 472Kcal/1989kJ; Protein 20.2g; Carbohydrate 63g, of which sugars 1g; Fat 17.4g, of which saturates 2.8g; Cholesterol 240mg; Calcium 127mg; Fibre 0.9g; Sodium 437mg.

Corn fritters

Sometimes it is the simplest dishes that taste the best. These fritters, packed with crunchy corn, are very easy to prepare and cook quickly in a hot wok.

MAKES 12

3 corn cobs, total weight about 250g/9oz
1 garlic clove, crushed
small bunch fresh coriander
    (cilantro), chopped
1 small fresh red or green chilli, seeded
    and finely chopped
1 spring onion (scallion), finely chopped
15ml/1 tbsp soy sauce
75g/3oz/2/3 cup rice flour or plain
    (all-purpose) flour
2 eggs, lightly beaten
60ml/4 tbsp water
oil, for shallow-frying
salt and ground black pepper
sweet chilli sauce, to serve

1 Using a sharp knife, slice the kernels from the cobs and place them in a large bowl. Add the garlic, chopped coriander, red or green chilli, spring onion, soy sauce, flour, beaten eggs and water, and mix well. Season with salt and pepper to taste and mix again. The mixture should be firm enough to hold its shape, but not stiff.

2 Heat the oil in a wok. Add spoonfuls of the corn mixture, gently spreading each one out with the back of the spoon to make a circular fritter. Cook for 1–2 minutes on each side.

3 Drain on kitchen paper and keep hot. Fry more fritters in batches and serve hot with sweet chilli sauce.

Nutritional information per portion: Energy 77Kcal/322kJ; Protein 2.3g; Carbohydrate 7.8g, of which sugars 0.6g; Fat 4.1g, of which saturates 0.6g; Cholesterol 32mg; Calcium 24mg; Fibre 0.8g; Sodium 104mg.

Crisp-fried crab claws

Crab claws are readily available from the freezer cabinet of many Asian stores and supermarkets. Thaw them thoroughly and dry on kitchen paper before coating them.

SERVES 4

50g/2oz/¹/₃ cup rice flour
15ml/1 tbsp cornflour (cornstarch)
2.5ml/¹/₂ tsp granulated (white) sugar
1 egg
60ml/4 tbsp cold water
1 lemon grass stalk
15ml/1 tbsp fresh coriander (cilantro)
1–2 fresh red chillies
2 garlic cloves, finely chopped
5ml/1 tsp Thai fish sauce
vegetable oil, for deep-frying
12 half-shelled crab claws, thawed if frozen
ground black pepper

FOR THE CHILLI VINEGAR DIP

45ml/3 tbsp granulated (white) sugar
120ml/4fl oz/¹/₂ cup water
120ml/4fl oz/¹/₂ cup red wine vinegar
15ml/1 tbsp Thai fish sauce
2–4 fresh red chillies, seeded and chopped

1 First make the chilli vinegar dip. Mix the sugar and water in a pan. Heat gently, stirring until the sugar has dissolved, then bring to the boil. Lower the heat and simmer for 5–7 minutes. Stir in the rest of the ingredients, pour into a serving bowl and set aside.

2 Combine the rice flour, cornflour and sugar in a bowl. Beat the egg with the cold water, then stir the egg and water mixture into the flour mixture and beat well until it forms a light batter.

3 Cut off the lower 5cm/2in of the lemon grass stalk and chop it finely. Chop the coriander, and seed and finely chop the red chillies. Add the lemon grass, coriander and chillies to the batter, with the garlic and fish sauce. Stir in pepper to taste.

4 Heat the oil in a wok or deep-fryer to 190°C/375°F or until a cube of bread browns in about 40 seconds. Dip the crab claws into the batter, then fry, in batches, until golden. Serve with the dip.

Nutritional information per portion: Energy 222Kcal/926kJ; Protein 10.1g; Carbohydrate 16.9g, of which sugars 0g; Fat 12.8g, of which saturates 1.7g; Cholesterol 78mg; Calcium 62mg; Fibre 0.3g; Sodium 256mg.

Tempura seafood

This quintessentially Japanese dish actually has its origins in the West, as tempura was introduced to Japan by Portuguese traders in the 17th century.

SERVES 4

8 large raw prawns (shrimp), heads
   and shells removed, tails intact
130g/4^1/$_2$oz squid body, cleaned
   and skinned
115g/4oz whiting fillets
4 fresh shiitake mushrooms,
   stalks removed
8 okra
^{1}/$_8$ nori sheet, 5 x 4cm/2 x 1^1/$_2$in
20g/^{3}/$_4$oz dried harusame noodles
   (a packet is a 150–250g/5–9oz mass)
vegetable oil and sesame oil,
   for deep-frying
plain (all-purpose) flour, for dusting
salt

FOR THE DIPPING SAUCE
400ml/14fl oz/1^2/$_3$ cups second dashi stock,
   made using water and instant dashi powder
200ml/7fl oz/scant 1 cup shoyu
200ml/7fl oz/scant 1 cup mirin

FOR THE CONDIMENT
450g/1lb mooli (daikon), peeled
4cm/1^1/$_2$in fresh root ginger

FOR THE TEMPURA BATTER
ice-cold water
1 large (US extra large) egg, beaten
200g/7oz/2 cups plain (all-purpose) flour, sifted
2–3 ice cubes

1 Devein the prawns, then make 4 x 3mm/^{1}/$_8$in deep cuts across the belly to stop them curling up. Snip the tips of the tails and gently squeeze out any liquid. Pat dry. Cut open the squid body. Lay it flat, inside down, on a chopping board, and make shallow criss-cross slits on the outside. Cut into 2.5 x 6cm/1 x 2^1/$_2$in rectangular strips. Cut the whiting fillets into similar-size strips.

2 Make two notched slits on the shiitake caps, in the form of a cross. Rub some salt over the okra, then wash under running water to clean the surface. Cut the nori into four long strips lengthways. Loosen the harusame noodles from the block and cut both ends with scissors to get a few strips. Make four bunches and tie them in the middle by wrapping with a nori strip. Wet the end to fix it.

3 Make the dipping sauce. In a pan, mix all the dipping sauce ingredients and bring to the boil, then immediately remove from the heat. Set aside and keep warm.

4 Prepare the condiment. Grate the daikon very finely. Drain in a sieve (strainer), then squeeze out any excess water by hand. Peel and grate the ginger. Lay clear film (plastic wrap) over an egg cup and press about 2.5ml/^{1}/$_2$ tsp grated ginger into the bottom. Add 30ml/2 tbsp grated daikon. Press and invert on to a small plate. Make three more ginger and daikon moulds in the same way.

5 Half-fill a wok with 3 parts vegetable oil to 1 part sesame oil. Bring to 175°C/347°F over a medium heat. Meanwhile, make the tempura batter. Add enough ice-cold water to the egg to make 150ml/¹/₄ pint/²/₃ cup, then pour into a large bowl. Add the flour and mix roughly with chopsticks. Do not beat; leave the batter lumpy. Add some ice cubes later to keep the temperature cool.

6 Dip the okra into the batter and deep-fry until golden, then drain. Batter the underside of the shiitake and deep-fry. Increase the heat a little, then fry the harusame by holding the nori tie with chopsticks and dipping them into the oil for a few seconds. Drain on kitchen paper and sprinkle with salt.

7 Hold the tail of a prawn, dust with flour, then dip into the batter. Do not put batter on the tail. Slide the prawn into the hot oil very slowly. Deep-fry one to two prawns at a time until crisp. Dust the whiting strips, dip into the batter, then deep-fry until golden. Wipe the squid strips well with kitchen paper, dust with flour, then dip in batter. Deep-fry until the batter is crisp. Drain the tempura on a wire rack and reheat the dipping sauce. Serve immediately.

Nutritional information per portion: Energy 401Kcal/1683kJ; Protein 27.3g; Carbohydrate 42.8g, of which sugars 4.1g; Fat 14.5g, of which saturates 2.2g; Cholesterol 231mg; Calcium 167mg; Fibre 3.2g; Sodium 1080mg.

Firecrackers

It's easy to see how these pastry-wrapped prawn snacks got their name. Not only do they whiz around in the wok like rockets, they explode with flavour in your mouth.

MAKES 16

16 large, raw king prawns (jumbo
    shrimp), heads and shells removed
    but tails left on
5ml/1 tsp red curry paste
15ml/1 tbsp Thai fish sauce
16 small wonton wrappers, about
    8cm/3$^1/_4$in square, thawed
    if frozen
16 fine egg noodles, soaked
oil, for deep-frying
lime wedges, to serve

1 Place the prawns on their sides and cut two slits through the underbelly of each, one about 1cm/$^1/_2$in from the head end and the other about 1cm/$^1/_2$in from the first cut, cutting across the prawn. This will prevent the prawns from curling when they are cooked.

2 Mix the curry paste with the fish sauce in a dish. Add the prawns and coat them in the mixture. Cover and leave to marinate for 10 minutes.

3 Place a wonton wrapper on the work surface at an angle so that it forms a diamond shape, then fold the top corner over so that the point is in the centre. Place a prawn, slits down, on the wrapper, with the tail projecting from the folded end, then fold the bottom corner over the other end of the prawn.

4 Fold each side of the wrapper over in turn to make a tightly folded roll. Tie a noodle in a bow around the roll and set it aside. Repeat with the remaining prawns and wrappers.

5 Heat the oil in a wok to 190°C/ 375°F or until a cube of bread browns in about 40 seconds. Fry the prawns, in batches, for 5–8 minutes, until golden brown and cooked through. Drain on kitchen paper. Serve with lime wedges.

Nutritional information per portion: Energy 71Kcal/298kJ; Protein 3.2g; Carbohydrate 7.1g, of which sugars 0.2g; Fat 3.5g, of which saturates 0.5g; Cholesterol 25mg; Calcium 20mg; Fibre 0.3g; Sodium 30mg.

Deep-fried small prawns and corn

Inspired by Japanese tempura, this simple snack food is a good way of using up small quantities of vegetables and prawns. It is easy to cook in a wok.

SERVES 4

200g/7oz small prawns (shrimp),
    cooked and peeled
4–5 button (white) mushrooms
4 spring onions (scallions)
75g/3oz/1/2 cup canned, drained
    or frozen corn, thawed
30ml/2 tbsp frozen peas, thawed
vegetable oil, for deep-frying
chives, to garnish

FOR THE TEMPURA BATTER

300ml/1/2 pint/11/4 cups ice-cold water
2 eggs, beaten
150g/5oz/11/4 cups plain (all-purpose) flour
1.5ml/1/4 tsp baking powder

FOR THE DIPPING SAUCE

400ml/14fl oz/12/3 cups second dashi
    stock, made with instant dashi powder
    and water
100ml/31/2fl oz/scant 1/2 cup shoyu
100ml/31/2fl oz/scant 1/2 cup mirin
15ml/1 tbsp chopped chives

1 Roughly chop half the prawns. Cut the mushrooms into small cubes. Slice the white part from the spring onions and chop this roughly.

2 To make the tempura batter, in a medium mixing bowl, mix the cold water and eggs. Add the flour and baking powder, and very roughly fold in with a pair of chopsticks or a fork. Do not beat. The batter should still be quite lumpy. Heat plenty of oil in a wok to 170°C/338°F.

3 Mix the prawns and vegetables into the batter.

4 Pour a quarter of the batter into a small bowl, then drop gently into the oil. Using wooden spoons, gather the scattered batter to form a fist-size ball. Deep-fry until golden. Drain on kitchen paper. Repeat to make three more fritters.

5 To make the dipping sauce, mix all the liquid ingredients together in a small pan and bring to the boil. Immediately turn off the heat. Sprinkle with the chopped chives.

6 Garnish the fritters with chives, and serve with the dipping sauce.

Nutritional information per portion: Energy 246Kcal/1039kJ; Protein 17.6g; Carbohydrate 37.4g, of which sugars 4.7g; Fat 4g, of which saturates 1g; Cholesterol 193mg; Calcium 117mg; Fibre 2g; Sodium 1963mg.

Satay prawns

This delicious dish is inspired by the classic Indonesian satay. The combination of mild peanuts, aromatic spices, sweet coconut milk and zesty lemon juice goes perfectly with succulent prawns.

SERVES 4–6

450g/1lb king prawns (jumbo shrimp)
25ml/1¹/₂ tbsp vegetable oil

FOR THE PEANUT SAUCE
25ml/1¹/₂ tbsp vegetable oil
15ml/1 tbsp chopped garlic
1 small onion, chopped
3–4 fresh red chillies, seeded and chopped
3 kaffir lime leaves, torn
1 lemon grass stalk, bruised and chopped
5ml/1 tsp medium curry paste
250ml/8fl oz/1 cup coconut milk
1cm/¹/₂in piece cinnamon stick

75g/3oz/¹/₃ cup crunchy peanut butter
45ml/3 tbsp tamarind juice, made by mixing
    tamarind paste with warm water
30ml/2 tbsp Thai fish sauce
30ml/2 tbsp palm sugar (jaggery) or
    light muscovado (brown) sugar
juice of ¹/₂ lemon

FOR THE GARNISH
spring onions (scallions), cut diagonally
¹/₂ bunch fresh coriander (cilantro)
    leaves (optional)
4 fresh red chillies, finely sliced (optional)

1 Remove the heads from the prawns and peel, leaving the tail ends intact. Slit each prawn along the back with a small, sharp knife and remove the black vein. Rinse under cold running water, pat dry, and set aside.

2 Make the peanut sauce. Heat half the oil in a wok or large, heavy frying pan. Add the garlic and onion and cook over a medium heat, stirring occasionally, for 3–4 minutes, until the mixture has softened but not browned. Add the chillies, kaffir lime leaves, lemon grass and curry paste. Stir well and cook for 2–3 minutes. Stir in the coconut milk, cinnamon stick, peanut butter, tamarind juice, fish sauce, sugar and lemon juice. Cook, stirring, until blended.

3 Bring to the boil, then reduce the heat to low and simmer gently for 15–20 minutes, until the sauce thickens. Stir occasionally with a wooden spoon to prevent the sauce from sticking to the base of the wok or frying pan.

4 Shallow fry the prawns until they turn pink. Alternatively, thread the prawns on to skewers and cook under a hot grill (broiler) for 2 minutes on each side.

5 Remove the cinnamon stick from the sauce and discard. Arrange the prawns on a warmed platter, garnish with spring onions, coriander leaves and sliced red chillies, if you like.

VARIATIONS

• *For a curry-style dish, heat the oil in a wok or large frying pan. Add the prawns (shrimp) and stir-fry for 3–4 minutes, or until pink. Mix the prawns with the sauce and serve with jasmine rice.*

• *You can use this basic sauce for satay pork or chicken, too. With a sharp knife, cut pork fillet (tenderloin) or skinless, boneless chicken breast portions into long thin strips and stir-fry in hot oil until golden brown all over and cooked through. Then stir into the sauce, instead of the king prawns.*

Nutritional information per portion: Energy 1042Kcal/4361kJ; Protein 59.7g; Carbohydrate 61.7g, of which sugars 53.1g; Fat 63.7g, of which saturates 13.1g; Cholesterol 472mg; Calcium 408mg; Fibre 7.5g; Sodium 3255mg.

Green curry puffs

Shrimp paste and green curry sauce, used judiciously, give these puffs their distinctive, spicy, savoury flavour, and the addition of chilli steps up the heat.

MAKES 24

24 small wonton wrappers, about 8cm/3¼ in square, thawed if frozen
15ml/1 tbsp cornflour (cornstarch), mixed to a paste with 30ml/2 tbsp water
oil, for deep-frying

FOR THE FILLING
1 small potato, about 115g/4oz, boiled
25g/1oz/3 tbsp cooked petits pois (baby peas)
25g/1oz/3 tbsp cooked corn
few sprigs fresh coriander (cilantro), chopped
1 small fresh red chilli, seeded and finely chopped
½ lemon grass stalk, finely chopped
15ml/1 tbsp soy sauce
5ml/1 tsp shrimp paste or fish sauce
5ml/1 tsp Thai green curry paste

1 To make the filling, first mash the boiled potato. Then combine all of the filling ingredients in a large bowl.

2 Lay out one wonton wrapper and place a teaspoon of the filling in the centre.

3 Brush a little of the cornflour paste along two sides of the square. Fold the other two sides over to meet them, then press together to make a triangular pastry and seal in the filling. Repeat this with the remaining wrappers, making more pastries in the same way.

4 Heat the oil in a wok to 190°C/375°F or until a cube of bread browns in about 40 seconds. Add the puffs to the oil, a few at a time, and fry them in batches for about 5 minutes, until they are golden brown.

5 Remove the puffs from the wok using a slotted spoon and leave to drain on kitchen paper. If you intend serving the puffs hot, place them in a low oven while you cook successive batches in the same way. The puffs also taste good when served cold.

Nutritional information per portion: Energy 69Kcal/291kJ; Protein 1.4g; Carbohydrate 9.9g, of which sugars 0.4g; Fat 3g, of which saturates 0.4g; Cholesterol 1mg; Calcium 22mg; Fibre 0.5g; Sodium 58mg.

Crispy salt and pepper squid

These delicious morsels of squid look stunning – perfect served with drinks, or as an appetizer. The crisp, golden coating contrasts beautifully with the succulent squid inside.

SERVES 4

750g/1lb 10oz fresh squid, cleaned
juice of 4–5 lemons
15ml/1 tbsp ground black pepper
15ml/1 tbsp sea salt
10ml/2 tsp caster (superfine) sugar
115g/4oz/1 cup cornflour (cornstarch)
3 egg whites, lightly beaten
vegetable oil, for deep-frying
chilli sauce or sweet-and-sour sauce,
    for dipping
skewers or toothpicks, to serve

1 Cut the squid into large bitesize pieces and score a diamond pattern on each piece, using a sharp knife or a cleaver. Trim the tentacles. Place in a large mixing bowl and pour over the lemon juice. Cover and marinate for 10–15 minutes. Drain well and pat dry.

2 In a separate bowl, mix together the pepper, salt, sugar and cornflour.

3 Dip the squid pieces in the egg whites and then toss lightly in the seasoned flour, shaking off any excess.

4 Fill a wok one-third full of oil and heat to 180°C/350°F or until a cube of bread browns in about 45 seconds. Deep-fry the squid, in batches, for 1 minute. Drain on kitchen paper and serve threaded on to skewers with chilli or sweet-and-sour sauce.

Nutritional information per portion: Energy 346Kcal/1462kJ; Protein 31.2g; Carbohydrate 31.3g, of which sugars 2.6g; Fat 11.6g, of which saturates 1.8g; Cholesterol 422mg; Calcium 32mg; Fibre 0g; Sodium 1741mg.

Fiery tuna spring rolls

This modern take on the classic spring roll is substantial enough to serve as a main meal with noodles and stir-fried greens. The tuna and wasabi filling tastes fantastic.

SERVES 4

1 large chunk of very fresh thick tuna steak
45ml/3 tbsp light soy sauce
30ml/2 tbsp wasabi
16 mangetouts (snow peas), trimmed
8 spring roll wrappers
sunflower oil, for deep-frying
soft noodles and stir-fried Asian greens, to serve
soy sauce and sweet chilli sauce, for dipping

1 Using a sharp knife cut the tuna into eight slices, each measuring about 12 x 2.5cm/4$^{1}/_{2}$ x 1in. Place in a large, non-metallic dish in a single layer.

2 Mix together the soy sauce and the wasabi and spoon evenly over the fish. Cover and marinate for 10–15 minutes. Meanwhile, blanch the mangetouts in boiling water for about 1 minute. Drain, refresh under cold water and pat dry.

3 Place a spring roll wrapper on a clean surface and put a piece of tuna in the centre. Top the tuna with two mangetouts, fold over the sides and roll up. Brush the edges of the wrapper with water to seal. Repeat with the remaining wrappers.

4 Fill a large wok one-third full with oil and heat to 180°C/350°F or until a cube of bread browns in about 45 seconds. Working in batches, deep-fry the rolls for 1–2 minutes, until crisp and golden.

5 Drain the rolls on kitchen paper and serve immediately with soft noodles, Asian greens and side dishes of soy sauce and sweet chilli sauce for dipping.

Nutritional information per portion: Energy 171Kcal/717kJ; Protein 14g; Carbohydrate 11.4g, of which sugars 1.7g; Fat 8g, of which saturates 1.3g; Cholesterol 14mg; Calcium 36mg; Fibre 0.8g; Sodium 825mg.

Thai spring rolls

Crunchy spring rolls are as popular in Thailand as they are in China. This Thai version is filled with a delicious garlic, pork and noodle mixture, and served with a sweet chilli dipping sauce.

MAKES 24

4–6 Chinese dried mushrooms,
50g/2oz cellophane noodles
30ml/2 tbsp vegetable oil
2 garlic cloves, chopped
2 fresh red chillies, seeded and chopped
225g/8oz minced (ground) pork
50g/2oz peeled cooked prawns (shrimp),
  thawed if frozen
30ml/2 tbsp Thai fish sauce
5ml/1 tsp granulated (white) sugar
50g/2oz piece of canned bamboo shoot
15ml/1 tbsp fresh coriander (cilantro)
1 carrot, grated
50g/2oz/²/₃ cup beansprouts
2 spring onions (scallions), finely chopped
24 x 15cm/6in square spring roll wrappers
30ml/2 tbsp plain (all-purpose) flour
vegetable oil, for deep-frying
ground black pepper
sweet chilli dipping sauce, to serve

1 Soak the mushrooms for 30 minutes in warm water. Drain, cut off and discard the stems, then chop the caps finely. Place the noodles in a large bowl, cover with boiling water and soak for 10 minutes. Drain and snip into 5cm/2in lengths.

2 Heat the oil in a wok, add the garlic and chillies and stir-fry for 30 seconds. Transfer to a plate. Add the pork to the wok and stir-fry until browned. Add the mushrooms, noodles, prawns, fish sauce, sugar and pepper to taste. Transfer to a bowl. Chop the bamboo shoot and coriander. Stir them into the mixture with the grated carrot, beansprouts, spring onions and reserved chilli mixture. Mix well.

3 Take a spring roll wrapper and cover the others with a dampened dish towel. Put the flour in a bowl with a little water to make a paste. Put a spoonful of filling in the centre of the wrapper, turn the bottom edge over and fold in the sides. Roll it almost to the top, brush the top edge with the flour paste and seal.

4 Fill the remaining wrappers. Heat the oil in a wok to 190°C/375°F or until a cube of bread browns in about 40 seconds. Fry the spring rolls, in batches, until crisp and golden. Drain on kitchen paper and serve hot with sweet chilli sauce.

Nutritional information per portion: Energy 74Kcal/310kJ; Protein 3.1g; Carbohydrate 7.2g, of which sugars 0.7g; Fat 3.8g, of which saturates 0.7g; Cholesterol 10mg; Calcium 13mg; Fibre 0.4g; Sodium 12mg.

Soups and Appetizers

For swift soups, such as those made with ready-made stock, a wok is ideal. The large surface area means rapid evaporation, so you need to keep an eye on liquid levels. An electric wok can work wonders – any preliminary cooking can be done at a high heat, then the thermostat can be turned down to a simmer. A variety of appetizers can be cooked in a wok, from Steamed Pork Buns to Salmon, Sesame and Ginger Fish Cakes.

Tofu and beansprout soup

This light and refreshing soup is quick and easy to make in the wok. The aromatic spicy broth is simmered briefly and then the tofu, beansprouts and noodles are quickly cooked. Use firm tofu as the softer variety will disintegrate during cooking.

SERVES 4

150g/5oz dried thick rice noodles

1 litre/1³⁄₄ pints/4 cups vegetable stock

1 fresh red chilli, seeded and finely sliced

15ml/1 tbsp light soy sauce

juice of 1 small lime

10ml/2 tsp palm sugar (jaggery)

5ml/1 tsp thinly sliced garlic

5ml/1 tsp finely chopped fresh root ginger

200g/7oz firm tofu

90g/3¹⁄₂ oz mung beansprouts

30ml/2 tbsp chopped fresh mint

15ml/1 tbsp chopped fresh
     coriander (cilantro)

15ml/1 tbsp chopped fresh sweet basil

50g/2oz/¹⁄₂ cup roasted peanuts

spring onion (scallion) slivers and red (bell)
     pepper slivers, to garnish (optional)

1 Place the dried thick rice noodles in a bowl and pour over enough boiling water to cover. Soak for 10–15 minutes, until soft. Drain, rinse and set aside.

2 Place the vegetable stock, finely sliced red chilli, soy sauce, lime juice, palm sugar, thinly sliced garlic and chopped fresh root ginger in a wok over a high heat.

3 Bring to the boil, then cover and reduce to a low heat. Simmer for 10–12 minutes.

4 Meanwhile, cut the firm tofu into neat cubes, using a sharp knife or cleaver. Add the tofu to the soup.

5 Add the drained noodles and mung bean sprouts to the soup and cook gently for just 2–3 minutes. Remove from the heat and stir in the herbs.

6 Roughly chop the peanuts. Ladle the soup into four individual bowls and scatter the peanuts over the top. Serve immediately, garnished with the spring onion and red pepper slivers, if you like.

Nutritional information per portion: Energy 266Kcal/1108kJ; Protein 10.5g; Carbohydrate 35.1g, of which sugars 3g; Fat 8.8g, of which saturates 1.4g; Cholesterol 0mg; Calcium 321mg; Fibre 2.4g; Sodium 115mg.

Chinese leaf, meatball and noodle broth

This wonderfully fragrant combination of spiced meatballs, noodles and vegetables cooked slowly in a richly flavoured broth makes for a very hearty, warming soup. Serve it as a main course on a cold winter evening, drizzled with chilli oil for a little extra heat.

SERVES 4

10 dried shiitake mushrooms
90g/3¹/₂oz bean thread noodles
675g/1¹/₂lb minced (ground) beef
10ml/2 tsp finely grated garlic
10ml/2 tsp finely grated fresh root ginger
1 fresh red chilli, seeded and chopped
6 spring onions (scallions), finely sliced
1 egg white
15ml/1 tbsp cornflour (cornstarch)
15ml/1 tbsp Chinese rice wine
30ml/2 tbsp sunflower oil
1.5 litres/2¹/₂ pints/6¹/₄ cups chicken
**   or beef stock**
50ml/2fl oz/¹/₄ cup light soy sauce
5ml/1 tsp caster (superfine) sugar
150g/5oz enoki mushrooms, trimmed
200g/7oz Chinese leaves (Chinese
**   cabbage) very thinly sliced**
salt and ground black pepper
sesame oil and chilli oil, to drizzle (optional)

1 Soak the dried mushrooms in 250ml/8fl oz/1 cup boiling water for 30 minutes and then squeeze dry, reserving the soaking liquid. Cut off the stems and discard, then thickly slice the caps and set aside.

2 Soak the noodles in boiling water for 3–4 minutes. Drain, rinse and set aside.

3 Process the beef, garlic, ginger, chilli, spring onions, egg white, cornflour, rice wine and seasoning in a food processor. Transfer the mixture to a bowl and divide into 30 portions, then shape each one into a ball.

4 Heat a wok over a high heat and add the oil. Fry the meatballs, in batches, for 2–3 minutes on each side until lightly browned. Drain on kitchen paper.

5 Wipe the wok clean and place over a high heat. Add the stock, soy sauce, sugar and shiitake mushrooms with the reserved soaking liquid and bring to the boil. Add the meatballs, reduce the heat and cook for 20–25 minutes.

6 Add the noodles, enoki mushrooms and cabbage and cook gently for 4–5 minutes. Serve, drizzled with sesame oil and chilli oil, if you like.

Nutritional information per portion: Energy 548Kcal/2279kJ; Protein 36.8g; Carbohydrate 24.9g, of which sugars 3g; Fat 33.3g, of which saturates 12.4g; Cholesterol 101mg; Calcium 52mg; Fibre 1.7g; Sodium 161mg.

Hot and sour soup

One of China's most popular soups, this is famed for its clever balance of flavours. The essential flavour contrast is provided by the 'hot' coming from pepper and the 'sour' from vinegar.

SERVES 6

4–6 Chinese dried mushrooms
2–3 small pieces of cloud ear (wood ear)
   mushrooms and a few golden needles
   (lily buds) (optional)
115g/4oz pork fillet (tenderloin)
45ml/3 tbsp cornflour (cornstarch)
150ml/¹/₄ pint/²/₃ cup water
15–30ml/1–2 tbsp sunflower oil
1 small onion, finely chopped
1.5 litres/2¹/₂ pints/6¹/₄ cups good
   quality beef or chicken stock, or
   2 x 300g/11oz cans consommé made
   up to the full quantity with water
150g/5oz fresh firm tofu, diced
60ml/4 tbsp rice vinegar
15ml/1 tbsp light soy sauce
1 egg, beaten
5 ml/1 tsp sesame oil
salt and ground white or black pepper
2–3 spring onions (scallions), shredded,
   to garnish

1 Place the dried mushrooms in a bowl, with the pieces of cloud ear and the golden needles, if using. Cover with warm water and leave to soak for about 30 minutes. Drain, reserving the soaking water. Cut off and discard the stems and slice the caps finely. Trim away any tough stem from the wood ears, then chop them finely. Using kitchen string, tie the golden needles into a bundle.

2 Cut the pork fillet into fine strips. Lightly dust the strips with some of the cornflour; mix the remaining cornflour with the water to form a smooth paste.

3 Heat the oil in a wok and fry the onion until soft. Increase the heat and fry the pork until it changes colour. Add the stock or consommé, mushrooms, soaking water, and cloud ears and golden needles, if using. Bring to the boil, then simmer for 15 minutes. Discard the golden needles, lower the heat and stir in the cornflour paste to thicken. Add the tofu, vinegar, soy sauce, and salt and pepper.

4 Bring the soup to just below boiling point, then drizzle in the beaten egg by letting it drop from a whisk so that it forms threads in the soup. Stir in the sesame oil and serve at once, garnished with spring onion shreds.

Nutritional information per portion: Energy 103Kcal/429kJ; Protein 7.3g; Carbohydrate 7.3g, of which sugars 0.3g; Fat 5.1g, of which saturates 1g; Cholesterol 44mg; Calcium 135mg; Fibre 0g; Sodium 208mg.

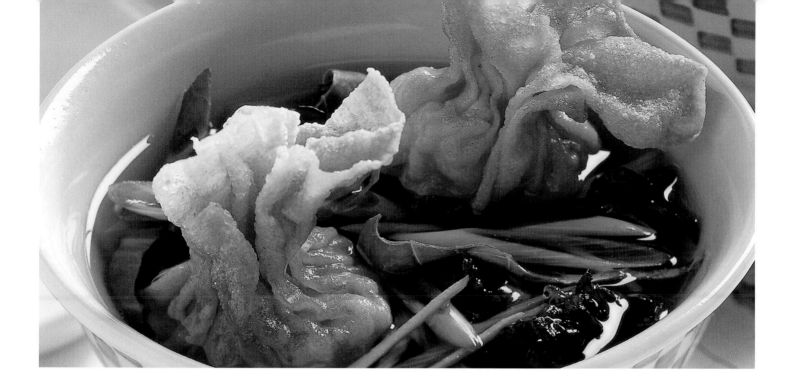

Crispy wonton soup

The freshly cooked crispy wontons are supposed to sizzle and 'sing' as the hot fat hits the soup, so add them just before you take the bowls to the table.

SERVES 6

2 cloud ear (wood ear) mushrooms,
  soaked for 30 minutes in warm water
50g/2oz canned bamboo shoots
2 rich-green inner spring greens leaves
1.2 litres/2 pints/5 cups home-made
  chicken stock
2.5cm/1in piece fresh root ginger, peeled
  and grated
4 spring onions (scallions), chopped
25ml/1¹/₂ tbsp dark soy sauce
2.5ml/¹/₂ tsp sesame oil
salt and ground black pepper

FOR THE FILLED WONTONS
5ml/1 tsp sesame oil
¹/₂ small onion, finely chopped
10 canned water chestnuts, drained
  and finely chopped
115g/4oz finely minced (ground) pork
24 wonton wrappers
groundnut (peanut) oil, for deep-frying

1 Make the filled wontons. Heat the sesame oil in a small pan, add the onion, water chestnuts and pork and fry, stirring occasionally, until the meat is no longer pink. Transfer into a bowl, season to taste and leave to cool.

2 Dampen the edges of a wonton wrapper. Place the other wrappers under a slightly dampened dish towel so that they don't dry out. Place about 5ml/1 tsp of the filling in the centre of the wrapper. Gather it up like a purse and twist the top or roll up like a baby spring roll. Repeat for the remaining wontons.

3 To make the soup, drain the cloud ears, discarding the soaking liquid. Trim away any rough stems, then slice thinly. Slice the bamboo shoots and finely shred the spring greens. Bring the stock to the boil, add the ginger and spring onions and simmer for 3 minutes. Add the cloud ears, spring greens, bamboo shoots and soy sauce. Simmer for 10 minutes, then stir in the sesame oil. Season with salt and pepper, cover and keep hot.

4 Heat the oil in a wok to 190°C/375°F and deep-fry the wontons for 3–4 minutes, until crisp and golden. Share among bowls of the soup and serve.

Nutritional information per portion: Energy 108Kcal/456kJ; Protein 6.3g; Carbohydrate 14.4g, of which sugars 1.4g; Fat 3.3g, of which saturates 0.9g; Cholesterol 13mg; Calcium 69mg; Fibre 1.4g; Sodium 249mg.

Balinese vegetable soup

The Balinese base this popular soup on beans, but any seasonal vegetables can be added or substituted. The recipe also includes shrimp paste, which is known locally as terasi.

SERVES 8

225g/8oz green beans

1.2 litres/2 pints/5 cups lightly salted water

1 garlic clove, roughly chopped

2 macadamia nuts or 4 almonds, finely chopped

1cm/¹/₂in cube shrimp paste

10–15ml/2–3 tsp coriander seeds, dry-fried

30ml/2 tbsp vegetable oil

1 onion, finely sliced

400ml/14fl oz can coconut milk

2 bay leaves

225g/8oz/4 cups beansprouts

8 thin lemon wedges

30ml/2 tbsp lemon juice

salt and ground black pepper

1 Trim the beans, reserving a few whole for garnish, and cut into small pieces. Bring the salted water to the boil, add the beans and cook for 3–4 minutes. Drain, reserving the cooking water.

2 Finely grind the chopped garlic, macadamia nuts or almonds, shrimp paste and coriander seeds to a paste using a pestle and mortar or in a food processor.

3 Heat a wok, add the oil, and fry the onion until transparent. Remove with a slotted spoon. Add the nut mixture to the wok and fry for 2 minutes. Do not let it brown. Pour in the reserved vegetable water. Spoon off 45–60ml/3–4 tbsp of the cream from the coconut milk. Set aside. Add the remaining milk to the wok, bring to the boil and add the bay leaves. Cook, uncovered, for 15–20 minutes.

4 Just before serving, reserve a few fried onions and beansprouts and stir the rest into the soup along with the trimmed beans. Add the lemon wedges, reserved coconut cream, lemon juice and seasoning; warm through, stirring well. Serve in individual bowls, garnished with the reserved beans, onion and beansprouts.

Nutritional information per portion: Energy 63Kcal/263kJ; Protein 2.2g; Carbohydrate 5.2g, of which sugars 4.2g; Fat 3.9g, of which saturates 0.5g; Cholesterol 3mg; Calcium 43mg; Fibre 1.2g; Sodium 84mg.

Steamed oysters with tomato and cucumber salsa

A plate of steamed fresh oysters makes a delicious and impressive appetizer and is surprisingly easy to prepare. The zesty, aromatic salsa complements the delicate oysters perfectly.

SERVES 4

30ml/2 tbsp sunflower oil
1 garlic clove, crushed
15ml/1 tbsp light soy sauce
12–16 oysters
sea salt, to serve

FOR THE SALSA
1 ripe plum tomato, seeds removed
1/2 small cucumber
1/4 small red onion
15ml/1 tbsp very finely chopped coriander (cilantro)
1 small red chilli, seeded and very finely chopped
juice of 1–2 limes
salt and ground black pepper

1 First prepare the salsa. Finely dice the tomato, cucumber and red onion. Place in a bowl with the chopped coriander and red chilli. Add the lime juice to the bowl and season to taste. Set aside (at room temperature) for 15–20 minutes.

2 In a separate bowl, mix together the sunflower oil, garlic and soy sauce.

3 Carefully open the oysters using a special oyster knife or a strong knife with a short, blunt blade. Arrange the oysters in their half shells in a bamboo steamer and spoon over the sauce. Cover the steamer and place over a wok of simmering water. Steam the oysters for 2–3 minutes. Serve the oysters on a bed of sea salt, topped with a teaspoonful of salsa each.

COOK'S TIP
To de-seed the tomato, cut it in half around the middle rather than over the top, and then scoop out the seeds using a teaspoon.

Nutritional information per portion: Energy 82Kcal/339kJ; Protein 4.5g; Carbohydrate 2.4g, of which sugars 1.3g; Fat 6.1g, of which saturates 0.8g; Cholesterol 21mg; Calcium 60mg; Fibre 0.4g; Sodium 461mg.

Parchment-wrapped prawns

These succulent pink prawns coated in a fragrant spice paste make the perfect dish for informal entertaining. Serve the prawns in their paper parcels and allow your guests to unwrap them at the table and enjoy the aroma of Thai spices as the parcel is opened.

SERVES 4

2 lemon grass stalks, very finely chopped
5ml/1 tsp galangal, very finely chopped
4 garlic cloves, finely chopped
finely grated rind and juice of 1 lime
4 spring onions (scallions), chopped
10ml/2 tsp palm sugar (jaggery)
15ml/1 tbsp soy sauce
5ml/1 tsp Thai fish sauce
5ml/1 tsp chilli oil
45ml/3 tbsp chopped fresh coriander (cilantro) leaves
30ml/2 tbsp chopped fresh Thai basil leaves
1kg/2¼lb raw tiger prawns (jumbo shrimp), heads and shells removed but with tails left on
basil leaves and lime wedges, to garnish

1 Place the lemon grass, galangal, garlic, lime rind and juice and spring onions in a food processor or blender. Blend in short bursts until the mixture forms a coarse paste.

2 Transfer the paste to a large bowl and stir in the palm sugar, soy sauce, fish sauce, chilli oil and herbs.

3 Add the prawns to the paste and toss to coat evenly. Cover and marinate in the refrigerator for 30 minutes–1 hour.

4 Cut out eight 20cm/8in squares of baking parchment. Place one-eighth of the prawn mixture in the centre of each one, then fold over the edges and twist together to create a sealed parcel.

5 Place the parcels in a large bamboo steamer, cover and steam over a wok of simmering water for 10 minutes, or until the prawns are just cooked through. Serve immediately garnished with basil leaves and lime wedges.

Nutritional information per portion: Energy 169Kcal/713kJ; Protein 35.4g; Carbohydrate 2.4g, of which sugars 2.4g; Fat 2g, of which saturates 0.3g; Cholesterol 390mg; Calcium 163mg; Fibre 0.2g; Sodium 381mg.

Seaweed-wrapped prawn rolls

Japanese nori seaweed is used to enclose the fragrant filling of prawns, water chestnuts, and fresh herbs and spices in these pretty steamed rolls. Ideal for entertaining, the rolls can be prepared in advance and stored in the refrigerator until ready to steam.

SERVES 4

675g/1½lb raw tiger prawns (jumbo shrimp), peeled and deveined
5ml/1 tsp finely chopped kaffir lime leaves
1 red chilli, seeded and chopped
5ml/1 tsp finely grated garlic clove
5ml/1 tsp finely grated root ginger
5ml/1 tsp finely grated lime rind
60ml/4 tbsp fresh coriander (cilantro), very finely chopped
1 egg white, lightly beaten
30ml/2 tbsp chopped water chestnuts
4 sheets of nori
salt and ground black pepper
kecap manis or soy sauce, to serve

1 Put the prawns in a food processor with the lime leaves, red chilli, garlic, ginger, lime rind and coriander. Process until smooth, add the egg white and water chestnuts, season and process again until combined. Transfer to a bowl, and chill, covered, for 3–4 hours.

2 Lay the nori sheets on a clean, dry surface and spread the prawn mixture over each sheet, leaving a 2cm/¾in border at one end. Roll up to form tight rolls, wrap in clear film (plastic wrap) and chill for 2–3 hours.

3 Unwrap the rolls and place on a board. Using a sharp knife, cut each roll into 2cm/¾in lengths. Place the slices in a baking parchment-lined bamboo steamer, cover and place over a wok of simmering water (making sure the water does not touch the steamer).

4 Steam the rolls for 6–8 minutes, or until cooked through. Serve the prawn rolls warm or at room temperature with a dish of kecap manis or soy sauce for dipping.

Nutritional information per portion: Energy 136Kcal/574kJ; Protein 30.8g; Carbohydrate 0.4g, of which sugars 0.4g; Fat 1.2g, of which saturates 0.2g; Cholesterol 329mg; Calcium 162mg; Fibre 0.7g; Sodium 345mg.

Crab dim sum with Chinese chives

These delectable Chinese-style dumplings have a wonderfully sticky texture and make a perfect appetizer. You can make them in advance, storing them in the refrigerator until ready to cook.

SERVES 4

150g/5oz fresh white crab meat
115g/4oz minced (ground) pork
30ml/2 tbsp chopped Chinese chives
15ml/1 tbsp finely chopped red (bell) pepper
30ml/2 tbsp sweet chilli sauce
30ml/2 tbsp hoisin sauce
24 fresh dumpling wrappers (available from Asian stores)
Chinese chives, to garnish
chilli oil and soy sauce, to serve

1 Place the crab meat, pork and chopped chives in a bowl. Add the red pepper, sweet chilli and hoisin sauces.

2 Working with two to three wrappers at a time, put a spoonful of the mixture on to each wrapper. Brush the edges of the wrapper with water and fold over to form a half-moon shape. Press and pleat the edges to seal, and flatten. Cover with a clean, damp dish towel and make the rest.

3 Put the dumplings on three lightly oiled plates and fit inside three tiers of a bamboo steamer. Cover the steamer and place over a wok of simmering water (making sure the water doesn't touch the steamer) for 8–10 minutes, or until the dumplings are cooked through and slightly translucent.

4 Serve the dumplings garnished with Chinese chives and with chilli oil and soy sauce for dipping.

Nutritional information per portion: Energy 166Kcal/700kJ; Protein 14.7g; Carbohydrate 20.5g, of which sugars 1.4g; Fat 3.3g, of which saturates 1.1g; Cholesterol 46mg; Calcium 83mg; Fibre 0.8g; Sodium 287mg.

Lemon, chilli and herb steamed razor clams

Razor clams have beautiful tubular shells and make a wonderful, unusual starter. Here they are lightly steamed and tossed in a fragrant Italian-style dressing. Serve with crusty bread to mop up the juices.

SERVES 4

12 razor clams
90–120ml/6–8 tbsp extra virgin olive oil
finely grated rind and juice of
    1 small lemon
2 garlic cloves, very finely grated
1 red chilli, seeded and very
    finely chopped
60ml/4 tbsp chopped flat leaf parsley
salt and ground black pepper
mixed salad leaves and crusty bread,
    to serve

1 Wash the razor clams well in plently of cold running water. Drain and arrange half the clams in a steamer, with the hinge side down.

2 Pour 5cm/2in water into a wok and bring to the boil. Carefully balance the steamer over the water and cover tightly. Steam for 3–4 minutes until the clams have opened. Keep them warm while you steam the rest.

3 In a bowl, mix together the olive oil, grated lemon rind and juice, grated garlic, chopped red chilli and flat leaf parsley.

4 Season the dressing well with salt and pepper. Arrange the steamed razor clams on plates and spoon the mixture over. Serve them immediately with a crisp mixed-leaf salad and crusty bread.

Nutritional information per portion: Energy 188Kcal/775kJ; Protein 6.1g; Carbohydrate 2.9g, of which sugars 0.5g; Fat 16.9g, of which saturates 2.4g; Cholesterol 20mg; Calcium 47mg; Fibre 1.1g; Sodium 364mg.

Herb and chilli fish custards

These pretty little custards make an unusual, beautifully presented and rather exotic appetizer for a dinner party, and they cook perfectly in the wok.

SERVES 4

2 eggs
200ml/7fl oz/scant 1 cup
   coconut cream
60ml/4 tbsp chopped fresh
   coriander (cilantro)
1 fresh red chilli, seeded and sliced
15ml/1 tbsp finely chopped lemon grass
2 kaffir lime leaves, finely shredded
30ml/2 tbsp Thai red curry paste
1 garlic clove, crushed

5ml/1 tsp finely grated ginger
2 spring onions (scallions), finely sliced
300g/11oz mixed firm white fish fillets
   (cod, halibut or haddock), skinned
200g/7oz raw tiger prawns (jumbo shrimp),
   peeled and deveined
4–6 pandanus leaves
salt and ground black pepper
shredded cucumber, steamed rice and
   soy sauce, to serve

1 Beat the eggs in a bowl, then stir in the coconut cream, coriander, chilli, lemon grass, lime leaves, curry paste, garlic, ginger and spring onions. Finely chop the fish and roughly chop the prawns and add to the egg mixture. Stir well and season.

2 Grease four ramekins and line them with the pandanus leaves. Divide the fish mixture between them, then arrange in a bamboo steamer.

3 Pour 5cm/2in water into a wok and bring to the boil. Suspend the steamer over the water, cover, reduce the heat to low and steam for 25–30 minutes, or until the fish is cooked through.

4 Serve the custards immediately with shredded cucumber, a little steamed rice and soy sauce.

COOK'S TIP
Pandanus leaves keep the custards from drying out, and have a floral flavour that is transferred to the food, but they are not edible and should be discarded after the cooking.

Nutritional information per portion: Energy 150Kcal/632kJ; Protein 26.2g; Carbohydrate 2.8g, of which sugars 2.8g; Fat 3.9g, of which saturates 1g; Cholesterol 227mg; Calcium 100mg; Fibre 0.6g; Sodium 234mg.

Salmon, sesame and ginger fish cakes

These light fish cakes are scented with the exotic flavours of sesame, lime and ginger. They make a tempting appetizer served simply with a wedge of lime for squeezing over, but are also perfect for a light lunch or supper, served with a crunchy, refreshing salad.

MAKES 25

500g/1¼lb salmon fillet, skinned
  and boned
45ml/3 tbsp dried breadcrumbs
30ml/2 tbsp mayonnaise
30ml/2 tbsp sesame seeds
30ml/2 tbsp light soy sauce
finely grated rind of 2 limes
10ml/2 tsp finely grated fresh root ginger
4 spring onions (scallions), finely sliced
vegetable oil, for shallow-frying
salt and ground black pepper
spring onions (scallions), to garnish
lime wedges, to serve

1 Finely chop the salmon and place in a bowl. Add the breadcrumbs, mayonnaise, sesame seeds, soy sauce, lime rind, ginger and spring onions and use your fingers to mix well.

2 With wet hands, divide the mixture into 25 portions and shape each into a small round cake. Place the cakes on a baking sheet, lined with baking parchment. Cover and chill for at least two hours. They can be left overnight.

3 When you are ready to cook the fish cakes, heat about 5cm/2in vegetable oil in a wok and fry the fish cakes, in batches, over a medium heat, for 2–3 minutes on each side.

4 Drain the fish cakes well on kitchen paper and serve either warm or at room temperature, garnished with spring onion slivers, with plenty of lime wedges for squeezing over.

Nutritional information per portion: Energy 83Kcal/343kJ; Protein 4.6g; Carbohydrate 1.6g, of which sugars 0.2g; Fat 6.5g, of which saturates 0.9g; Cholesterol 11mg; Calcium 16mg; Fibre 0.2g; Sodium 117mg.

Lettuce parcels

Known as Sang Choy in Hong Kong, this is a popular 'assemble-it-yourself' treat. The filling – an imaginative blend of textures and flavours – is served with crisp lettuce leaves, which are spread with hoisin sauce and used as wrappers.

SERVES 6

2 boneless chicken breast portions, total weight about 350g/12oz

4 Chinese dried mushrooms, soaked for 30 minutes in warm water to cover

30ml/2 tbsp vegetable oil

2 garlic cloves, crushed

6 drained canned water chestnuts, thinly sliced

30ml/2 tbsp light soy sauce

5ml/1 tsp Sichuan peppercorns, dry fried and crushed

4 spring onions (scallions), finely chopped

5ml/1 tsp sesame oil

vegetable oil, for deep-frying

50g/2oz cellophane noodles

salt and ground black pepper (optional)

1 crisp lettuce and 60ml/4 tbsp hoisin sauce, to serve

1 Remove the skin from the chicken breasts, pat dry and set aside. Chop the chicken into thin strips. Drain the soaked mushrooms. Cut off and discard the mushroom stems; slice the caps finely and set aside.

2 Heat the oil in a wok. Add the garlic, then add the chicken and stir-fry until the pieces are cooked through and no longer pink. Add the sliced mushrooms, water chestnuts, soy sauce and peppercorns. Toss for 2–3 minutes, then season, if needed. Stir in half of the spring onions, then the sesame oil. Remove from the heat and keep warm.

3 Heat the oil for deep-frying to 190°C/375°F. Cut the chicken skin into strips, deep-fry until very crisp then drain on kitchen paper. Add the noodles to the hot oil, deep-fry until crisp. Drain on kitchen paper.

4 Crush the noodles and put in a serving dish. Top with the chicken skin, chicken mixture and remaining spring onions. Toss to mix. Arrange the lettuce leaves on a platter.

5 Guests can take one or two lettuce leaves, spread the inside with hoisin sauce and add a spoonful of filling, rolling them into a parcel.

Nutritional information per portion: Energy 195Kcal/821kJ; Protein 28.7g; Carbohydrate 7.5g, of which sugars 0.6g; Fat 5.5g, of which saturates 0.9g; Cholesterol 82mg; Calcium 11mg; Fibre 0.1g; Sodium 428mg.

Son-in-law eggs

The fascinating name of this dish comes from a story about a prospective bridegroom who, wanting to impress his future mother-in-law, devised a recipe based on the only dish he could make – boiled eggs.

SERVES 4–6

30ml/2 tbsp vegetable oil
6 shallots, thinly sliced
6 garlic cloves, thinly sliced
6 fresh red chillies, sliced
oil, for deep-frying
6 hard-boiled eggs, shelled
salad leaves, to serve
sprigs of fresh coriander (cilantro),
    to garnish

FOR THE SAUCE

75g/3oz/6 tbsp palm sugar (jaggery)
    or light muscovado (brown) sugar
75ml/5 tbsp Thai fish sauce
90ml/6 tbsp tamarind juice, made by
    mixing tamarind paste with a little
    warm water

1 Make the sauce. Put the sugar, Thai fish sauce and tamarind juice in a pan. Bring to the boil, stirring until the sugar dissolves, then lower the heat and simmer for 5 minutes. Taste and add more sugar, fish sauce or tamarind juice, if needed. Transfer the sauce to a bowl.

2 Heat the vegetable oil in a frying pan and cook the sliced shallots, garlic and chillies for 5 minutes. Transfer to a bowl.

3 Heat the oil in a wok to 190°C/375°F or until a cube of bread, added to the oil, browns in about 40 seconds. Deep-fry the eggs until golden. Remove and drain on kitchen paper.

4 Cut the eggs into quarters and arrange them on a bed of leaves. Drizzle with the sauce and sprinkle over the shallot mixture. Garnish with coriander sprigs and serve immediately.

Nutritional information per portion: Energy 180Kcal/752kJ; Protein 7.3g; Carbohydrate 18g, of which sugars 17.1g; Fat 9.4g, of which saturates 2g; Cholesterol 190mg; Calcium 50mg; Fibre 0.5g; Sodium 666mg.

Steamed pork buns

These deliciously light stuffed buns are a popular street snack sold throughout China. They make an unusual alternative to rice and, once cooked, can be reheated in a steamer.

SERVES 4

30ml/2 tbsp golden caster
   (superfine) sugar
10ml/2 tsp dried yeast
300g/11oz/2³/₄ cups plain
   (all-purpose) flour
30ml/2 tbsp sunflower oil
10ml/2 tsp baking powder

FOR THE FILLING
250g/9oz sausage meat from
   pork sausages
15ml/1 tbsp barbecue sauce
30ml/2 tbsp oyster sauce
15ml/1 tbsp sweet chilli sauce
15ml/1 tbsp Chinese rice wine
15ml/1 tbsp hoisin sauce
5ml/1 tsp chilli oil

1 To make the dough, pour 250ml/8fl oz/1 cup warm water into a mixing bowl. Add the sugar and stir to dissolve. Stir in the yeast, cover and leave in a warm place for 15 minutes. Sift the flour into a large mixing bowl and make a well in the centre. Add the sugar and yeast mixture to it with the sunflower oil. Stir the mixture together using your fingers and turn out on to a lightly floured surface.

2 Knead the dough for 8–10 minutes until elastic. Put in a lightly oiled bowl, cover with a dish towel and leave to rise in a warm place for 3–4 hours. When risen, place the dough on a lightly floured surface and shape into a large circle. Sprinkle the baking powder in the centre, bring in all the edges and knead for 6–8 minutes. Divide into 12 balls, cover with a damp dish towel and set aside.

3 Put the sausage meat into a bowl and mix in the other filling ingredients with your fingers. Press each dough ball into a 12cm/4¹/₂ in round. Spoon the mixture in the centre of each round, bring the edges up to the centre, and seal.

4 Steam the buns in a covered bamboo steamer over a wok of simmering water for 20–25 minutes, until they are puffed up and the pork is cooked through.

Nutritional information per portion: Energy 588Kcal/2468kJ; Protein 14g; Carbohydrate 76.4g, of which sugars 14g; Fat 27.3g, of which saturates 8.5g; Cholesterol 29mg; Calcium 137mg; Fibre 2.8g; Sodium 722mg.

Stuffed Thai omelettes

Omelettes are usually cooked in a flat pan, but a wok works equally well. The hot chilli in this recipe makes an interesting contrasting flavour to the delicate egg.

SERVES 4

30ml/2 tbsp groundnut (peanut) oil
2 garlic cloves, finely chopped
1 small onion, finely chopped
225g/8oz minced (ground) pork
30ml/2 tbsp Thai fish sauce
5ml/1 tsp granulated (white) sugar
2 tomatoes, peeled and chopped
15ml/1 tbsp chopped fresh
    coriander (cilantro)
ground black pepper
fresh coriander (cilantro) sprigs and
    sliced fresh red chillies, to garnish

FOR THE OMELETTES

5 eggs
15ml/1 tbsp Thai fish sauce
30ml/2 tbsp groundnut (peanut) oil

1 Heat the oil in a wok, add the garlic and onion and cook over a medium heat for 3–4 minutes, until soft. Add the pork and cook until lightly browned.

2 Stir in the Thai fish sauce, sugar and tomatoes and season with pepper. Simmer over a low heat until thickened. Mix in the coriander. Remove from the heat and cover.

3 Make the omelettes. Put the eggs and Thai fish sauce in a bowl and beat lightly with a fork. Heat 15ml/ 1 tbsp of the oil in a frying pan or wok over a medium heat.

4 When the oil is very hot, but not smoking, add half the egg mixture and immediately tilt the wok, spreading it into a thin, even layer over the base. Cook over a medium heat until just set and the underside is golden.

5 Spoon half the filling into the centre of the omelette. Fold into a square parcel by bringing the opposite sides of the omelette together. Slide on to a serving dish, folded side down. Make another parcel in the same way.

6 Halve the omelettes to serve and garnish with the coriander and chillies.

Nutritional information per portion: Energy 305Kcal/1267kJ; Protein 19.2g; Carbohydrate 4.8g, of which sugars 4.5g; Fat 23.6g, of which saturates 5.7g; Cholesterol 275mg; Calcium 48mg; Fibre 0.7g; Sodium 130mg.

Golden corn cakes with aioli

East meets West in these crisp, mouthwatering cakes that bring together creamy goat's cheese and tangy Mediterranean peppers in the Asian wok.

SERVES 4

300g/11oz/scant 2 cups fresh
   corn kernels
200g/7oz/scant 1 cup ricotta cheese
200g/7oz/scant 1 cup goat's
   cheese, crumbled
30ml/2 tbsp thyme leaves
50g/2oz/½ cup plain (all-purpose) flour
1 large (US extra large) egg,
   lightly beaten
150g/5oz natural dried breadcrumbs
vegetable oil, for deep-frying
salt and ground black pepper

FOR THE AIOLI

2 red (bell) peppers, halved and seeded
2 garlic cloves, crushed
250ml/8fl oz/1 cup mayonnaise

1 Make the aioli. Preheat the grill (broiler) to medium-high and cook the peppers, skin-side up, for 8–10 minutes, until the skins blister. Put them in a plastic bag for 10 minutes and then peel away the skin. Place the flesh in a food processor with the garlic and mayonnaise and blend until fairly smooth. Transfer to a bowl and chill.

2 In a bowl, combine the corn, cheeses and thyme, then stir in the flour and egg and season well.

3 Place the breadcrumbs on a plate. Roll 15ml/1 tbsp of the corn mixture into a ball, flatten slightly and coat in the breadcrumbs. Place on baking parchment and chill for 30 minutes.

4 Fill a wok one-third full of oil and heat to 180°C/350°F (or until a cube of bread, dropped into the oil, browns in about 45 seconds). Working in batches, deep-fry the corn cakes for 1–2 minutes, until golden. Drain well on kitchen paper and serve with the aioli.

Nutritional information per portion: Energy 1048Kcal/4363kJ; Protein 26.1g; Carbohydrate 68.2g, of which sugars 17.3g; Fat 76.5g, of which saturates 22g; Cholesterol 162mg; Calcium 156mg; Fibre 3.9g; Sodium 1091mg.

Shellfish and Fish

Some of the finest wok recipes feature fish and shellfish, since they lend themselves so perfectly to steaming, stir-frying and deep-frying. Whether it's fish in a creamy sauce, or something with a crispy coating, the wok is the perfect utensil. With a large wok, you can steam fish whole, wrapped in banana leaves to seal in the flavours. For smaller portions, use a bamboo steamer, and steam your vegetables at the same time.

Stir-fried prawns with tamarind

This dish perfectly illustrates the versatility of the wok, used first for deep-frying, then dry-frying, and then stir-frying. Leave a few prawns in their shells for visual effect.

SERVES 4–6

15ml/1 tbsp chopped garlic
30ml/2 tbsp sliced shallots
vegetable oil, for deep-frying
6 dried red chillies
30ml/2 tbsp vegetable oil
30ml/2 tbsp chopped onion
30ml/2 tbsp palm sugar (jaggery)
    or light muscovado (brown) sugar
30ml/2 tbsp chicken stock or water
15ml/1 tbsp Thai fish sauce
90ml/6 tbsp tamarind juice, made
    by mixing tamarind paste with
    warm water
450g/1lb prawns (shrimp), peeled
2 spring onions (scallions), chopped,
    to garnish

1 Deep-fry the garlic and sliced shallots, drain and set aside. Drain the oil from the wok and wipe clean.

2 Add the dried chillies and dry-fry by pressing them against the surface of the wok with a spatula, turning them occasionally. Do not let them burn. Set aside to cool slightly.

3 Add the vegetable oil to the wok and reheat. Add the onion and cook over a medium heat, stirring occasionally, for 2–3 minutes, until softened and golden brown.

4 Add the sugar, chicken stock or water, Thai fish sauce, dry-fried red chillies and tamarind juice, stirring the mixture until all of the sugar has dissolved. Bring the mixture to the boil, then lower the heat slightly.

5 Add the prawns, and deep-fried garlic and shallots to the wok. Toss them over the heat for 3–4 minutes, until the prawns are pink and cooked through. Garnish with the spring onions and serve.

Nutritional information per portion: Energy 117Kcal/493kJ; Protein 13.6g; Carbohydrate 6.8g, of which sugars 6.4g; Fat 4.2g, of which saturates 0.5g; Cholesterol 146mg; Calcium 69mg; Fibre 0.3g; Sodium 144mg.

Fragrant tiger prawns with dill

This elegant dish has a fresh, light flavour and can be served for a dinner party but is equally good as a simple supper. The delicate fresh prawns are complemented by mild cucumber and fragrant dill.

SERVES 4–6

500g/1¼lb raw tiger prawns
(jumbo shrimp), heads and shells
removed but tails left on
500g/1¼lb cucumber
30ml/2 tbsp butter
15ml/1 tbsp olive oil
15ml/1 tbsp finely chopped garlic
45ml/3 tbsp chopped fresh dill
juice of 1 lemon
salt and ground black pepper
steamed rice or noodles, to serve

1 Using a small, sharp knife, carefully make a shallow slit along the back of each prawn and use the point of the knife to remove the black vein. Set the prawns aside.

2 Peel the cucumber and slice in half lengthways. Using a small teaspoon, gently scoop out all the seeds and discard. Cut the cucumber into 4 x 1cm/1½ x ½in sticks.

3 Heat a wok over a high heat, then add the butter and oil.

4 When the butter has melted, add the cucumber and garlic and fry over a high heat, stirring, for 2–3 minutes.

5 Add the prawns and stir-fry over a high heat for 3–4 minutes, until the prawns turn pink and are just cooked through, then remove from the heat.

6 Add the fresh dill and lemon juice to the wok and toss to combine. Season well with salt and ground black pepper and serve immediately with steamed rice or noodles.

Nutritional information per portion: Energy 192Kcal/798kJ; Protein 23.2g; Carbohydrate 2.5g, of which sugars 1.9g; Fat 9.8g, of which saturates 4.4g; Cholesterol 260mg; Calcium 123mg; Fibre 0.9g; Sodium 287mg.

Curried seafood with coconut milk

This quick curry is based on a Thai classic. The lovely green colour comes from the finely chopped chilli and fresh herbs added during the last few moments of cooking.

SERVES 4

225g/8oz small ready-prepared squid
225g/8oz raw tiger prawns (jumbo shrimp)
400ml/14fl oz/1²/₃ cups coconut milk
2 kaffir lime leaves, finely shredded
30ml/2 tbsp Thai fish sauce
450g/1lb firm white fish fillets, skinned,
    boned and cut into chunks
2 fresh green chillies, seeded and
    finely chopped
30ml/2 tbsp torn fresh basil or coriander
    (cilantro) leaves
squeeze of fresh lime juice
cooked Thai jasmine rice, to serve

FOR THE CURRY PASTE

6 spring onions (scallions), coarsely chopped
4 fresh coriander (cilantro) stems, coarsely
    chopped, plus 45ml/3 tbsp chopped fresh
    coriander (cilantro)
4 kaffir lime leaves, shredded
8 fresh green chillies, seeded and
    coarsely chopped
1 lemon grass stalk, coarsely chopped
2.5cm/1in piece fresh root ginger, peeled
    and coarsely chopped
45ml/3 tbsp chopped fresh basil
15ml/1 tbsp vegetable oil

1 Put all the curry paste ingredients, except the oil, in a food processor and process to a paste. Alternatively, pound together using a pestle and mortar. Stir in the oil. Rinse the squid and pat dry with kitchen paper. Cut the bodies into rings and halve the tentacles, if necessary.

2 Heat a wok until hot, add the prawns and stir-fry, without any oil, for about 4 minutes, until they turn pink. Remove the prawns from the wok and leave to cool slightly, then peel off the shells, saving a few with shells on for the garnish. Make a slit along the back of each one and remove the black vein.

3 Pour the coconut milk into the wok, then bring to the boil over a medium heat, stirring constantly. Add 30ml/2 tbsp of curry paste, the shredded lime leaves and fish sauce and stir well. Reduce the heat and simmer gently for about 10 minutes. Add the squid, prawns and chunks of fish and cook for about 2 minutes, until tender. Take care not to overcook the squid as it will become tough very quickly.

4 Just before serving, stir in the chillies and basil or coriander. Taste and adjust the flavour with a squeeze of lime juice. Garnish with the prawns left in their shells, and serve with Thai jasmine rice.

Nutritional information per portion: Energy 238Kcal/1005kJ; Protein 40.6g; Carbohydrate 7g, of which sugars 6.2g; Fat 5.5g, of which saturates 0.9g; Cholesterol 288mg; Calcium 145mg; Fibre 1.4g; Sodium 622mg.

Curried prawns in coconut milk

If you use canned coconut milk and bought curry paste, this is one of the quickest and easiest dishes there is. Served with noodles, it makes the perfect light supper.

SERVES 4–6

600ml/1 pint/2¹/₂ cups coconut milk

30ml/2 tbsp yellow curry paste
(see cook's tip)

15ml/1 tbsp Thai fish sauce

2.5ml/¹/₂ tsp salt

5ml/1 tsp caster (superfine) sugar

450g/1lb raw king prawns (jumbo
shrimp) peeled, thawed if frozen

225g/8oz cherry tomatoes

¹/₂ fresh yellow and orange (bell) pepper,
seeded and cut into thin strips, plus
chives and juice of ¹/₂ lime, to garnish

1 Put half the coconut milk in a wok and bring to the boil. Add the yellow curry paste, stir well, then lower the heat and simmer for about 10 minutes.

2 Add the Thai fish sauce, salt, sugar and remaining coconut milk. Simmer for 5 minutes more, stirring frequently. Add the prawns and cherry tomatoes. Simmer very gently for about 5 minutes until the prawns are pink and tender.

3 Serve, sprinkled with lime juice and garnished with the pepper and chives.

COOK'S TIP

To make yellow curry paste, put into a food processor or blender 6–8 fresh yellow chillies, the chopped base of 1 lemon grass stalk, 4 chopped shallots, 4 chopped garlic cloves, 15ml/1 tbsp chopped peeled fresh root ginger, 5ml/1 tsp coriander seeds, 5ml/1 tsp mustard powder, 5ml/1 tsp salt, 2.5ml/¹/₂ tsp ground cinnamon, 15ml/1 tbsp soft light brown sugar and 30ml/2 tbsp sunflower oil. Process to a paste, scrape into a glass jar, cover and keep in the refrigerator.

Nutritional information per portion: Energy 99Kcal/421kJ; Protein 13.8g; Carbohydrate 6.9g, of which sugars 6.9g; Fat 2g, of which saturates 0.5g; Cholesterol 146mg; Calcium 92mg; Fibre 0.4g; Sodium 375mg.

Sambal goreng with prawns

Sambal goreng is an immensely adaptable sauce. It is used here with prawns and green pepper, but you could add fine strips of calf's liver, chicken livers, tomatoes, green beans or hard-boiled eggs.

SERVES 4–6

350g/12oz peeled cooked prawns (shrimp)
1 green (bell) pepper, seeded and sliced
60ml/4 tbsp tamarind juice
pinch of caster (superfine) sugar
45ml/3 tbsp coconut milk or coconut cream
strips of lime rind and red onion slices,
    to garnish
boiled or steamed rice

FOR THE SAMBAL GORENG

2.5cm/1in cube shrimp paste
2 onions, roughly chopped
2 garlic cloves, roughly chopped
2.5cm/1in piece fresh galangal
10ml/2 tsp chilli sambal or 2 fresh red
    chillies, seeded and sliced
1.5ml/¼ tsp salt
30ml/2 tbsp vegetable oil
45ml/3 tbsp tomato purée (paste)
600ml/1 pint/2½ cups vegetable stock
    or water

1 Make the sambal goreng. Grind the shrimp paste with the onions and garlic using a mortar and pestle. Alternatively, put in a food processor and process to a paste. Peel and slice the galangal, and add it to the mixture with the chilli sambal or sliced chillies and salt. Process or pound to a fine paste.

2 Heat the oil in a wok or frying pan and fry the paste for 1–2 minutes, without browning, until the mixture gives off a rich aroma. Stir in the tomato purée and the stock or water and cook for 10 minutes. Ladle half the sauce into a bowl and leave to cool. Save the leftover sauce for another recipe.

3 Add the prawns and green pepper to the remaining sauce. Cook over a medium heat for 3–4 minutes, then stir in the tamarind juice, sugar and coconut milk or cream. Spoon into warmed serving bowls and garnish with strips of lime rind and sliced red onion. Serve at once with boiled or steamed rice.

COOK'S TIP

Store the sauce in the refrigerator for up to 3 days, or freezer for up to 3 months.

Nutritional information per portion: Energy 108Kcal/452kJ; Protein 11.8g; Carbohydrate 5.9g, of which sugars 5.1g; Fat 4.3g, of which saturates 0.5g; Cholesterol 118mg; Calcium 72mg; Fibre 1.2g; Sodium 175mg.

Thai fried noodles

This tasty dish is often served for breakfast in Thailand, so if you fancy an early morning workout with a wok, give it a try. It also makes a great evening meal.

SERVES 4–6

16 raw tiger prawns (jumbo shrimp)

350g/12oz thick rice noodles

45ml/3 tbsp vegetable oil

15ml/1 tbsp chopped garlic

2 eggs, lightly beaten

15ml/1 tbsp dried shrimp, rinsed

30ml/2 tbsp pickled mooli (daikon)

50g/2oz fried tofu, cut into small slivers

2.5ml/½ tsp dried chilli flakes

1 large bunch garlic chives, about
   115g/4oz, cut into 5cm/2in lengths

225g/8oz/4 cups beansprouts

50g/2oz/½ cup roasted peanuts,
   coarsely ground

5ml/1 tsp granulated (white) sugar

15ml/1 tbsp dark soy sauce

30ml/2 tbsp Thai fish sauce

30ml/2 tbsp tamarind juice, made
   by mixing tamarind paste with
   warm water

fresh coriander (cilantro) leaves and
   lime wedges to garnish

1 Peel the prawns, leaving the tails intact. Carefully cut along the back of each prawn and remove the dark vein. Soak the rice noodles in a large bowl of warm water for 20–30 minutes, then drain thoroughly and set aside.

2 Heat 15ml/1 tbsp of the oil in a wok. Stir-fry the garlic until golden. Stir in the prawns and cook them for 1–2 minutes, until pink. Remove the prawns and set aside.

3 Heat 15ml/1 tbsp of the remaining oil in the wok. Add the eggs and tilt the wok to make a thin layer. Stir to scramble and break up. Remove from the wok and set aside.

4 Heat the remaining oil in the same wok. Add the dried shrimp, pickled mooli, tofu slivers and dried chilli flakes. Stir briefly. Add the noodles and stir-fry for about 5 minutes. Add the garlic chives, half the beansprouts and half the peanuts. Add the sugar, then season with soy sauce, fish sauce and tamarind juice. Mix well and cook until the noodles are heated through. Mix in the prawns and egg mixture.

5 Serve topped with the remaining beansprouts and peanuts. Garnish with coriander and lime wedges.

Nutritional information per portion: Energy 372Kcal/1553kJ; Protein 14.2g; Carbohydrate 51.1g, of which sugars 2.3g; Fat 11.6g, of which saturates 2g; Cholesterol 128mg; Calcium 57mg; Fibre 1.1g; Sodium 274mg.

Fried jasmine rice with prawns

Strips of omelette are used to garnish this rice dish. Use your wok for frying the omelette – the sloping sides make it easy to spread the beaten egg thinly and then to slide it out.

SERVES 4–6

45ml/3 tbsp vegetable oil
1 egg, beaten
1 onion, chopped
15ml/1 tbsp chopped garlic
15ml/1 tbsp shrimp paste
1kg/2¼lb/4 cups cooked jasmine rice
350g/12oz cooked shelled prawns (shrimp)
50g/2oz thawed frozen peas
oyster sauce, to taste
2 spring onions (scallions), chopped
15–20 Thai basil leaves, roughly snipped,
    plus an extra sprig, to garnish

1 Heat 15ml/1 tbsp of the oil in a wok or frying pan. Add the egg and swirl it around to set like a thin pancake. Cook (on one side only) over a gentle heat until golden. Slide the pancake on to a board, roll up and cut into thin strips. Set aside.

2 Heat the remaining oil in the wok, add the onion and garlic and stir-fry for 2–3 minutes. Stir in the shrimp paste and mix well until combined.

3 Add the rice, prawns and peas, and toss and stir together, until everything is heated through.

4 Season with oyster sauce to taste, taking great care as the shrimp paste is salty. Mix in the spring onions and basil leaves.

5 Transfer to a serving dish and top with the strips of egg pancake. Serve, garnished with a sprig of basil.

Nutritional information per portion: Energy 357Kcal/1508kJ; Protein 17.6g; Carbohydrate 54.6g, of which sugars 1.7g; Fat 9.2g, of which saturates 1.5g; Cholesterol 154mg; Calcium 111mg; Fibre 1g; Sodium 198mg.

Goan prawn curry with mango

This sweet, spicy, hot-and-sour curry comes from the shores of western India. It's simple to make, and the addition of mango and tamarind produces a very full, rich flavour.

SERVES 4

1 green mango
5ml/1 tsp hot chilli powder
15ml/1 tbsp paprika
2.5ml/½ tsp ground turmeric
4 garlic cloves, crushed
10ml/2 tsp finely grated ginger
30ml/2 tbsp ground coriander
10ml/2 tsp ground cumin
15ml/1 tbsp palm sugar (jaggery)
400g/14oz can coconut milk
10ml/2 tsp salt
15ml/1 tbsp tamarind paste
1kg/2¼lb large prawns (shrimp)
chopped coriander (cilantro), to garnish
steamed white rice, chopped tomato,
    cucumber and onion salad, to serve

1 Wash, stone and slice the mango and set aside. In a large bowl, mix the chilli powder, paprika, turmeric, garlic, ginger, ground coriander, ground cumin and palm sugar. Add 400ml/14fl oz/1⅔ cups cold water to the bowl and stir to combine.

2 Transfer the spice mixture to a wok, place over a high heat and bring to the boil. Cover the wok with a lid, reduce the heat to low and simmer gently for 8–10 minutes.

3 Add the mango, coconut milk, salt and tamarind paste to the wok and stir to combine. Bring the mixture back to a simmer and add the prawns.

4 Cover the wok and cook gently for 10–12 minutes, or until the prawns have turned pink and are cooked.

5 Serve the curry garnished with chopped coriander, accompanied by steamed white rice and a tomato, cucumber and onion salad.

Nutritional information per portion: Energy 151Kcal/648kJ; Protein 22.1g; Carbohydrate 14.1g, of which sugars 14g; Fat 1.1g, of which saturates 0.5g; Cholesterol 263mg; Calcium 143mg; Fibre 1g; Sodium 2102mg.

Spiced scallops and sugar snap peas on crispy noodle cakes

Tender, juicy scallops and sugar snap peas cooked in spices and served on a bed of fried noodles is a winning combination. It's simple and stylish and makes a great dish for entertaining.

SERVES 4

45ml/3 tbsp oyster sauce
10ml/2 tsp soy sauce
5ml/1 tsp sesame oil
5ml/1 tsp golden caster (superfine) sugar
30ml/2 tbsp sunflower oil
2 fresh red chillies, finely sliced
4 garlic cloves, finely chopped
10ml/2 tsp finely chopped fresh
   root ginger

250g/9oz sugar snap peas, trimmed
500g/1¼lb king scallops, cleaned, roes
   discarded and sliced in half
3 spring onions (scallions), finely shredded

FOR THE NOODLE CAKES
250g/9oz fresh thin egg noodles
10ml/2 tsp sesame oil
120ml/4fl oz/½ cup sunflower oil

1 Cook the noodles in a wok of boiling water for 1 minute, or until tender. Drain well and put in a bowl with the sesame oil and 15ml/1 tbsp of the sunflower oil. Spread them out on a baking sheet and leave to dry in a warm place for 1 hour.

2 To cook the noodle cakes, heat the remaining sunflower oil in a non-stick wok over a high heat. Divide the noodle mixture into four portions and add one portion to the wok. Using a spatula, flatten it out and shape it into a cake.

3 Reduce the heat slightly and cook for about 5 minutes on each side, until golden and crisp. Drain on kitchen paper. Keep warm while making the remaining cakes.

4 Mix together the oyster sauce, soy sauce, sesame oil and sugar in a small bowl, stirring until the sugar has dissolved completely.

5 Heat a wok over medium heat with the sunflower oil. Add the chillies, garlic and ginger, and stir-fry for 30 seconds. Add the sugar snap peas and stir-fry for 1–2 minutes. Add the scallops and spring onions and stir-fry over a high heat for 1 minute. Stir in the oyster sauce mixture and cook for a further minute.

6 To serve, place a noodle cake on each of four warmed plates and top with the scallop mixture.

Nutritional information per portion: Energy 689Kcal/2888kJ; Protein 41.4g; Carbohydrate 59.9g, of which sugars 6.2g; Fat 33.3g, of which saturates 5.4g; Cholesterol 78mg; Calcium 73mg; Fibre 5g; Sodium 700mg.

Steamed scallops with ginger

It helps to have two woks when making this dish. If you are not doubly blessed, borrow an extra one from a friend, or use a large, heavy pan with a trivet for steaming the second plate of scallops. Take care not to overcook the tender seafood.

SERVES 4

24 king scallops in their shells, cleaned
15ml/1 tbsp very finely shredded fresh
  root ginger
5ml/1 tsp very finely chopped garlic
1 large fresh red chilli, seeded and
  very finely chopped
15ml/1 tbsp light soy sauce
15ml/1 tbsp Chinese rice wine
a few drops of sesame oil
2–3 spring onions (scallions), very
  finely shredded
15ml/1 tbsp very finely chopped
  fresh chives
noodles or rice, to serve

1 Remove the scallops from their shells, then remove the membrane and hard white muscle from each one. Arrange the scallops on two plates. Rinse the shells, dry and set aside.

2 Fill two woks with 5cm/2in water and place a trivet in the base of each one. Bring to the boil.

3 Mix together the ginger, garlic, chilli, soy sauce, rice wine, sesame oil, spring onions and chives. Spoon over the scallops. Lower a plate into each wok. Turn the heat to low, cover and steam for 10–12 minutes.

4 Divide the scallops among four, or eight, of the reserved shells. Serve immediately with noodles or rice.

Nutritional information per portion: Energy 167Kcal/708kJ; Protein 29.8g; Carbohydrate 7g, of which sugars 2.6g; Fat 2g, of which saturates 0.6g; Cholesterol 59mg; Calcium 53mg; Fibre 0.8g; Sodium 496mg.

Herb- and chilli-seared scallops

Tender, succulent scallops taste simply divine when marinated in fresh chilli, fragrant mint and aromatic basil, then quickly seared in a piping hot wok. If you can't find king scallops for this recipe, use twice the quantity of smaller queen scallops.

SERVES 4

20–24 king scallops, cleaned
120ml/4fl oz/¹/₂ cup olive oil
finely grated rind and juice of 1 lemon
30ml/2 tbsp finely chopped mixed
    fresh mint and basil
1 fresh red chilli, seeded and
    finely chopped
salt and ground black pepper
500g/1¹/₄lb pak choi (bok choy)

1 Place the scallops in a shallow, non-metallic bowl in a single layer. In another clean bowl, mix together half the oil, the lemon rind and juice, chopped herbs and chilli and spoon over the scallops. Season well with salt and black pepper, cover and set aside. Using a sharp knife, cut each pak choi lengthways into four pieces.

2 Heat a wok over a high heat. When hot, drain the scallops (reserving the marinade) and add to the wok. Cook for 1 minute on each side, or until cooked to your liking.

3 Pour the marinade over the scallops and remove the wok from the heat. Transfer the scallops and juices to a platter and keep warm. Wipe out the wok with kitchen paper.

4 Place the wok over a high heat. When all moisture has evaporated, add the remaining oil. When the oil is hot add the pak choi and stir-fry over a high heat for 2–3 minutes, until the leaves wilt. Divide the greens among four warmed serving plates, then top with the scallops and their juices and serve.

Nutritional information per portion: Energy 410Kcal/1714kJ; Protein 44.5g; Carbohydrate 8.3g, of which sugars 2.1g; Fat 22.3g, of which saturates 3.5g; Cholesterol 82mg; Calcium 286mg; Fibre 3.2g; Sodium 494mg.

Langoustines with lemon grass risotto

The wok is wonderful for making risotto. For this version, the traditional Italian risotto is given a subtle Asian twist with the addition of fragrant lemon grass, Thai fish sauce and Chinese chives: the perfect accompaniment to simply steamed langoustines.

SERVES 4

8 fresh langoustines

30ml/2 tbsp olive oil

15ml/1 tbsp butter

1 onion, finely chopped

1 carrot, finely diced

1 celery stick, finely diced

30ml/2 tbsp very finely chopped
    lemon grass

300g/11oz/1¹⁄₂ cups arborio or other
    risotto rice

200ml/7fl oz/scant 1 cup dry white wine

1.5 litres/2¹⁄₂ pints/6¹⁄₄ cups boiling
    vegetable stock

50ml/2fl oz/¹⁄₄ cup Thai fish sauce

30ml/2 tbsp finely chopped Chinese chives

salt and ground black pepper

1 Place the langoustines in a baking parchment-lined bamboo steamer, cover and place over a wok of simmering water. Steam for 6–8 minutes, remove from the heat and keep warm.

2 Heat the olive oil and butter in a wok and add the vegetables. Cook over a high heat for 2–3 minutes. Add the lemon grass and risotto rice and stir-fry for 2 minutes.

3 Add the wine to the wok, reduce the heat and slowly stir until the wine is absorbed. Add about two thirds of the stock and cook gently, stirring constantly until absorbed. Continue adding the stock, stirring until absorbed before adding more.

4 When the rice is tender, stir in the fish sauce and Chinese chives, check the seasoning and serve immediately, topped with the langoustines.

Nutritional information per portion: Energy 467Kcal/1949kJ; Protein 23.8g; Carbohydrate 64.2g, of which sugars 3.4g; Fat 8.9g, of which saturates 2.3g; Cholesterol 201mg; Calcium 114mg; Fibre 0.9g; Sodium 218mg.

Steamed mussels in coconut milk

Mussels steamed in coconut milk and fresh aromatic herbs and spices make an ideal dish for informal entertaining. It is quick and easy to make in a wok, and is great for a relaxed dinner with friends. Serve with plenty of crusty bread.

SERVES 4

15ml/1 tbsp sunflower oil

6 garlic cloves, roughly chopped

15ml/1 tbsp finely chopped fresh
    root ginger

2 large fresh red chillies, seeded and
    finely sliced

6 spring onions (scallions), finely chopped

400ml/14fl oz/1²/₃ cups coconut milk

45ml/3 tbsp light soy sauce

2 limes

5ml/1 tsp caster (superfine) sugar

1.6kg/3¹/₂lb mussels, scrubbed
    and beards removed

a large handful of chopped
    coriander (cilantro)

salt and ground black pepper

1 Heat the wok over a high heat and then add the oil. Stir in the garlic, ginger, chillies and spring onions and stir-fry for 30 seconds. Pour in the coconut milk, then add the soy sauce.

2 Grate the zest of the limes into the coconut milk mixture and add the sugar. Stir to mix and bring to the boil.

3 Add the cleaned mussels. Return to the boil, cover and cook briskly for 5–6 minutes, or until all the mussels have opened. Discard any mussels that remain closed.

4 Remove the wok from the heat and stir the chopped coriander into the mussel mixture. Season the mussels well with salt and pepper. Ladle into warmed bowls and serve immediately.

COOK'S TIP
For an informal supper with friends, take the wok to the table rather than serving in individual bowls. A wok makes a great serving dish, and there's something utterly irresistible about eating the mussels straight from it.

Nutritional information per portion: Energy 165Kcal/702kJ; Protein 21.9g; Carbohydrate 7.7g, of which sugars 7.6g; Fat 5.6g, of which saturates 1g; Cholesterol 48mg; Calcium 276mg; Fibre 0.3g; Sodium 1165mg.

Crab and tofu stir-fry

For a light meal suitable for serving at any time, this speedy stir-fry is the ideal choice. As you need only a little crab meat – and you could use the canned variety – this is a very economical dish. The tofu boosts the protein content.

SERVES 2

250g/9oz firm tofu
60ml/4 tbsp vegetable oil
2 garlic cloves, finely chopped
115g/4oz white crab meat
130g/4$\frac{1}{2}$oz/generous 1 cup baby corn, halved lengthways
2 spring onions (scallions), chopped
1 fresh red chilli, seeded and finely chopped
30ml/2 tbsp soy sauce
15ml/1 tbsp Thai fish sauce
5ml/1 tsp palm sugar (jaggery) or light muscovado (brown) sugar
juice of 1 lime
small bunch fresh coriander (cilantro), chopped, to garnish

1 Using a sharp knife, cut the firm tofu into 1cm/$\frac{1}{2}$in cubes.

2 Heat the vegetable oil in a wok or large, heavy frying pan. Add the tofu cubes and stir-fry until they are golden all over, taking care not to break them up. Remove the tofu cubes with a slotted spoon and set aside.

3 Add the chopped garlic to the wok or pan and stir-fry until golden. Add the crab meat, tofu, corn, spring onions, chilli, soy sauce, fish sauce and sugar. Cook, stirring constantly, until the vegetables are just tender.

4 Stir in the lime juice, transfer to warmed bowls, sprinkle with the coriander and serve immediately.

Nutritional information per portion: Energy 365Kcal/1514kJ; Protein 23.1g; Carbohydrate 5.8g, of which sugars 4.8g; Fat 27.9g, of which saturates 3.3g; Cholesterol 41mg; Calcium 719mg; Fibre 1.2g; Sodium 2131mg.

Stir-fried squid with ginger

There's an ancient belief that a well-loved wok holds the memory of all the dishes that have ever been cooked in it. Give yours something to remember by introducing it to this classic combination of baby squid in soy sauce, ginger and lemon juice.

SERVES 2

4 ready-prepared baby squid,
    total weight about 250g/9oz
15ml/1 tbsp vegetable oil
2 garlic cloves, finely chopped
30ml/2 tbsp soy sauce
2.5cm/1in piece fresh root ginger,
    peeled and finely chopped
juice of 1/2 lemon
5ml/1 tsp granulated (white) sugar
2 spring onions (scallions), chopped
noodles, to serve

1 Rinse the squid well and pat dry with kitchen paper. Cut the bodies into rings and halve the tentacles, if necessary.

2 Heat the oil in a wok or frying pan and cook the garlic until golden brown, but do not let it burn.

3 Add the squid to the wok or frying pan and stir-fry for 30 seconds over a high heat.

4 Add the soy sauce, ginger, lemon juice, sugar and spring onions. Stir-fry for a further 30 seconds. Serve with noodles.

Nutritional information per portion: Energy 165Kcal/694kJ; Protein 19.7g; Carbohydrate 4.8g, of which sugars 3.2g; Fat 7.6g, of which saturates 1.2g; Cholesterol 281mg; Calcium 20mg; Fibre 0g; Sodium 1206mg.

Deep-fried plaice

In this dish the flesh of the fish and also the skeleton is deep-fried to such crispness that you can eat the bones, tails and heads, if you like.

SERVES 4

4 small plaice or flounder, about
    500–675g/1¼–1½lb total weight,
    gutted, not trimmed, and washed
    under cold running water
60ml/4 tbsp cornflour (cornstarch)
vegetable oil, for deep-frying
salt

FOR THE CONDIMENT
130g/4½oz mooli (daikon), peeled
4 dried chillies, seeded
1 bunch of chives, finely chopped
    (to make 50ml/2fl oz/¼ cup)

FOR THE SAUCE
20ml/4 tsp rice vinegar
20ml/4 tsp shoyu

1 Use a sharp knife to make deep cuts around the gills and across the tail of the fish. Cut through the skin from the head to the tail along the centre of the fish. Slide the knife under the cut near the head and cut the fillet from the bone. Repeat for the other half, turn the fish over and repeat to get four fillets from each fish. Transfer to a dish and sprinkle salt on both sides. Keep the skeletons.

2 Pierce the mooli with a skewer in four places. Insert the chillies into the holes. After 15 minutes, grate the mooli finely and squeeze out the moisture. Scoop a quarter into an egg cup, then press with your fingers. Turn out the cup on to a plate. Make three more mounds. Mix the rice vinegar and shoyu in a bowl.

3 Cut the fish fillets into four slices crossways and put in a plastic bag with the cornflour. Shake gently to coat. Heat the oil in a wok or pan to 175°C/347°F. Deep-fry the fillets in batches until golden brown. Heat the oil to 180°C/350°F. Dust the skeletons with cornflour and slide into the oil. Cook until golden, drain for 5 minutes, then fry again until crisp. Drain and sprinkle with salt. Serve the fish and skeletons with the mooli and chives. Have small plates for the sauce.

Nutritional information per portion: Energy 331Kcal/1378kJ; Protein 19.7g; Carbohydrate 16.2g, of which sugars 1.2g; Fat 21.2g, of which saturates 2.6g; Cholesterol 0mg; Calcium 120mg; Fibre 1.2g; Sodium 640mg.

Sweet and sour fish

When fish such as red mullet or snapper is deep-fried in oil the skin becomes crisp, while the flesh inside remains moist and juicy. The sweet and sour sauce perfectly complements the fish.

SERVES 4–6

1 large or 2 medium fish, such as snapper
   or mullet, cleaned, with heads removed
20ml/4 tsp cornflour (cornstarch)
120ml/4fl oz/¹/₂ cup vegetable oil
15ml/1 tbsp chopped garlic
15ml/1 tbsp chopped fresh ginger
30ml/2 tbsp chopped shallots
225g/8oz cherry tomatoes
30ml/2 tbsp red wine vinegar
30ml/2 tbsp granulated (white) sugar
30ml/2 tbsp tomato ketchup
15ml/1 tbsp Thai fish sauce
45ml/3 tbsp water
salt and ground black pepper
shredded spring onions (scallions),
   to garnish

1 Rinse and dry the fish. Score the skin diagonally on both sides, then coat the fish lightly all over with 15ml/1 tbsp of the cornflour. Shake off any excess. Heat the oil in a wok or large frying pan. Add the fish and cook over a medium heat for 6–7 minutes. Turn the fish over and cook for 6–7 minutes more, until it is crisp and brown.

2 Remove the fish with a metal spatula or fish slice and place on a large platter. Pour off all but 30ml/2 tbsp of the oil from the wok and reheat. Add the garlic, ginger and shallots and cook over a medium heat, stirring occasionally, for 3–4 minutes, until golden. Add the cherry tomatoes and cook until they burst open. Stir in the vinegar, sugar, tomato ketchup and fish sauce. Lower the heat and simmer gently for 1–2 minutes, then taste and adjust the seasoning, adding more vinegar, sugar and/or fish sauce, if necessary.

3 In a cup, mix the remaining 5ml/1 tsp cornflour to a paste with the water. Stir into the sauce. Heat, stirring, until it thickens. Pour the sauce over the fish, garnish with shredded spring onions and serve.

Nutritional information per portion: Energy 245Kcal/1023kJ; Protein 16.2g; Carbohydrate 14.8g, of which sugars 10.6g; Fat 13.8g, of which saturates 1.6g; Cholesterol 38mg; Calcium 27mg; Fibre 1.1g; Sodium 138mg.

Steamed fish with chilli sauce

A large wok is ideal for steaming fish. By leaving the fish whole and on the bone, maximum flavour is retained and the flesh remains beautifully moist. The banana leaf is both authentic and attractive, but you can use baking parchment to wrap your fish instead.

SERVES 4

1 large or 2 medium firm fish such as sea
    bass or grouper, scaled and cleaned
30ml/2 tbsp rice wine
3 fresh red chillies, seeded and thinly sliced
2 garlic cloves, finely chopped
2cm/³/₄in piece fresh root ginger,
    peeled and finely shredded
2 lemon grass stalks, crushed
    and finely chopped
2 spring onions (scallions), chopped
30ml/2 tbsp Thai fish sauce
juice of 1 lime
1 fresh banana leaf

FOR THE CHILLI SAUCE

10 fresh red chillies, seeded and chopped
4 garlic cloves, chopped
60ml/4 tbsp Thai fish sauce
15ml/1 tbsp granulated (white) sugar
75ml/5 tbsp fresh lime juice

1 Thoroughly rinse the fish under cold running water. Pat it dry with kitchen paper. With a sharp knife, slash the skin of the fish a few times on both sides.

2 Mix together the rice wine, chillies, garlic, shredded ginger, lemon grass and spring onions in a non-metallic bowl. Add the fish sauce and lime juice and mix to a paste. Place the fish on the banana leaf and spread the spice paste evenly over it, rubbing it in well where the skin has been slashed.

3 Put a rack in the base of a wok. Pour in boiling water to a depth of 5cm/2in. Lift the banana leaf, together with the fish, and put it on the rack. Cover and steam for 10–15 minutes, or until cooked.

4 Put all the chilli sauce ingredients in a food processor and process until smooth. If it seems too thick, add a little cold water. Transfer into a serving bowl.

5 Serve the fish hot, on the banana leaf, if you like, with the sweet chilli sauce to spoon over the top.

Nutritional information per portion: Energy 228Kcal/960kJ; Protein 35.2g; Carbohydrate 12g, of which sugars 10.1g; Fat 4.7g, of which saturates 0.7g; Cholesterol 140mg; Calcium 254mg; Fibre 1.6g; Sodium 392mg.

Fragrant red snapper in banana leaves

Shiny, dark green banana leaves make a really good wrapping for fish that is steamed in the wok. Here, whole snappers are infused with a delightful mix of coconut cream, mint, coriander, kaffir lime leaves, lemon grass and chilli to make an impressive main course.

SERVES 4

**4 small red snapper, grouper, tilapia
   or red bream, gutted and cleaned**
**4 large squares of banana leaf
   (approximately 30cm/12in square)**
50ml/2fl oz/¹⁄₄ cup coconut cream
90ml/6 tbsp chopped coriander (cilantro)
90ml/6 tbsp chopped mint
juice of 3 limes
3 spring onions (scallions), finely sliced
4 kaffir lime leaves, finely shredded
2 red chillies, seeded and finely sliced
4 lemon grass stalks, split lengthways
salt and ground black pepper
coriander (cilantro) leaves, to garnish
**steamed rice and steamed Asian greens,
   to serve**

1 Using a small sharp knife, score the fish diagonally on each side. Half fill a wok with water and bring to the boil. Dip each square of banana leaf into the water for 15–20 seconds until pliable. Rinse under cold water and dry with kitchen paper. Place the coconut cream, chopped herbs, lime juice, spring onions, lime leaves and chillies in a bowl and stir well. Season with salt and pepper.

2 Lay each banana leaf out flat and place a fish and a split lemon grass stalk in the centre of each. Spread the herb mixture over each fish. Wrap the banana leaf around each one to form four neat parcels. Secure each parcel tightly with a bamboo skewer or a cocktail stick (toothpick).

3 Place the parcels in a single layer in one or two tiers of a large bamboo steamer and place over a wok of simmering water. Cover tightly and steam for 15–20 minutes, or until the fish is cooked through.

4 Remove the fish from the steamer and serve in their banana-leaf wrappings, garnished with coriander, with steamed rice and steamed Asian greens.

Nutritional information per portion: Energy 185Kcal/781kJ; Protein 39.4g; Carbohydrate 0.9g, of which sugars 0.8g; Fat 2.7g, of which saturates 0.6g; Cholesterol 74mg; Calcium 87mg; Fibre 0.1g; Sodium 168mg.

Deep-fried skate wings with wasabi

Whole skate wings dipped in a tempura batter and deep-fried until crisp and golden look stunning and taste wonderful. The creamy, zesty mayonnaise flavoured with soy sauce, fiery wasabi paste and spring onions makes a great accompaniment.

SERVES 4

4 x 250g/9oz skate wings
65g/2½oz/9 tbsp cornflour (cornstarch)
65g/2½oz/9 tbsp plain (all-purpose) flour
5ml/1 tsp salt
5ml/1 tsp Chinese five-spice powder
15ml/1 tbsp sesame seeds
200ml/7fl oz/scant 1 cup ice-cold
    soda water
sunflower oil, for deep-frying

FOR THE MAYONNAISE
200ml/7fl oz/scant 1 cup mayonnaise
15ml/1 tbsp light soy sauce
finely grated rind and juice of 1 lime
5ml/1 tsp wasabi paste
15ml/1 tbsp finely chopped spring
    onion (scallion)

1 Using scissors, trim the frill from the edges of the skate wings and discard.

2 In a mixing bowl, combine the cornflour, plain flour, salt, five-spice powder and sesame seeds. Gradually stir in the soda water. (The mixture will be quite lumpy.)

3 Fill a large wok one-third full of sunflower oil and heat to 190°C/375°F or until a cube of bread browns in 40 seconds. One at a time, dip the skate wings in the batter, lower them carefully into the wok and deep-fry for 4–5 minutes, until cooked and crispy. Drain on kitchen paper. Set aside and keep warm.

4 Meanwhile, mix together all the mayonnaise ingredients and divide among four small bowls. Serve immediately with the skate wings.

COOK'S TIP
Look for packets of tempura batter mix at Asian markets.

Nutritional information per portion: Energy 705Kcal/2921kJ; Protein 31.9g; Carbohydrate 11.7g, of which sugars 1.2g; Fat 59.3g, of which saturates 11g; Cholesterol 38mg; Calcium 112mg; Fibre 0.5g; Sodium 792mg.

Fish moolie

This is a very popular South-east Asian fish curry in a coconut sauce, which is truly delicious.
Choose a firm-textured fish so that the pieces stay intact during the brief cooking process.
You could use halibut instead of monkfish.

SERVES 4

500g/1¼lb monkfish or other
**   firm-textured fish fillets, skinned**
**   and cut into 2.5cm/1in cubes**
2.5ml/½ tsp salt
50g/2oz/⅔ cup desiccated (dry,
**   unsweetened, shredded) coconut**
2 lemon grass stalks, trimmed
6 shallots or small onions, chopped
6 blanched almonds
2–3 garlic cloves, roughly chopped
2.5cm/1in piece fresh root ginger,
**   peeled and sliced**
10ml/2 tsp ground turmeric
45ml/3 tbsp vegetable oil
2 x 400ml/14fl oz cans coconut milk
1–3 fresh chillies, seeded and sliced
salt and ground black pepper
fresh chives, to garnish
boiled rice, to serve

1 Lay the pieces of fish in a shallow dish and sprinkle with the salt. Dry-fry the coconut in a wok or large frying pan over medium heat, stirring constantly, until crisp. Put in a food processor, process to an oily paste and transfer to a bowl.

2 Chop the lower 5cm/2in of the lemon grass stalks and put in the processor with the shallots or onions, almonds, garlic and ginger. Process to a paste. Add the turmeric and process briefly. Bruise the remaining lemon grass and set aside.

3 Heat the oil in a wok. Add the onion mixture and cook for a few minutes without browning. Stir in the coconut milk and, stirring constantly to prevent curdling, bring to the boil. Add the fish, most of the sliced chilli and the bruised lemon grass stalks. Cook for 3–4 minutes. Stir in the onion and coconut paste and cook for 2–3 minutes more. Do not overcook. Adjust the seasoning to taste.

4 Remove the lemon grass. Transfer to a hot serving dish and sprinkle with the remaining chilli. Garnish with chives and serve with boiled rice.

Nutritional information per portion: Energy 319Kcal/1335kJ; Protein 22.4g; Carbohydrate 16.7g, of which sugars 14.9g; Fat 18.6g, of which saturates 8.3g; Cholesterol 18mg; Calcium 96mg; Fibre 3g; Sodium 249mg.

Mackerel with mushrooms and black beans

Earthy-tasting shiitake mushrooms, zesty fresh ginger and pungent salted black beans are the perfect partners for robustly flavoured mackerel fillets. The striking combination of flavours all come together beautifully in this deliciously tasty meal.

SERVES 4

8 x 115g/4oz mackerel fillets

20 dried shiitake mushrooms

15ml/1 tbsp fresh root ginger,
    finely julienned

3 star anise

45ml/3 tbsp dark soy sauce

15ml/1 tbsp Chinese rice wine

15ml/1 tbsp salted black beans

6 spring onions (scallions), finely shredded

30ml/2 tbsp sunflower oil

5ml/1 tsp sesame oil

4 garlic cloves, very thinly sliced

sliced cucumber and steamed basmati rice,
    to serve

1 Divide the mackerel fillets between two lightly oiled heatproof plates, skin-side up. Using a small, sharp knife, make 3–4 diagonal slits in each one. Set aside. Place the dried shiitake mushrooms in a large bowl and pour over enough boiling water to cover. Leave to soak for 20–25 minutes. Drain, reserving the soaking liquid, discard the stems and slice the caps thinly.

2 Place a trivet or a steamer rack in a large wok and pour in 5cm/2in of the mushroom liquid (top up with water if necessary). Add half the ginger and the star anise. Push the remaining ginger strips into the slits in the mackerel and scatter over the sliced mushrooms. Bring the liquid in the wok to a boil, then lower one of the prepared plates on to the trivet.

3 Cover the wok, reduce the heat and steam for 10–12 minutes, or until the mackerel is cooked. Remove the plate and repeat with the second plate of fish, adding liquid to the wok if necessary. Transfer the steamed fish to a serving platter and keep warm. Ladle 105ml/7 tbsp of the steaming liquid into a clean wok with the soy sauce, wine and black beans, place over a gentle heat and bring to a simmer. Spoon over the fish and sprinkle over the spring onions.

4 Wipe the wok with kitchen paper and place over a medium heat. Add the oils and garlic and stir-fry for a few minutes until the garlic is lightly golden. Pour over the fish and serve with sliced cucumber and steamed basmati rice.

Nutritional information per portion: Energy 573Kcal/2378kJ; Protein 43.9g; Carbohydrate 3.2g, of which sugars 1.1g; Fat 42.7g, of which saturates 8.2g; Cholesterol 122mg; Calcium 37mg; Fibre 1.2g; Sodium 678mg.

Spiced halibut and tomato curry and ginger

The chunky cubes of white fish contrast visually with the rich red spicy tomato sauce and taste just as good as they look. Halibut is used here, but you can use any type of firm white fish.

SERVES 4

1 lemon
60ml/4 tbsp rice wine vinegar
30ml/2 tbsp cumin seeds
5ml/1 tsp ground turmeric
5ml/1 tsp chilli powder
5ml/1 tsp salt
750g/1lb 11oz thick halibut fillets,
    skinned and cubed
60ml/4 tbsp sunflower oil
1 onion, finely chopped
3 garlic cloves, finely grated
30ml/2 tbsp finely grated fresh root ginger
10ml/2 tsp black mustard seeds
2 x 400g/14oz cans chopped tomatoes
5ml/1 tsp sugar
chopped coriander (cilantro) and sliced
    fresh green chilli, to garnish
natural (plain) yogurt, to drizzle (optional)
basmati rice, pickles and poppadums,
    to serve

1 Squeeze the lemon and pour 60ml/4tbsp of the juice into a shallow glass bowl. Add the vinegar, cumin seeds, turmeric, chilli powder and salt. Add the cubed fish to the bowl and coat evenly. Cover the bowl with clear film (plastic wrap) and refrigerate for 25–30 minutes.

2 Meanwhile, heat a wok over a high heat and add the oil. When hot, add the onion, garlic, ginger and mustard seeds. Reduce the heat to low and cook very gently for about 10 minutes, stirring occasionally.

3 Add the tomatoes and sugar, bring to the boil, reduce the heat, cover and cook gently for 15–20 minutes, stirring occasionally. Add the fish and its marinade to the wok, stir gently to mix, then cover and simmer gently for 15–20 minutes, or until the fish is cooked through and flakes easily with a fork.

4 Ladle the curry into shallow bowls, garnish with fresh coriander and green chillies, and drizzle over some natural yogurt, if you like. Serve with basmati rice, pickles and poppadums.

Nutritional information per portion: Energy 335Kcal/1409kJ; Protein 41.9g; Carbohydrate 8.4g, of which sugars 8.1g; Fat 15.2g, of which saturates 2.1g; Cholesterol 66mg; Calcium 73mg; Fibre 2.2g; Sodium 622mg.

Steamed fish skewers on rice noodles

Fresh trout is perfect for summer entertaining. Here, succulent fillets are marinated in a tangy citrus spice blend, then steamed in the wok before serving on a bed of fragrant herb noodles.

SERVES 4

4 trout fillets, skinned
2.5ml/1/2 tsp turmeric
15ml/1 tbsp mild curry paste
juice of 2 lemons
15ml/1 tbsp sunflower oil
45ml/3 tbsp chilli-roasted peanuts,
  roughly chopped
salt and ground black pepper
chopped fresh mint, to garnish

FOR THE NOODLES

300g/11oz thick rice noodles
15ml/1 tbsp sunflower oil
1 red chilli, seeded and finely sliced
4 spring onions (scallions), cut into slivers
60ml/4 tbsp roughly chopped fresh mint
60ml/4 tbsp roughly chopped fresh
  sweet basil

1 Trim each fillet and place in a large bowl. Mix together the turmeric, curry paste, lemon juice and oil and pour over the fish. Season with salt and black pepper and toss to mix well.

2 Place the rice noodles in a bowl and pour over enough boiling water to cover. Leave for 3–4 minutes and then drain. Refresh in cold water, drain and set aside.

3 Thread two bamboo skewers through each trout fillet and arrange in two tiers of a bamboo steamer lined with baking parchment. Cover the steamer and place over a wok of simmering water (making sure the water doesn't touch the steamer). Steam for 5–6 minutes, or until the fish is just cooked through.

4 Meanwhile, in a clean wok heat the oil. Add the chilli, spring onions and drained noodles. Stir-fry for about 2 minutes and then stir in the chopped herbs. Season with salt and ground black pepper and divide among four bowls. Top each bowl of noodles with a steamed fish skewer and scatter over the chilli-roasted peanuts. Serve immediately.

Nutritional information per portion: Energy 555Kcal/2317kJ; Protein 36g; Carbohydrate 62.8g, of which sugars 1g; Fat 16.6g, of which saturates 1.6g; Cholesterol 0mg; Calcium 52mg; Fibre 1.3g; Sodium 97mg.

Poultry Dishes

The wok is an excellent cooking vessel for poultry – fast cooking keeps it moist and flavoursome. Poultry's mild taste also makes it a good protein to mix with robust oriental flavours. This chapter ranges from fast and simple stir-fries, such as Cashew Chicken, to slow-cooked dishes, like Southern Thai Chicken Curry. The wok serves as a steamer for Orange and Ginger Glazed Poussins, and as a deep-fryer for Lemon and Sesame Chicken.

Chicken and lemon grass curry

Quick-cook curries, such as this Thai speciality, work well in a wok, especially if you use an electric appliance, which allows you to adjust the heat for successful simmering.

SERVES 4

45ml/3 tbsp vegetable oil

2 garlic cloves, crushed

500g/1¼lb skinless, chicken thighs, boned and chopped into small pieces

45ml/3 tbsp Thai fish sauce

120ml/4fl oz/½ cup chicken stock

5ml/1 tsp granulated (white) sugar

1 lemon grass stalk, chopped into 4 sticks and lightly crushed

5 kaffir lime leaves, rolled into cylinders and thinly sliced across, plus extra to garnish

chopped roasted peanuts and chopped fresh coriander (cilantro), to garnish

FOR THE CURRY PASTE

1 lemon grass stalk, coarsely chopped

2.5cm/1in piece fresh galangal, peeled and coarsely chopped

2 kaffir lime leaves, chopped

3 shallots, coarsely chopped

6 coriander (cilantro) roots, coarsely chopped

2 garlic cloves

2 fresh green chillies, seeded and coarsely chopped

5ml/1 tsp shrimp paste

5ml/1 tsp ground turmeric

1 Make the curry paste. Place all the ingredients in a large mortar and pound with the pestle, or process to a smooth paste using a food processor.

2 Heat the vegetable oil in a wok or large, heavy frying pan, add the garlic and cook over a low heat, stirring frequently, until golden brown. Be careful not to let the garlic burn or it will taste bitter. Add the curry paste and stir-fry with the garlic for about 30 seconds more.

3 Add the chicken pieces to the wok or pan and stir until thoroughly coated with the curry paste. Stir in the Thai fish sauce and chicken stock, with the sugar, and cook, stirring constantly, for 2 minutes more.

4 Add the lemon grass and lime leaves, reduce the heat and simmer for 10 minutes. If the mixture begins to dry out, add a little more stock or water.

5 Remove the lemon grass, if you like. Spoon the curry into four dishes, garnish with the lime leaves, peanuts and coriander, and serve immediately.

Nutritional information per portion: Energy 229Kcal/959kJ; Protein 31.3g; Carbohydrate 4.3g, of which sugars 3.4g; Fat 9.7g, of which saturates 1.4g; Cholesterol 94mg; Calcium 32mg; Fibre 0.5g; Sodium 397mg.

Yellow chicken curry

The pairing of slightly sweet coconut milk and fruit with savoury chicken and spices is at once a comforting, refreshing and exotic combination.

SERVES 4

300ml/½ pint/1¼ cups chicken stock
30ml/2 tbsp tamarind juice, made by
    mixing tamarind paste with a little
    warm water
15ml/1 tbsp granulated (white) sugar
200ml/7fl oz/scant 1 cup coconut milk
1 green papaya, peeled and seeded
250g/9oz skinless chicken breast fillets
juice of 1 lime
lime slices and coriander (cilantro)
    leaves, to garnish

FOR THE CURRY PASTE
1 fresh red chilli, seeded
    and coarsely chopped
4 garlic cloves, coarsely chopped
3 shallots, coarsely chopped
2 lemon grass stalks, sliced
5cm/2in piece fresh turmeric, coarsely
    chopped, or 5ml/1 tsp ground turmeric
5ml/1 tsp shrimp paste
5ml/1 tsp salt

1 Make the yellow curry paste. Put the red chilli, garlic, shallots, lemon grass and turmeric in a mortar or food processor. Add the shrimp paste and salt. Pound or process to a paste, adding a little water if needed.

2 Pour the stock into a wok or pan and bring to the boil. Stir in the curry paste and bring back to the boil. Add the tamarind juice, sugar and coconut milk.

3 Thinly slice the papaya, and dice the chicken breast fillets. Add to the wok and cook over a medium to high heat for about 15 minutes, stirring frequently, until the chicken is cooked.

4 Stir the lime juice into the wok. Transfer the curry on to four warmed dishes and serve immediately, garnished with the lime slices and coriander leaves.

Nutritional information per portion: Energy 149Kcal/633kJ; Protein 17.2g; Carbohydrate 18.9g, of which sugars 17.2g; Fat 1.1g, of which saturates 0.3g; Cholesterol 50mg; Calcium 70mg; Fibre 2.8g; Sodium 153mg.

Southern Thai chicken curry

This is a mild coconut curry flavoured with turmeric, coriander and cumin seeds, combining the culinary influences of Malaysia and neighbouring Thailand.

SERVES 4

1 chicken, weighing about 1.5kg/3–3¹/₂lb
60ml/4 tbsp vegetable oil
1 large garlic clove, crushed
400ml/14fl oz/1²/₃ cups coconut cream
250ml/8fl oz/1 cup chicken stock
30ml/2 tbsp Thai fish sauce
30ml/2 tbsp sugar
juice of 2 limes
1 bunch spring onions (scallions)
**   and 2 small fresh red chillies,**
**   seeded, to garnish**
thick rice noodles, to serve

FOR THE CURRY PASTE
5ml/1 tsp dried chilli flakes
2.5ml/¹/₂ tsp salt
5cm/2in piece fresh turmeric or
**   5ml/1 tsp ground turmeric**
2.5ml/¹/₂ tsp coriander seeds
2.5ml/¹/₂ tsp cumin seeds
5ml/1 tsp shrimp paste

1 First make the curry paste. Put all the ingredients into a mortar or food processor, and pound or process to a smooth paste.

2 Chop the chicken into 12 large pieces. Heat the oil in a wok or frying pan and cook the garlic until golden. Add the chicken and cook until golden. Remove the chicken and set aside.

3 Reheat the oil, add the curry paste and then half the coconut cream. Cook for a few minutes until fragrant.

4 Return the chicken to the wok or pan, add the stock, mixing well, then add the remaining coconut cream, the fish sauce, sugar and lime juice. Stir well and bring to the boil, then lower the heat and simmer for 15 minutes.

5 Thinly slice the spring onions and chop the chillies and set aside.

6 Turn the curry into four warm serving bowls and sprinkle with the chopped chillies and sliced spring onions to garnish. Serve immediately with thick rice noodles.

Nutritional information per portion: Energy 686Kcal/2849kJ; Protein 46.8g; Carbohydrate 12.8g, of which sugars 12.8g; Fat 50g, of which saturates 12.8g; Cholesterol 246mg; Calcium 67mg; Fibre 0g; Sodium 352mg.

Stir-fried chicken with basil and chilli

This quick and easy chicken dish from Thailand owes its spicy flavour to fresh chillies and its pungency to Thai basil, which has a lovely aroma with hints of aniseed.

SERVES 4–6

45ml/3 tbsp vegetable oil

4 garlic cloves, thinly sliced

2–4 fresh red chillies, seeded and
    finely chopped

450g/1lb skinless chicken breast
    fillets, cut into bitesize pieces

45ml/3 tbsp Thai fish sauce

10ml/2 tsp dark soy sauce

5ml/1 tsp granulated (white) sugar

10–12 fresh Thai basil leaves

2 fresh red chillies, seeded and finely
    chopped, and about 20 deep-fried
    Thai basil leaves, to garnish

1 Heat the oil in a wok or large, heavy frying pan. Add the garlic and chillies and stir-fry over a medium heat for 1–2 minutes until the garlic is golden. Take care not to let the garlic burn, otherwise it will taste bitter.

2 Add the pieces of chicken to the wok or pan, in batches if necessary, and stir-fry until the chicken changes colour.

3 Stir in the fish sauce, soy sauce and sugar. Continue to stir-fry the mixture for 3–4 minutes, or until the chicken is fully cooked and golden brown.

4 Stir in the fresh Thai basil leaves. Spoon the mixture on to a warm platter, or into individual dishes. Garnish with the chopped chillies and deep-fried Thai basil and serve immediately.

Nutritional information per portion: Energy 138Kcal/576kJ; Protein 18.3g; Carbohydrate 1.9g, of which sugars 1.8g; Fat 6.4g, of which saturates 0.9g; Cholesterol 53mg; Calcium 6mg; Fibre 0.1g; Sodium 579mg.

Cashew chicken

A popular item on any Chinese restaurant menu, this dish is easy to recreate at home. It is important to have the wok very hot before adding the chicken.

SERVES 4–6

450g/1lb skinless chicken breast fillets
1 red (bell) pepper
2 garlic cloves
4 dried red chillies
30ml/2 tbsp vegetable oil
30ml/2 tbsp oyster sauce
15ml/1 tbsp soy sauce
pinch of granulated (white) sugar
1 bunch spring onions (scallions),
**   cut into 5cm/2in lengths**
175g/6oz/1½ cups cashews, roasted

1 Trim off any excess fat from the chicken breast fillets. With a sharp knife, cut the chicken into bitesize pieces. Set aside.

2 Halve the red pepper, discard the seeds and membranes, then cut the flesh into 2cm/¾in dice. Peel and thinly slice the garlic and chop the dried chillies.

3 Preheat a wok and then drizzle a 'necklace' of oil around the inner rim of the wok, so that it coats the entire inner surface. Swirl the wok to make sure it is even.

4 Add the garlic and dried chillies to the wok and stir-fry over a medium heat until golden. Do not let the garlic burn, otherwise it will taste bitter.

5 Add the chicken breast pieces and stir-fry until cooked through, then add the red pepper. If the mixture is very dry, add a little water. Stir in the oyster sauce, soy sauce and sugar. Add the spring onions and cashew nuts.

6 Stir-fry for a further 1–2 minutes, until heated through, and then serve immediately.

Nutritional information per portion: Energy 314Kcal/1307kJ; Protein 24.7g; Carbohydrate 10.2g, of which sugars 6.2g; Fat 19.6g, of which saturates 3.7g; Cholesterol 53mg; Calcium 24mg; Fibre 1.7g; Sodium 268mg.

Lemon and sesame chicken

These delicate strips of chicken are at their best if you have time to leave them to marinate overnight so that they can really soak up the flavours. The subtle fragrance of lemon perfectly complements the rich taste of fried chicken and the nutty sesame seeds.

SERVES 4

4 large chicken breast portions,
   skinned and cut into strips
15ml/1 tbsp light soy sauce
15ml/1 tbsp Chinese rice wine
2 garlic cloves, crushed
10ml/2 tsp finely grated fresh
   root ginger
1 egg, lightly beaten
150g/5oz cornflour (cornstarch)
sunflower oil, for deep-frying
toasted sesame seeds, to sprinkle
rice or noodles, to serve

FOR THE SAUCE

15ml/1 tbsp sunflower oil
2 spring onions (scallions),
   finely sliced
1 garlic clove, crushed
10ml/2 tsp cornflour (cornstarch)
90ml/6 tbsp chicken stock
10ml/2 tsp finely grated lemon rind
30ml/2 tbsp lemon juice
10ml/2 tsp caster (superfine) sugar
2.5ml/½ tsp sesame oil
pinch of salt

1 Place the chicken strips in a large, non-metallic bowl. Mix together the light soy sauce, rice wine, garlic and ginger and pour over the chicken. Toss together to combine.

2 Cover the bowl of chicken with clear film (plastic wrap) and place in the refrigerator for 8–10 hours, or overnight if possible.

3 When ready to cook, add the beaten egg to the chicken and mix well, then tip the mixture into a colander to drain off any excess marinade and egg.

4 Place the cornflour in a large plastic bag and add the chicken pieces. Shake it vigorously to coat the chicken strips thoroughly.

5 Fill a wok one-third full of sunflower oil and heat to 180°C/350°F or until a cube of bread, dropped into the oil, browns in about 45 seconds.

6 Deep-fry the chicken, in batches, for 3–4 minutes. Lift out the chicken using a slotted spoon and drain on kitchen paper. Reheat the oil and deep-fry the chicken once more, in batches, for 2–3 minutes. Remove with a slotted spoon and drain on kitchen paper. Pour the oil out and wipe out the wok with kitchen paper.

7 To make the sauce, heat the wok, then add the sunflower oil. When the oil is hot, add the spring onions and garlic and stir-fry for 1–2 minutes. Mix together the cornflour, stock, lemon rind and juice, sugar, sesame oil and salt and pour into the wok.

8 Cook over a high heat for 2–3 minutes until thickened. Return the chicken to the wok, toss lightly to coat with sauce, and sprinkle over the toasted sesame seeds. Serve with rice or noodles.

Nutritional information per portion: Energy 229Kcal/959kJ; Protein 31.3g; Carbohydrate 4.3g, of which sugars 3.4g; Fat 9.7g, of which saturates 1.4g; Cholesterol 94mg; Calcium 32mg; Fibre 0.5g; Sodium 397mg.

Crispy five-spice chicken

Tender strips of chicken, with a delicately spiced rice flour coating, turn deliciously crisp and golden when shallow-fried. Serve on a bed of stir-fried noodles with sweet peppers and broccoli.

SERVES 4

200g/7oz thin egg noodles
30ml/2 tbsp sunflower oil
2 garlic cloves, very thinly sliced
1 fresh red chilli, seeded and sliced
**1/2 red (bell) pepper, seeded and very
    thinly sliced**
**300g/11oz carrots, peeled and cut
    into thin strips**
**300g/11oz Chinese broccoli or Chinese
    greens, roughly sliced**
45ml/3 tbsp hoisin sauce
45ml/3 tbsp soy sauce
15ml/1 tbsp caster (superfine) sugar
**4 skinless chicken breast fillets, cut
    into strips**
2 egg whites, lightly beaten
115g/4oz/1 cup rice flour
15ml/1 tbsp five-spice powder
salt and ground black pepper
vegetable oil, for shallow-frying

1 Cook the noodles in boiling water for 2–4 minutes, or according to the packet instructions, drain and set aside.

2 Heat a wok, add the sunflower oil, and when it is hot add the garlic, chilli, red pepper, carrots and the broccoli or greens. Stir-fry over a high heat for 2–3 minutes. Add the sauces and sugar and cook for a further 2–3 minutes. Add the drained noodles, toss to combine, then remove from the heat, cover and keep warm.

3 Dip the chicken strips into the egg white. Combine the rice flour and five-spice powder in a shallow dish and season. Add the chicken strips to the flour mixture and toss to coat.

4 Heat about 2.5cm/1in oil in a clean wok. When hot, shallow-fry the chicken for 3–4 minutes until crisp and golden.

5 Divide the noodle mixture among plates, and serve the chicken on top.

Nutritional information per portion: Energy 679Kcal/2849kJ; Protein 43.9g; Carbohydrate 75.8g, of which sugars 17g; Fat 23.2g, of which saturates 3.7g; Cholesterol 103mg; Calcium 96mg; Fibre 6.3g; Sodium 1207mg.

Scented chicken wraps

For sheer sophistication, these leaf-wrapped chicken bites can't be beaten. They are surprisingly easy to make and can be deep-fried in minutes in the wok.

SERVES 4

400g/14oz skinless chicken thighs, boned
45ml/3 tbsp soy sauce
30ml/2 tbsp finely grated garlic
15ml/1 tbsp cumin
15ml/1 tbsp ground coriander
15ml/1 tbsp golden caster
   (superfine) sugar
5ml/1 tsp finely grated fresh root ginger
1 fresh bird's eye chilli
30ml/2 tbsp oyster sauce
15ml/1 tbsp Thai fish sauce
1 bunch of pandanus leaves, to wrap
vegetable oil, for deep-frying
sweet chilli sauce, to serve

1 Using a cleaver or sharp knife, cut the chicken into bitesize pieces and place in a large mixing bowl.

2 Place the soy sauce, garlic, cumin, coriander, sugar, ginger, chilli, oyster sauce and fish sauce in a blender and process until smooth. Pour over the chicken, cover and leave to marinate in the refrigerator for 6–8 hours.

3 When ready to cook, drain the chicken from the marinade and wrap each piece in a pandanus leaf (you will need to cut the leaves to size) and secure with a cocktail stick (toothpick).

4 Fill a wok one-third full of oil and heat to 180°C/350°F or until a cube of bread browns in about 45 seconds. Carefully add the chicken parcels, three or four at a time, and deep-fry for 3–4 minutes, or until cooked through. Drain on kitchen paper and serve with the chilli sauce. (Do not eat the leaves.)

Nutritional information per portion: Energy 159Kcal/669kJ; Protein 24.5g; Carbohydrate 6.8g, of which sugars 6.6g; Fat 3.9g, of which saturates 0.6g; Cholesterol 70mg; Calcium 10mg; Fibre 0.1g; Sodium 1055mg.

Fragrant tarragon chicken

Chicken thighs have a particularly good flavour and stand up well to the robust ingredients used in this dish. Few people think of using a wok for braising, but it actually works extremely well, provided you have a suitable lid that fits snugly.

SERVES 4

3 heads of garlic, cloves separated but still in their skins

2 onions, quartered

8 chicken thighs

90ml/6 tbsp chopped fresh tarragon leaves

30–45ml/2–3 tbsp olive oil

8 small pickled lemons

750ml/1¼ pints/3 cups dessert wine

250ml/8fl oz/1 cup chicken stock

salt and ground black pepper

sautéed potatoes and steamed yellow or green beans, to serve

1 Arrange the garlic cloves and quartered onions in the base of a large wok and lay the chicken thighs over the top in a single layer. Sprinkle the tarragon over the top of the chicken, season well with salt and ground black pepper and drizzle over the olive oil.

2 Chop the pickled lemons and add to the wok. Pour the wine and stock over and bring to the boil. Cover the wok tightly, reduce the heat to low and simmer for 1½ hours. Remove from the heat, and leave to stand, covered, for 10 minutes. Serve with sautéed potatoes and steamed beans.

Nutritional information per portion: Energy 390Kcal/1630kJ; Protein 24g; Carbohydrate 21.8g, of which sugars 17.2g; Fat 8.8g, of which saturates 1.6g; Cholesterol 105mg; Calcium 86mg; Fibre 2.7g; Sodium 122mg.

Spiced coconut chicken with cardamom

You need to plan ahead to make this luxurious chicken curry. The chicken legs are marinated overnight in an aromatic blend of yogurt and spices before being gently simmered with hot green chillies in creamy coconut milk. Serve with rice.

SERVES FOUR

1.6kg/3¹/₂lb large chicken drumsticks
30ml/2 tbsp sunflower oil
400ml/14fl oz/1²/₃ cups coconut milk
4–6 large green chillies, halved
45ml/3 tbsp finely chopped
    coriander (cilantro)
salt and ground black pepper
natural (plain) yogurt, to drizzle

FOR THE MARINADE
15ml/1 tbsp cardamom pods
15ml/1 tbsp grated fresh root ginger
10ml/2 tsp crushed garlic
105ml/7 tbsp natural (plain) yogurt
2 fresh green chillies, seeded and chopped
5ml/1 tsp ground coriander
5ml/1 tsp ground cumin
5ml/1 tsp ground turmeric
finely grated rind and juice of 1 lime

1 Make the marinade. Smash the cardamom pods in a mortar using a pestle so that the seeds separate from the husks. Discard the husks. Put the ginger, cardamom seeds, garlic, half the yogurt, green chillies, coriander, cumin, turmeric and lime rind and juice in a blender. Process until smooth, season and pour into a large glass bowl.

2 Add the chicken to the bowl and toss to coat. Cover and marinate in the refrigerator for 6–8 hours, or overnight.

3 Heat the oil in a large, non-stick wok over a low heat. Add the chicken, reserving the marinade, and brown all over. Then add the coconut milk, remaining yogurt, reserved marinade and green chillies and bring to the boil.

4 Reduce the heat and simmer gently, uncovered, for 30–35 minutes. Check the seasoning, adding more if needed. Stir in the chopped coriander and ladle into warmed bowls. Serve immediately, drizzled with yogurt.

Nutritional information per portion: Energy 691Kcal/2906kJ; Protein 107.7g; Carbohydrate 6.2g, of which sugars 6.1g; Fat 26.5g, of which saturates 6.5g; Cholesterol 540mg; Calcium 142mg; Fibre 0.6g; Sodium 805mg.

Tangy chicken salad

When you've got a wok, making a fresh and lively dish like this one is easy. The salad is ideal for a light lunch on a hot and lazy summer's day. The dressing is delicious.

SERVES 4–6

4 skinless chicken breast fillets
2 garlic cloves, crushed
30ml/2 tbsp soy sauce
30ml/2 tbsp vegetable oil
120ml/4fl oz/¹/₂ cup coconut cream
30ml/2 tbsp Thai fish sauce
juice of 1 lime
30ml/2 tbsp palm sugar (jaggery) or
   light muscovado (brown) sugar
50g/2oz/¹/₂ cup cashew nuts, roasted
115g/4oz/¹/₂ cup water chestnuts, sliced
4 shallots, thinly sliced
4 kaffir lime leaves, thinly sliced
1 lemon grass stalk, thinly sliced
5ml/1 tsp chopped fresh galangal
2 spring onions (scallions), thinly sliced
10–12 fresh mint leaves, torn
1 large fresh red chilli, seeded
2 fresh red chillies, to garnish
1 lettuce, separated into leaves, to serve

1 Place the chicken in a large dish. Rub with the garlic and soy sauce and drizzle with 15ml/1 tbsp of the oil. Cover and marinate for 1–2 hours.

2 Heat the remaining oil in a wok or frying pan and stir-fry the chicken for 3–4 minutes on each side, or until cooked. Remove and set aside to cool.

3 In a pan, heat the coconut cream, fish sauce, lime juice and sugar. Stir until the sugar has dissolved; set aside.

4 Tear the cooked chicken into strips and put it in a bowl. Coarsely chop the roasted cashew nuts and add to the bowl with the water chestnuts, shallots, kaffir lime leaves, lemon grass, galangal, spring onions and mint leaves. Finely chop the red chilli and add to the bowl.

5 Pour the coconut dressing over the mixture and toss well to coat. Seed and finely slice the red chillies. Serve the chicken on a bed of lettuce leaves, garnished with the sliced chillies.

Nutritional information per portion: Energy 216Kcal/905kJ; Protein 26.2g; Carbohydrate 7.8g, of which sugars 6.6g; Fat 9.1g, of which saturates 1.6g; Cholesterol 70mg; Calcium 23mg; Fibre 0.7g; Sodium 453mg.

Hijiki seaweed and chicken

The taste of hijiki is somewhere between rice and vegetable. It goes well with meat or tofu products, especially when it's stir-fried in the wok first with a little oil.

SERVES 2

90g/3¹/₂oz dried hijiki seaweed

150g/5oz chicken breast portion

15ml/1 tbsp vegetable oil

¹/₂ small carrot, about 5cm/2in, peeled and chopped into long, narrow matchsticks

100ml/3¹/₂fl oz/scant ¹/₂ cup instant dashi powder plus 1.5ml/¹/₄ tsp dashi-no-moto

30ml/2 tbsp sake

30ml/2 tbsp caster (superfine) sugar

45ml/3 tbsp shoyu

a pinch of cayenne pepper

1 Soak the hijiki in cold water for 30 minutes. When ready to cook, it crushes easily between the fingers. Wash under running water in a sieve (strainer). Drain.

2 Peel the skin from the chicken and par-boil the skin in rapidly boiling water for 1 minute, then drain. With a sharp knife, remove and discard the yellow fat from the skin. Discard the clear membrane between the fat and the skin as well. Cut the skin into thin strips about 5mm/¹/₄in wide and 2.5cm/1in long. Cut the meat into bitesize chunks.

3 Heat the oil in a wok or frying pan and stir-fry the strips of chicken skin for 5 minutes, or until golden and curled up. Add the chicken meat and keep stirring until the colour changes. Add the hijiki and carrot, then stir-fry for a further minute. Add the remaining ingredients. Lower the heat and toss over the heat for 5 minutes more.

4 Remove the wok from the heat and leave to stand for about 10 minutes. Serve in small individual bowls. Sprinkle with cayenne pepper.

Nutritional information per portion: Energy 224Kcal/942kJ; Protein 19g; Carbohydrate 19.8g, of which sugars 19.4g; Fat 6.4g, of which saturates 1g; Cholesterol 52mg; Calcium 24mg; Fibre 0.6g; Sodium 1658mg.

Lotus leaf parcels filled with chicken, rice and vegetables

The lotus leaves impart a delicious smoky flavour to the rice in this dish. You can buy the dried leaves from Asian supermarkets. The parcels make a great lunch or evening meal.

SERVES 4

2 large lotus leaves
300g/11oz/1½ cups Thai jasmine rice
400ml/14fl oz/1⅔ cups vegetable or
  chicken stock
8 dried shiitake mushrooms
15ml/1 tbsp sunflower oil
200g/7oz skinless chicken thigh fillets
50g/2oz pancetta, cubed

3 garlic cloves, finely sliced
10ml/2 tsp finely grated fresh root ginger
50g/2oz carrots, cut into thin batons
50g/2oz mangetouts (snow peas), sliced
  down the middle
60ml/4 tbsp light soy sauce
15ml/1 tbsp Chinese rice wine
5ml/1 tsp cornflour (cornstarch)

1 Soak the lotus leaves in a large bowl of hot water for 1½ hours. Drain, cut in half, and set aside. Put the rice in a wok and add the stock. Bring to the boil, then reduce the heat, cover and cook gently for 10 minutes. Remove from the heat.

2 Soak the mushrooms in boiling water for 15 minutes, drain, reserving the liquid. Squeeze them dry, then discard the stems and thinly slice the caps. Cut the chicken into small cubes.

3 Add the oil to a clean wok and place over a high heat. Add the chicken and pancetta and stir-fry for 2–3 minutes, until lightly browned. Add the garlic, ginger, carrots, mangetouts and mushrooms and stir-fry for 30 seconds.

4 Add half the soy sauce, the rice wine and 60ml/4 tbsp of the reserved mushroom liquid to the wok. Combine the cornflour with 15ml/1 tbsp cold water, add to the wok and cook for a few minutes until the mixture thickens. Add the rice and the remaining soy sauce and mix well.

5 Place the lotus leaves on a clean work surface (brown side down) and divide the chicken mixture among them. Fold in the sides of the leaves, then roll up and place the parcels, seam side down, in a baking parchment-lined bamboo steamer. Place the steamer, covered, over a wok of simmering water for 20 minutes (replenishing the water if necessary). Serve immediately and unwrap at the table.

Nutritional information per portion: Energy 377Kcal/1581kJ; Protein 20.7g; Carbohydrate 63.7g, of which sugars 2.4g; Fat 4g, of which saturates 1.2g; Cholesterol 43mg; Calcium 31mg; Fibre 0.8g; Sodium 1082mg.

Chiang mai noodles

An interesting noodle dish from Thailand that combines soft, boiled noodles with crisp deep-fried ones and adds the classic Thai contrast of sweet, hot and sour flavours.

SERVES 4

250ml/8fl oz/1 cup coconut cream
15ml/1 tbsp magic paste
5ml/1 tsp Thai red curry paste
450g/1lb chicken thigh meat, chopped
   into small pieces
30ml/2 tbsp dark soy sauce
2 red (bell) peppers, seeded and
   finely diced
600ml/1 pint/2½ cups chicken or
   vegetable stock
90g/3½oz fresh or dried rice noodles

FOR THE NOODLE GARNISH
vegetable oil, for deep-frying
90g/3½oz thin dried rice noodles
2 pickled garlic cloves, chopped
small bunch fresh coriander
   (cilantro), chopped
2 limes, cut into wedges

1 Pour the coconut cream into a large wok and bring to the boil over a medium heat. Continue to boil, stirring frequently, for 8–10 minutes, until the milk separates and an oily sheen appears on the surface. Add the magic paste and red curry paste and cook, stirring constantly, for 3–5 seconds, until fragrant.

2 Add the chicken and toss over the heat until sealed on all sides. Stir in the soy sauce and peppers and stir-fry for 3–4 minutes. Add the stock. Bring to the boil, then lower the heat and simmer for 10–15 minutes, until the chicken is cooked.

3 Meanwhile, make the noodle garnish. Heat the oil in a wok to 190°C/375°F or until a cube of bread browns in about 40 seconds. Break the noodles in half, then divide them into four portions. Add one portion at a time to the hot oil. They will puff up on contact. As soon as they are crisp, remove and drain.

4 Cook the noodles in a pan of boiling water until tender, following the packet instructions. Drain, divide among four dishes, then spoon the curry sauce over. Top each with a cluster of fried noodles. Sprinkle the chopped pickled garlic and coriander on top and serve immediately, offering lime wedges for squeezing.

Nutritional information per portion: Energy 245Kcal/1034kJ; Protein 29.4g; Carbohydrate 27.6g, of which sugars 9g; Fat 1.8g, of which saturates 0.6g; Cholesterol 79mg; Calcium 35mg; Fibre 1.4g; Sodium 677mg.

Curried chicken and rice

This simple one-wok meal is perfect for casual entertaining. It can be made using virtually any tender pieces of meat or stir-fry vegetables that you have to hand.

SERVES 4

60ml/4 tbsp vegetable oil
4 garlic cloves, finely chopped
1 chicken (about 1.5kg/3–3½lb) or
   chicken pieces, skinned and boned
   and cut into bitesize pieces
5ml/1 tsp garam masala
450g/1lb/2⅔ cups jasmine rice, rinsed
   and drained
10ml/2 tsp salt
1 litre/1¾ pints/4 cups chicken stock
small bunch fresh coriander (cilantro),
   chopped, to garnish

1 Heat the oil in a wok or flameproof casserole, which has a lid. Add the garlic and cook over a low to medium heat until golden. Add the chicken, increase the heat and brown the pieces on all sides. It's best to do this in batches.

2 Add the garam masala, stir well to coat the chicken all over in the spice, then add the drained rice. Add the salt and stir to mix.

3 Pour in the stock, stir well, then cover the wok or casserole and bring to the boil. Reduce the heat to low and simmer gently for 10 minutes, until the rice is cooked and tender.

4 Lift the wok or casserole off the heat, leaving the lid on, and leave for 10 minutes.

5 Fluff up the rice grains with a fork and spoon on to a platter. Sprinkle with the coriander and serve immediately.

Nutritional information per portion: Energy 715Kcal/2994kJ; Protein 56.3g; Carbohydrate 89.8g, of which sugars 0g; Fat 13.8g, of which saturates 1.9g; Cholesterol 140mg; Calcium 32mg; Fibre 0g; Sodium 1103mg.

Orange and ginger glazed poussins

These moist, succulent poussins coated in a spiced citrus and honey glaze make a great alternative to a traditional roast. Be sure to plan ahead – they need to be marinated for at least 6 hours.

SERVES 4

4 poussins, 300–350g/11–12oz each
juice and finely grated rind of 2 oranges
2 garlic cloves, crushed
15ml/1 tbsp grated fresh root ginger
90ml/6 tbsp soy sauce
75ml/5 tbsp clear honey
2–3 star anise
30ml/2 tbsp Chinese rice wine
about 20 kaffir lime leaves
a large bunch of spring onions
    (scallions), shredded
60ml/4 tbsp butter
1 large orange, segmented

1 Place the poussins in a deep, non-metallic dish. Combine the orange rind and juice, garlic, ginger, half the soy sauce, half the honey, star anise and rice wine, then pour the mixture over the poussins. Turn the poussins so they are coated all over in the marinade. Cover the dish with clear film (plastic wrap), and place in the refrigerator for at least 6 hours to marinate.

2 Line a large, heatproof plate with the kaffir lime leaves and spring onions. Lift the poussins from the marinade and lay on the leaves. Reserve the marinade.

3 Place a trivet or steamer rack in the base of a large wok and pour in 5cm/2in water. Bring to the boil and carefully lower the plate of poussins on to the trivet or rack. Cover, reduce the heat to low and steam for 45 minutes–1 hour, or until the poussins are cooked through and tender. (Add more water if necessary.)

4 Remove the poussins from the wok and keep warm. Wipe the wok and pour in the reserved marinade, butter and the remaining soy sauce and honey. Bring to the boil, reduce the heat and cook gently for 10–15 minutes, until thick. Spoon the glaze over the poussins and serve, garnished with orange segments.

Nutritional information per portion: Energy 568Kcal/2378kJ; Protein 67.3g; Carbohydrate 18.7g, of which sugars 18.5g; Fat 25.3g, of which saturates 11.1g; Cholesterol 32mg; Calcium 110mg; Fibre 0.7g; Sodium 1344mg.

Jungle curry of guinea fowl

A traditional country curry from the north-central region of Thailand, this dish can be made using any game, fish or chicken. Guinea fowl is not typically Thai, but is widely available in the West.

SERVES 4

1 guinea fowl or similar game bird

15ml/1 tbsp vegetable oil

10ml/2 tsp Thai green curry paste

15ml/1 tbsp Thai fish sauce

2.5cm/1in piece fresh galangal, peeled and finely chopped

15ml/1 tbsp fresh green peppercorns

3 kaffir lime leaves, torn

15ml/1 tbsp whisky, preferably Mekhong

300ml/½ pint/1¼ cups chicken stock

50g/2oz snake beans or yard-long beans, cut into 5cm/2in lengths (about ½ cup)

225g/8oz/3¼ cups chestnut mushrooms, sliced

1 piece drained canned bamboo shoot, about 50g/2oz, shredded

5ml/1 tsp dried chilli flakes, to garnish (optional)

1 Cut up the guinea fowl, remove and discard the skin, then take all the meat off the bones. Chop the meat into bitesize pieces and set aside.

2 Heat the oil in a wok or frying pan and add the curry paste. Stir-fry over a medium heat for 30 seconds, until fragrant. Add the fish sauce and the guinea fowl meat and stir-fry until the meat is browned all over. Add the galangal, peppercorns, lime leaves and whisky, then pour in the stock.

3 Bring to the boil. Add the vegetables, return to a simmer and cook gently for 2–3 minutes, until they are just cooked. Spoon into a dish, sprinkle with chilli flakes, if you like, and serve.

COOK'S TIPS

• *Guinea fowl range in size from 675g/1½lb to 2kg/4½lb, but about 1.2kg/2½lb is average. American readers could use two or three Cornish hens, depending on size.*

• *Fresh green peppercorns are simply unripe berries. They are sold on the stem and look like miniature Brussels sprout stalks. You can substitute bottled green peppercorns.*

Nutritional information per portion: Energy 321Kcal/1345kJ; Protein 42.2g; Carbohydrate 1.1g, of which sugars 0.7g; Fat 15g, of which saturates 4.4g; Cholesterol 0mg; Calcium 73mg; Fibre 1.1g; Sodium 127mg.

Chinese duck curry

This richly spiced curry illustrates how five-spice powder marries the flavours of duck, ginger and butternut squash. The duck tastes good even if you only have time to marinate it briefly.

SERVES 4

4 duck breast portions, skinned
30ml/2 tbsp five-spice powder
30ml/2 tbsp sesame oil
grated rind and juice of 1 orange
1 medium butternut squash,
**   peeled and cubed**
10ml/2 tsp Thai red curry paste
30ml/2 tbsp Thai fish sauce
15ml/1 tbsp palm sugar (jaggery) or
**   light muscovado (brown) sugar**
300ml/1/2 pint/11/4 cups coconut milk
2 fresh red chillies, seeded
4 kaffir lime leaves, torn
small bunch coriander (cilantro),
**   chopped, to garnish**
noodles, to serve

1 Cut the duck meat into bitesize pieces and put in a bowl with the five-spice powder, sesame oil and orange rind and juice. Stir well to coat the duck in the marinade. Cover the bowl with clear film (plastic wrap) and set aside in a cool place to marinate for at least 15 minutes.

2 Meanwhile, bring a pan of water to the boil. Add the squash and cook for 10–15 minutes, until just tender. Drain well and set aside.

3 Pour the marinade from the duck into a wok and heat until boiling. Stir in the curry paste and cook for 2–3 minutes, until blended and fragrant. Add the duck and cook for 3–4 minutes, stirring, until browned on all sides.

4 Add the fish sauce and sugar and cook for 2 minutes more. Stir in the coconut milk until the mixture is smooth, then add the cooked squash, with the chillies and lime leaves. Simmer gently, stirring frequently, for 5 minutes, then spoon into a dish, sprinkle with the coriander and serve with noodles.

Nutritional information per portion: Energy 295Kcal/1241kJ; Protein 31.4g; Carbohydrate 13.3g, of which sugars 12.3g; Fat 15.9g, of which saturates 3.1g; Cholesterol 165mg; Calcium 102mg; Fibre 2g; Sodium 427mg.

Red duck curry with pea aubergines

This tasty curry is simmered and then left to stand to allow the flavours to blend beautifully. An electric wok will help to maintain the steady temperature needed for gentle simmering.

SERVES 4

400ml/14fl oz can coconut milk

200ml/7fl oz/scant 1 cup chicken stock

30ml/2 tbsp red Thai curry paste

8 spring onions (scallions), finely sliced

10ml/2 tsp grated fresh root ginger

30ml/2 tbsp Chinese rice wine

15ml/1 tbsp fish sauce

15ml/1 tbsp soy sauce

2 lemon grass stalks, halved lengthways

3–4 kaffir lime leaves

4 duck breast portions, cut into
    bitesize pieces

300g/11oz pea aubergines (eggplants)

10ml/2 tsp caster (superfine) sugar

salt and ground black pepper

10–12 fresh basil and mint leaves,
    to garnish

steamed jasmine rice, to serve

1 Place a wok over a low heat and add the coconut milk, stock, curry paste, spring onions, ginger, rice wine, fish and soy sauces, lemon grass and lime leaves. Stir well to mix, then bring to the boil over a medium heat.

2 Add the duck, pea aubergines and sugar to the wok and gently simmer for 25–30 minutes, stirring occasionally.

3 Remove the wok from the heat and leave to stand, covered, for about 15 minutes. Season to taste.

4 Serve the duck curry ladled into shallow bowls, garnished with fresh mint and basil leaves. Serve with steamed jasmine rice.

COOK'S TIP

Tiny pea aubergines are sold in Asian stores. If you can't find them, use regular aubergines cut into chunks.

Nutritional information per portion: Energy 241Kcal/1017kJ; Protein 31.1g; Carbohydrate 10.2g, of which sugars 10g; Fat 10.5g, of which saturates 2.3g; Cholesterol 165mg; Calcium 65mg; Fibre 1.8g; Sodium 546mg.

Shredded duck and noodle salad

This refreshing, piquant salad makes a mouthwatering first course or light meal. The moist marinated duck tastes superb with the fresh raw vegetables, noodles and zesty dressing.

SERVES 4

4 duck breast portions
30ml/2 tbsp Chinese rice wine
10ml/2 tsp finely grated fresh root ginger
60ml/4 tbsp soy sauce
15ml/1 tbsp sesame oil
15ml/1 tbsp clear honey
10ml/2 tsp Chinese five-spice powder

FOR THE NOODLES

150g/5oz cellophane noodles
small handful of fresh mint leaves
small handful of coriander (cilantro) leaves
1 red (bell) pepper, seeded and finely sliced
4 spring onions (scallions), finely sliced
50g/2oz mixed salad leaves

FOR THE DRESSING

45ml/3 tbsp light soy sauce
30ml/2 tbsp mirin
10ml/2 tsp golden caster (superfine) sugar
1 garlic clove, crushed
10ml/2 tsp chilli oil

1 Place the duck breast portions in a non-metallic bowl. Mix the rice wine, ginger, soy sauce, sesame oil, clear honey and five-spice powder. Toss to coat the duck, cover and marinate in the refrigerator for 3–4 hours.

2 Double over a large sheet of heavy foil and lay on a heatproof plate. Put the duck portions on it and spoon the marinade over. Enclose the duck in the foil, scrunching the edges to seal.

3 Place a trivet or steamer rack in a large wok and add water to a depth of about 5cm/2in. Bring to the boil and put the plate on the trivet.

4 Cover, reduce the heat and steam gently for 50–60 minutes. Remove and leave to rest for 15 minutes.

5 Soak the noodles in a large bowl of boiling water for 5–6 minutes. Refresh under cold water and drain again. Put in a bowl with the herbs, red pepper, spring onions and salad leaves.

6 Mix together all the dressing ingredients. Remove the skin from the duck and roughly shred the flesh using a fork. Divide the noodle salad among four bowls and top with the shredded duck. Spoon over the dressing and serve.

Nutritional information per portion: Energy 398Kcal/1671kJ; Protein 32.8g; Carbohydrate 41.7g, of which sugars 10.8g; Fat 11.6g, of which saturates 2.2g; Cholesterol 165mg; Calcium 40mg; Fibre 1g; Sodium 1688mg.

Duck and sesame stir-fry

This recipe comes from northern Thailand and is intended for game birds, as farmed duck has too much fat. Use wild duck if you can get it, but if using farmed duck, remove the skin and fat layer.

SERVES 4

250g/9oz boneless wild duck meat
15ml/1 tbsp sesame oil
15ml/1 tbsp vegetable oil
4 garlic cloves, finely sliced
2.5ml/¹/₂ tsp dried chilli flakes
15ml/1 tbsp Thai fish sauce
15ml/1 tbsp light soy sauce
120ml/4fl oz/¹/₂ cup water
1 head broccoli, cut into small florets
coriander (cilantro) and 15ml/1 tbsp
   toasted sesame seeds, to garnish

1 Cut the duck meat into bitesize pieces. Heat the wok, add the oils and, when hot, stir-fry the garlic over a medium heat until it is golden brown – do not let it burn.

2 Add the duck to the pan and stir-fry for a further 2 minutes, until the meat begins to brown.

3 Stir in the chilli flakes, fish sauce, soy sauce and water. Add the broccoli and continue to stir-fry for about 2 minutes, until the duck is just cooked through.

4 Serve on four warmed plates, garnished with coriander and sesame seeds.

Nutritional information per portion: Energy 192Kcal/798kJ; Protein 18.7g; Carbohydrate 2.7g, of which sugars 2.3g; Fat 12.9g, of which saturates 2.1g; Cholesterol 69mg; Calcium 104mg; Fibre 3.6g; Sodium 436mg.

Meat Dishes

Rich meat curries and gently simmered dishes lend themselves perfectly to the wok, with great depths of flavour coming from chillies, garlic, ginger or galangal. The robust tastes of fresh lemon grass and coriander can be added, married together by smooth, sweet coconut milk, which tames their stridency.

For an intense dish, try Beef Rendang, or for a milder dish, opt for Fried Rice with Pork, which is quick and easy to prepare.

Sweet and sour pork, Thai-style

It was the Chinese who originally created sweet and sour cooking, but the Thais also do it very well. This version has a fresh and clean flavour. Serve with rice for a substantial meal.

SERVES 4

350g/12oz lean pork
30ml/2 tbsp vegetable oil
4 garlic cloves, thinly sliced
1 small red onion, sliced
30ml/2 tbsp Thai fish sauce
15ml/1 tbsp granulated (white) sugar
1 red (bell) pepper, seeded and diced
1/2 cucumber, seeded and sliced
2 plum tomatoes, cut into wedges
115g/4oz piece of fresh pineapple,
    cut into small chunks
2 spring onions (scallions), cut into
    short lengths
ground black pepper
coriander (cilantro) leaves and spring
    onions (scallions), shredded to garnish

1 Place the pork in the freezer for 30–40 minutes, until firm. Using a sharp knife, cut it into thin strips.

2 Heat the oil in a wok or large frying pan. Add the garlic. Cook over a medium heat until golden, then add the pork and stir-fry for 4–5 minutes. Add the onion slices and toss to mix.

3 Add the fish sauce, sugar and ground black pepper to taste. Toss the mixture over the heat for 3–4 minutes more.

4 Stir in the red pepper, cucumber, tomatoes, pineapple and spring onions. Stir-fry for 3–4 minutes more, then spoon into a bowl. Garnish with the coriander and spring onions and serve.

Nutritional information per portion: Energy 211Kcal/881kJ; Protein 20.3g; Carbohydrate 11.8g, of which sugars 10.7g; Fat 9.5g, of which saturates 2g; Cholesterol 55mg; Calcium 31mg; Fibre 2g; Sodium 70mg.

Stir-fried pork with dried shrimp

Dried shrimps impart a delicious savoury taste, which goes very well with pork and wilted greens. This is good just as it is, but could be served with noodles or jasmine rice.

SERVES 4

250g/9oz pork fillet (tenderloin),
   thickly sliced
30ml/2 tbsp vegetable oil
2 garlic cloves, finely chopped
45ml/3 tbsp dried shrimps
10ml/2 tsp dried shrimp paste
30ml/2 tbsp soy sauce
juice of 1 lime
15ml/1 tbsp palm sugar (jaggery)
   or light muscovado (brown) sugar
1 small fresh red or green chilli,
   seeded and finely chopped
4 pak choi (bok choy) or 450g/1lb
   spring greens (collards), shredded

1 Place the pork in the freezer for about 30–40 minutes, until firm. Using a sharp knife, cut it into thin slices.

2 Heat the vegetable oil in a wok or frying pan and cook the garlic until golden brown. Add the pork and stir-fry for about 4 minutes, until just cooked through.

3 Add the dried shrimp, then stir in the shrimp paste, with the soy sauce, lime juice and sugar. Add the chilli and pak choi or spring greens and toss over the heat until the vegetables are just wilted.

4 Transfer the stir-fry to warmed individual bowls and serve immediately.

Nutritional information per portion: Energy 200Kcal/833kJ; Protein 23.1g; Carbohydrate 6.3g, of which sugars 6.2g; Fat 9.2g, of which saturates 1.7g; Cholesterol 96mg; Calcium 334mg; Fibre 2.4g; Sodium 1223mg.

Lemon grass pork

Chillies and lemon grass flavour this simple stir-fry, while chopped, unsalted peanuts add an interesting contrast in texture. Look out for jars of chopped lemon grass, which are handy when the fresh vegetable isn't available, and keep well in the refrigerator.

SERVES 4

675g/1¹/₂lb boneless pork loin
2 lemon grass stalks, finely chopped
4 spring onions (scallions),
   thinly sliced
5ml/1 tsp salt
12 black peppercorns, coarsely crushed
30ml/2 tbsp groundnut (peanut) oil
2 garlic cloves
2 fresh red chillies, seeded
5ml/1 tsp soft light brown sugar
30ml/2 tbsp Thai fish sauce
25g/1oz/¹/₄ cup roasted unsalted
   peanuts, chopped
ground black pepper
fresh coriander (cilantro) leaves,
   to garnish
cooked rice noodles, to serve

1 Trim any excess fat from the pork. Cut the meat across into 5mm/¹/₄in thick slices, then cut each slice into 5mm/¹/₄in strips. Put in a bowl with the lemon grass, spring onions, salt and crushed peppercorns; mix well. Cover with clear film (plastic wrap) and leave to marinate in a cool place for 30 minutes.

2 Preheat a wok, add the oil and swirl it around. Add the pork mixture and stir-fry over a medium heat for about 3 minutes, until browned all over.

3 Chop the garlic cloves and red chillies and add them to the wok. Stir-fry for a further 5–8 minutes over a medium heat, until the pork is cooked through and tender.

4 Add the sugar, fish sauce and chopped peanuts and toss to mix everything together. Season to taste with black pepper. Lay a bed of rice noodles on four plates, and serve the stir-fry immediately on top. Garnish with the fresh coriander leaves.

Nutritional information per portion: Energy 297Kcal/1240kJ; Protein 37.9g; Carbohydrate 2.1g, of which sugars 1.7g; Fat 15.2g, of which saturates 3.6g; Cholesterol 106mg; Calcium 20mg; Fibre 0.5g; Sodium 119mg.

Aromatic pork with basil

The combination of moist, juicy pork and mushrooms, crisp green mangetouts and fragrant basil in this ginger- and garlic-infused stir-fry is absolutely delicious. Served with simple steamed jasmine rice, it makes a perfect quick meal during the week.

SERVES 4

500g/1¼lb pork fillet (tenderloin)
40g/1½oz cornflour (cornstarch)
15ml/1 tbsp sunflower oil
10ml/2 tsp sesame oil
15ml/1 tbsp very finely shredded
   fresh root ginger
3 garlic cloves, thinly sliced
200g/7oz mangetouts (snow peas)
300g/11oz/generous 4 cups mixed
   mushrooms, such as shiitake, button
   (white) or oyster, sliced if large
120ml/4fl oz/½ cup Chinese cooking wine
45ml/3 tbsp soy sauce
a small handful of sweet basil leaves
salt and ground black pepper
steamed jasmine rice, to serve

1 Thinly slice the pork fillet. Place the cornflour in a strong plastic bag. Season well and add the sliced pork. Shake to coat the pork in flour and then remove the pork and shake off any excess flour. Set aside.

2 Preheat the wok over a high heat and add the oils. When very hot, stir in the ginger and garlic and cook for 30 seconds. Add the pork and cook for about 5 minutes, stirring, to seal.

3 Halve the mangetouts lengthways and add to the wok with the mixed mushrooms. Stir-fry for 2–3 minutes. Add the Chinese cooking wine and soy sauce, stir-fry for a further 2–3 minutes and then remove the wok from the heat.

4 Just before serving, stir the sweet basil leaves into the pork. Serve on individual plates with steamed jasmine rice.

Nutritional information per portion: Energy 298Kcal/1248kJ; Protein 30.4g; Carbohydrate 14.6g, of which sugars 4.8g; Fat 9.8g, of which saturates 2.4g; Cholesterol 79mg; Calcium 41mg; Fibre 2g; Sodium 903mg.

Sweet and sour pork

This classic Chinese-style dish, with its stunning colours, piquant sweet and sour sauce and gloriously sticky texture makes a tasty evening meal. Serve with fried rice and steamed Asian greens to create an authentic Chinese meal.

SERVES 4

1 carrot
1 red (bell) pepper
4 spring onions (scallions)
45ml/3 tbsp light soy sauce
15ml/1 tbsp Chinese rice wine
15ml/1 tbsp sesame oil
5ml/1 tsp freshly ground black pepper
500g/1¼lb pork loin, cut into
   1cm/½in cubes
65g/2½oz/9 tbsp cornflour (cornstarch)
65g/2½oz/9 tbsp plain (all-purpose) flour

5ml/1 tsp bicarbonate of soda (baking soda)
pinch of salt
sunflower oil, for deep-frying
10ml/2 tsp finely grated garlic
5ml/1 tsp finely grated fresh root ginger
60ml/4 tbsp tomato ketchup
30ml/2 tbsp caster (superfine) sugar
15ml/1 tbsp rice vinegar
15ml/1 tbsp cornflour (cornstarch) blended
   with 120ml/4fl oz/½ cup water
egg fried rice or noodles, to serve

1 Chop the carrots, pepper and spring onions into thin shreds. In a large mixing bowl, combine 15ml/1 tbsp of the soy sauce with the rice wine, sesame oil and pepper. Toss in the pork. Cover and chill for 3–4 hours.

2 Combine the cornflour, plain flour and bicarbonate of soda in a bowl. Add a pinch of salt and mix in 150ml/¼ pint/⅔ cup cold water to make a thick batter. Add the pork to the batter and mix well with your hands to coat evenly.

3 Fill a wok one-third full with the sunflower oil and heat to 180°C/350°F or until a cube of bread browns in 45 seconds. Deep-fry the pork cubes, in batches, for 1–2 minutes, or until golden. Remove and drain on kitchen paper.

4 Mix together the garlic, ginger, tomato ketchup, sugar, the remaining soy sauce, rice vinegar and cornflour mixture in a small pan. Place over a medium heat for 2–3 minutes, until thickened. Add the carrot, red pepper and spring onions, stir and remove from the heat.

5 Reheat the deep-frying oil to 180°C/350°F and then re-fry the pork, in batches, for 1–2 minutes, until golden and crisp. Drain, add to the sauce and toss to mix. Serve with egg-fried rice or noodles.

Nutritional information per portion: Energy 445Kcal/1873kJ; Protein 29.8g; Carbohydrate 52.2g, of which sugars 17.4g; Fat 13.9g, of which saturates 2.9g; Cholesterol 79mg; Calcium 55mg; Fibre 2g; Sodium 1154mg.

Cellophane noodles with pork

Simple, speedy and satisfying, this is the sort of dish the wok was made for. It looks spectacular, with the clear, glass-like noodles curling over the colourful vegetable mixture.

SERVES 2

200g/7oz dried cellophane noodles
30ml/2 tbsp vegetable oil
15ml/1 tbsp magic paste
200g/7oz minced (ground) pork
1 fresh green or red chilli, seeded and
    finely chopped
300g/11oz/3½ cups beansprouts
bunch spring onions (scallions),
    finely chopped
30ml/2 tbsp soy sauce
30ml/2 tbsp Thai fish sauce
30ml/2 tbsp sweet chilli sauce
15ml/1 tbsp palm sugar (jaggery)
    or light muscovado (brown) sugar
30ml/2 tbsp rice vinegar
30ml/2 tbsp roasted peanuts, chopped
    and small bunch fresh coriander
    (cilantro), chopped, to garnish

1 Place the noodles in a large bowl, cover with boiling water and soak for 10 minutes. Drain the noodles and set aside until ready to use.

2 Heat the oil in a wok or large, heavy frying pan. Add the magic paste and stir-fry for 2–3 seconds, then add the pork. Stir-fry the meat, breaking it up with a wooden spatula, for 2–3 minutes, until browned all over.

3 Add the chopped chilli and stir-fry for 3–4 seconds, then add the beansprouts and chopped spring onions, stir-frying for a few seconds after each addition.

4 Snip the noodles into shorter lengths and add to the wok, with the soy sauce, Thai fish sauce, sweet chilli sauce, sugar and rice vinegar.

5 Toss the ingredients together over the heat until well combined and the noodles have warmed through. Pile on to a platter or into a large bowl. Sprinkle over the peanuts and coriander and serve immediately.

Nutritional information per portion: Energy 755Kcal/3153kJ; Protein 39.8g; Carbohydrate 96.8g, of which sugars 14.6g; Fat 23.3g, of which saturates 4.2g; Cholesterol 63mg; Calcium 94mg; Fibre 4g; Sodium 1158mg.

Five-flavour noodles

The Japanese name for this dish translates as 'five different ingredients'; but you can add as many ingredients as you like to make an exciting and tasty noodle stir-fry.

SERVES 4

300g/11oz dried Chinese thin egg noodles
    or 500g/1¼lb fresh yaki-soba noodles
200g/7oz lean boneless pork, thinly sliced
22ml/4 tsp sunflower oil
10g/¼oz grated fresh root ginger
1 garlic clove, crushed
200g/7oz green cabbage, roughly chopped
1 green (bell) pepper, seeded
1 red (bell) pepper, seeded
115g/4oz/2 cups beansprouts
salt and ground black pepper
20ml/4 tsp ao-nori seaweed,
    to garnish (optional)

FOR THE SEASONING MIX

60ml/4 tbsp Worcestershire sauce
15ml/1 tbsp Japanese soy sauce
15ml/1 tbsp oyster sauce
15ml/1 tbsp sugar
2.5ml/½ tsp salt
ground white pepper

1 Cook the noodles according to the instructions on the packet. Drain well and set aside.

2 Cut the pork into 3–4cm/1¼–1½in strips and season with salt and pepper.

3 Heat 7.5ml/1½ tsp of the oil in a wok. Stir-fry the pork until just cooked, then remove it from the pan.

4 Once cooled, wipe the wok clean with kitchen paper, and heat the remaining oil in it. Add the ginger, garlic and cabbage and stir-fry for 1 minute.

5 Slice the green and red peppers into fine strips. Add the beansprouts to the wok, stir until softened, then add the sliced peppers and stir-fry for a further minute.

6 Return the pork to the pan and add the noodles. Stir in all the ingredients for the seasoning mix and stir-fry for 2–3 minutes. Serve immediately, sprinkled with ao-nori seaweed (if using).

Nutritional information per portion: Energy 471Kcal/1988kJ; Protein 22.8g; Carbohydrate 71g, of which sugars 17.4g; Fat 12.6g, of which saturates 3g; Cholesterol 54mg; Calcium 95mg; Fibre 5.2g; Sodium 652mg.

Spicy fried noodles

This is a wonderfully versatile dish because you can adapt it to include your favourite ingredients – just as long as you keep a balance of flavours, textures and colours.

SERVES 4

225g/8oz egg thread noodles
60ml/4 tbsp vegetable oil
175g/6oz pork fillet (tenderloin)
1 skinless, boneless chicken breast
    portion (about 175g/6oz)
2 garlic cloves, finely chopped
115g/4oz/1 cup cooked peeled
    prawns (shrimp)
juice of half a lemon
45ml/3 tbsp Thai fish sauce
30ml/2 tbsp soft light brown sugar
2 eggs, beaten
½ fresh red chilli, seeded
    and finely chopped
50g/2oz/⅔ cup beansprouts
60ml/4 tbsp roasted peanuts, chopped
3 spring onions (scallions), cut into
    5cm/2in lengths and shredded
45ml/3 tbsp chopped fresh
    coriander (cilantro)

1 Bring a large pan of water to the boil. Add the noodles, remove the pan from the heat and leave for 5 minutes.

2 Slice the pork and chicken into thin strips. Heat 45ml/3 tbsp of the oil in a wok or large frying pan, add the garlic and cook for 30 seconds. Add the chicken and pork and stir-fry until lightly browned. Add the prawns and stir-fry for 2 minutes. Add the lemon juice, fish sauce and sugar. Stir-fry until the sugar dissolves.

3 Drain the noodles and add to the wok with the remaining 15ml/1 tbsp oil. Toss all the ingredients together. Pour the beaten eggs over the noodles and stir-fry until almost set, then add the chilli and beansprouts.

4 Divide the roasted peanuts, spring onions and coriander leaves into two equal portions, add one portion to the pan and stir-fry for about 2 minutes.

5 Tip the noodle mixture on to a serving platter. Sprinkle on the remaining roasted peanuts, spring onions and chopped coriander and serve immediately.

Nutritional information per portion: Energy 597Kcal/2504kJ; Protein 39.3g; Carbohydrate 50.8g, of which sugars 10.3g; Fat 27.8g, of which saturates 5.5g; Cholesterol 226mg; Calcium 76mg; Fibre 2.9g; Sodium 250mg.

Crispy Thai noodle salad

Rice noodles puff up and become light and crispy when deep-fried and make a lovely base for this tangy, fragrant salad with its heady combination of flavours. Serve as a snack or light meal.

SERVES 4

sunflower oil, for deep-frying
115g/4oz thin rice noodles
45ml/3 tbsp groundnut (peanut) oil
2 eggs, lightly beaten with
    15ml/1 tbsp water
30ml/2 tbsp palm sugar (jaggery)
30ml/2 tbsp Thai fish sauce
15ml/1 tbsp rice wine vinegar
30ml/2 tbsp tomato ketchup
1 fresh red chilli, thinly sliced
3 garlic cloves, crushed
5ml/1 tsp finely grated fresh
    root ginger
200g/7oz minced (ground) pork
400g/14oz cooked peeled tiger
    prawns (shrimp)
4 spring onions (scallions),
    finely shredded
60ml/4 tbsp chopped coriander
    (cilantro) leaves

1 Fill a wok one-third full of sunflower oil and heat to 180°C/350°F or until a cube of bread browns in about 45 seconds. Working in batches, deep-fry the rice noodles, for 10–20 seconds, or until puffed up. Drain on kitchen paper.

2 Heat 15ml/1 tbsp of groundnut oil in a clean wok. Add half the egg mixture and swirl the wok to make an omelette. Cook gently for 2–3 minutes until just set, then transfer to a board. Repeat to make a second omelette. Place on top of the first one and roll into a cylinder. Cut crossways to make thin strips. Set aside.

3 In a bowl, mix together the sugar, fish sauce, rice wine vinegar, tomato ketchup, chilli, garlic and ginger. Stir half this mixture into the pork. Heat the remaining groundnut oil in the wok. When hot, add the pork mixture and stir-fry for 4–5 minutes until cooked through. Add the prawns and stir-fry for 1–2 minutes.

4 Remove the wok from the heat and add the remaining palm sugar mixture, fried vermicelli, spring onions and coriander and toss to combine. Divide among four warmed plates and serve topped with the shredded omelette.

Nutritional information per portion: Energy 508Kcal/2118kJ; Protein 35.1g; Carbohydrate 33.1g, of which sugars 10.5g; Fat 26.4g, of which saturates 5g; Cholesterol 371mg; Calcium 142mg; Fibre 0.8g; Sodium 405mg.

Curried pork with pickled garlic

This very rich curry is best accompanied by lots of plain rice and perhaps a light vegetable dish. Asian stores sell pickled garlic – it's well worth investing in a jar for its delicious sweet taste.

SERVES 2

130g/4½oz lean pork steaks
30ml/2 tbsp vegetable oil
1 garlic clove, crushed
15ml/1 tbsp Thai red curry paste
130ml/4½fl oz/generous ½ cup
 coconut cream
2.5cm/1in piece fresh root ginger,
 finely chopped
30ml/2 tbsp vegetable or chicken stock
30ml/2 tbsp Thai fish sauce
5ml/1 tsp granulated (white) sugar
2.5ml/½ tsp ground turmeric
10ml/2 tsp lemon juice
4 pickled garlic cloves, finely chopped
strips of lemon and lime rind,
 to garnish

1 Put the pork steaks in the freezer for 30–40 minutes, until firm, then, using a sharp knife, cut the meat into thin slices, trimming off any excess fat.

2 Heat the oil in a wok or large, heavy frying pan and cook the garlic over a low to medium heat until golden brown. Do not let it burn.

3 Add the Thai red curry paste and stir it in well.

4 Add the coconut cream and stir until the liquid begins to reduce and thicken.

5 Stir in the pork. Cook for 4 minutes, until the pork is cooked through.

6 Add the chopped ginger, stock, Thai fish sauce, sugar and ground turmeric, stirring constantly. Add the lemon juice and pickled garlic and heat through. Serve in bowls, garnished with strips of the rind.

Nutritional information per portion: Energy 227Kcal/947kJ; Protein 16.3g; Carbohydrate 9.8g, of which sugars 6.1g; Fat 14g, of which saturates 2.4g; Cholesterol 41mg; Calcium 30mg; Fibre 1g; Sodium 474mg.

Fried rice with pork

This is great for using up last night's leftover rice, but for safety's sake, it must have been cooled quickly and kept in the refrigerator, then fried until thoroughly heated.

SERVES 4–6

45ml/3 tbsp vegetable oil
1 onion, chopped
15ml/1 tbsp chopped garlic
115g/4oz pork, cut into small cubes
2 eggs, beaten
500g/2¼lb/4 cups cooked rice
30ml/2 tbsp Thai fish sauce
15ml/1 tbsp dark soy sauce
2.5ml/½ tsp caster (superfine) sugar
4 spring onions (scallions), finely sliced,
    sliced fresh red chillies, and 1 lime,
    cut into wedges, to serve

1 Heat the oil in a wok or large frying pan. Add the chopped onion and garlic and cook for about 2 minutes until softened.

2 Add the pork to the softened onion and garlic. Stir-fry until the pork is cooked through.

3 Add the eggs and cook until scrambled into small lumps.

4 Add the cooked rice and continue to stir and toss, to coat it all with the oil and prevent it from sticking.

5 Add the Thai fish sauce, soy sauce and sugar and mix well. Continue to fry until the rice is thoroughly heated. Spoon into warmed individual bowls and serve with sliced spring onions, chillies and lime wedges.

Nutritional information per portion: Energy 343Kcal/1448kJ; Protein 11.2g; Carbohydrate 54.3g, of which sugars 2.2g; Fat 10.6g, of which saturates 2g; Cholesterol 82mg; Calcium 51mg; Fibre 0.6g; Sodium 220mg.

Nasi goreng

One of the most popular dishes from Indonesia, this is a marvellous way to use up leftover rice, as well as meats such as pork and chicken. Always ensure leftover ingredients are thoroughly reheated.

SERVES 4–6

350g/12oz/1¾ cups basmati rice
   (dry weight), cooked and cooled
2 eggs
30ml/2 tbsp water
105ml/7 tbsp sunflower oil
2–3 fresh red chillies
10ml/2 tsp shrimp paste
2 garlic cloves, crushed
1 onion, sliced
225g/8oz pork fillet or fillet of beef,
   cut into strips
115g/4oz cooked, peeled prawns (shrimp)
225g/8oz cooked chicken, chopped
30ml/2 tbsp dark soy sauce
salt and freshly ground black pepper
crispy fried onions, to serve

1 Separate the grains of the cooked rice with a fork. Cover and set aside. Beat the eggs with the water, and season.

2 Heat 15ml/1 tbsp of the oil in a wok or frying pan, pour in half the egg mixture and cook until set, without stirring. Slide the omelette on to a plate, roll up and cut into strips. Set aside. Make another omelette in the same way.

3 Finely shred one of the chillies and set aside. Put the shrimp paste into a food processor, add the remaining chilli, garlic and onion. Process to a paste.

4 Heat the remaining oil in a wok. Fry the paste, without browning, until fragrant. Add the strips of pork or beef and toss over the heat, to seal in the juices. Cook for 2 minutes, stirring constantly. Add the prawns, cook for 2 minutes, stirring, then add the chicken, rice, and soy sauce and season to taste.

5 Serve garnished with the omelette strips, shredded chilli and onions.

Nutritional information per portion: Energy 463Kcal/1929kJ; Protein 27.3g; Carbohydrate 49.4g, of which sugars 2.1g; Fat 17.1g, of which saturates 2.7g; Cholesterol 151mg; Calcium 49mg; Fibre 0.5g; Sodium 288mg.

Spicy shredded beef

The essence of this recipe is that the beef is sliced into very fine strips for stir-frying. This is easier to achieve if the beef is placed in the freezer for at least 30 minutes until it is very firm.

SERVES 2

225g/8oz rump (round) steak

15ml/1 tbsp each light and dark
   soy sauce

15ml/1 tbsp rice wine or
   medium-dry sherry

5ml/1 tsp soft dark brown sugar
   or golden granulated sugar

90ml/6 tbsp vegetable oil

1 large onion, thinly sliced

2.5cm/1in piece fresh root ginger,
   peeled and grated

1–2 carrots, cut into matchsticks

2–3 fresh or dried chillies, halved,
   seeded (optional) and chopped

salt and ground black pepper

fresh chives, to garnish

1 With a sharp knife, slice the well-chilled beef very thinly, then cut each slice into fine strips or shreds. In a bowl, mix together the light and dark soy sauces with the rice wine or sherry and sugar. Add the strips of beef and stir well to ensure they are evenly coated with the marinade.

2 Heat a wok and add half the oil. When it is hot, stir-fry the onion and ginger for 3–4 minutes, then transfer to a plate. Add the carrot, stir-fry for 3–4 minutes until slightly softened, then transfer to a plate and keep warm.

3 Heat the remaining oil in the wok, then add the beef, with the marinade, followed by the chillies. Cook over high heat for 2 minutes, stirring constantly. Return the fried onion and ginger to the wok and stir-fry for 1 minute more.

4 Season with salt and pepper to taste, cover and cook for 30 seconds. Transfer the meat into two warmed bowls and add the strips of carrots. Garnish with fresh chives and serve.

Nutritional information per portion: Energy 532Kcal/2207kJ; Protein 27.3g; Carbohydrate 19.3g, of which sugars 15.4g; Fat 38.1g, of which saturates 5.8g; Cholesterol 66mg; Calcium 59mg; Fibre 3.3g; Sodium 1154mg.

Green beef curry with Thai aubergines

This is a very quick curry so be sure to use good quality meat. Sirloin is recommended, but tender rump steak could be used instead. Since it uses bought curry paste, there's very little preparation.

SERVES 4–6

450g/1lb sirloin steak
15ml/1 tbsp vegetable oil
45ml/3 tbsp Thai green curry paste
600ml/1 pint/2½ cups coconut milk
4 kaffir lime leaves, torn
15–30ml/1–2 tbsp Thai fish sauce
5ml/1 tsp palm sugar (jaggery) or
  light muscovado (brown) sugar
150g/5oz small Thai aubergines
  (eggplants), halved
small handful of fresh Thai basil
2 fresh green chillies, to garnish

1 Trim off any excess fat from the sirloin steak, then using a sharp knife, cut it into long, thin strips. This is easiest to do if it has been chilled in the freezer for 30–40 minutes. Set it aside.

2 Heat the oil in a wok. Add the curry paste and cook for 1–2 minutes, until fragrant. Stir in half the coconut milk, adding a little at a time. Cook, stirring frequently, for about 5–6 minutes, until an oily sheen appears on the surface of the liquid.

3 Add the beef to the pan with the kaffir lime leaves, Thai fish sauce, sugar and aubergine halves. Cook for 2–3 minutes, then stir in the remaining coconut milk.

4 Bring back to a simmer and cook until the meat and aubergines are cooked through. Stir in the Thai basil just before serving. Finely shred the green chillies and use to garnish the curry.

Nutritional information per portion: Energy 146Kcal/615kJ; Protein 18.2g; Carbohydrate 6.2g, of which sugars 6.1g; Fat 5.6g, of which saturates 1.9g; Cholesterol 38mg; Calcium 36mg; Fibre 0.5g; Sodium 163mg.

Beef rendang

In Indonesia, where this spicy dish originated, it is usually served with the meat quite dry; if you prefer more sauce, simply add more water when stirring in the potatoes.

SERVES 6–8

2 onions or 5–6 shallots, chopped

4 garlic cloves, chopped

2.5cm/1in piece fresh galangal, peeled and
    sliced, or 15ml/1 tbsp galangal paste

lower part of 1 lemon grass stem, sliced

2.5cm/1in piece fresh turmeric, peeled and
    sliced, or 5ml/1 tsp ground turmeric

2.5cm/1in piece fresh root ginger, peeled

4–6 fresh red chillies, seeded

1kg/2¼lb prime beef in one piece

5ml/1 tsp tamarind pulp

5ml/1 tsp coriander seeds, dry-fried

5ml/1 tsp cumin seeds, dry-fried

2 kaffir lime leaves, torn into pieces

2 x 400ml/14fl oz cans coconut milk

300ml/½ pint/1¼ cups water

30ml/2 tbsp dark soy sauce

8–10 small new potatoes, scrubbed

salt and ground black pepper

crispy fried onions, sliced fresh red chillies
    and spring onions (scallions), to garnish

1 Put the onions or shallots in a food processor. Add the garlic, galangal, lemon grass and turmeric. Slice the ginger, roughly chop the chillies and add to the food processor. Process to a fine paste. Alternatively, grind in a mortar, using a pestle.

2 Cut the meat into cubes using a large sharp knife, then place in a bowl. Soak the tamarind pulp in 60ml/4 tbsp warm water and set aside.

3 Grind the dry-fried coriander and cumin seeds, then add to the meat with the onion, chilli paste and kaffir lime leaves; stir well. Cover and leave in a cool place to marinate while you prepare the other ingredients.

4 Pour the coconut milk and water into a wok, then stir in the spiced meat and soy sauce. Strain the tamarind water and add to the wok. Stir over a medium heat until the liquid boils, then simmer gently, half-covered, for 1½ hours.

5 Add the potatoes and simmer for 20–25 minutes, or until the meat and the potatoes are tender. Add water if you prefer. Season and serve, garnished with the crispy fried onions, chillies and spring onions.

Nutritional information per portion: Energy 289Kcal/1210kJ; Protein 30.2g; Carbohydrate 15.4g, of which sugars 8.6g; Fat 12.2g, of which saturates 5g; Cholesterol 73mg; Calcium 63mg; Fibre 1.4g; Sodium 465mg.

Thick beef curry in sweet peanut sauce

This curry is deliciously rich and thicker than most other Thai curries. Serve it with boiled jasmine rice and salted duck eggs, if you like.

SERVES 4–6

600ml/1 pint/2¹/₂ cups coconut milk
45ml/3 tbsp Thai red curry paste
45ml/3 tbsp Thai fish sauce
30ml/2 tbsp palm sugar (jaggery) or
  light muscovado (brown) sugar
2 lemon grass stalks, bruised
450g/1lb rump (round) steak,
  cut into thin strips
75g/3oz/³/₄ cup roasted
  peanuts, ground
2 fresh red chillies, sliced
5 kaffir lime leaves, torn
salt and ground black pepper
2 salted eggs, cut in wedges,
  and 10–15 Thai basil leaves,
  to garnish

1 Pour half the coconut milk into a large, heavy pan. Place over a medium heat and bring to the boil, stirring constantly until the milk separates.

2 Stir in the Thai red curry paste and cook for 2–3 minutes until the mixture is fragrant and thoroughly blended. Add the Thai fish sauce, sugar and bruised lemon grass stalks. Mix well until combined.

3 Continue to cook until the colour deepens. Gradually add the remaining coconut milk, stirring constantly. Bring back to the boil.

4 Add the beef and peanuts. Cook, stirring constantly, for 8–10 minutes, or until most of the liquid has evaporated. Add the chillies and lime leaves. Season to taste and serve, garnished with wedges of salted eggs and Thai basil leaves.

Nutritional information per portion: Energy 310Kcal/1296kJ; Protein 29.1g; Carbohydrate 9.7g, of which sugars 8.5g; Fat 17.4g, of which saturates 5.3g; Cholesterol 69mg; Calcium 59mg; Fibre 1.2g; Sodium 215mg.

Stir-fried beef in oyster sauce

This simple recipe is often made with just one type of mushroom, but using a mixture makes the dish more interesting. Oyster sauce adds depth and is an essential ingredient.

SERVES 4–6

30ml/2 tbsp soy sauce

15ml/1 tbsp cornflour (cornstarch)

450g/1lb rump (round) or sirloin steak,
   placed in the freezer for 30-40 minutes
   and sliced diagonally into thin strips

45ml/3 tbsp groundnut (peanut) oil or
   vegetable oil for stir-frying

15ml/1 tbsp chopped garlic

15ml/1 tbsp chopped fresh root ginger

225g/8oz/3¼ cups mixed mushrooms
   such as shiitake, oyster and straw

30ml/2 tbsp oyster sauce

5ml/1 tsp granulated (white) sugar

4 spring onions (scallions),
   cut into short lengths

ground black pepper

2 fresh red chillies, seeded and cut
   into strips, to garnish

1 Mix the soy sauce and cornflour in a large bowl. Add the steak, coating well, cover with clear film (plastic wrap) and leave to marinate for 1–2 hours.

2 Heat half the oil in a wok or large, heavy frying pan. Add the garlic and ginger and cook for 1–2 minutes, until fragrant. Drain the steak, add to the wok and stir well. Cook, stirring, for 1–2 minutes, until browned. Remove and set aside.

3 Heat the remaining oil in the wok. Add the mushrooms. Stir-fry over a medium heat until golden brown.

4 Return the steak to the wok and mix it with the mushrooms. Add the oyster sauce and sugar, mix well, then add ground black pepper to taste. Toss the mixture over the heat until all the ingredients are thoroughly combined.

5 Stir the spring onions into the wok. Serve, garnished with the strips of red chilli.

Nutritional information per portion: Energy 160Kcal/670kJ; Protein 17.6g; Carbohydrate 2.9g, of which sugars 2.7g; Fat 8.8g, of which saturates 2g; Cholesterol 44mg; Calcium 10mg; Fibre 0.6g; Sodium 485mg.

Thai crispy noodles with beef

Rice vermicelli is something special – when it's added to hot oil it expands to four times its original size. The strands become crisp and crunchy, adding a great contrast to the beef and vegetables.

SERVES 4

450g/1lb rump (round) steak

teriyaki sauce, for brushing

175g/6oz rice vermicelli

groundnut (peanut) oil, for deep-frying
    and stir-frying

8 spring onions (scallions), diagonally sliced

2 garlic cloves, crushed

4–5 carrots, cut into julienne strips

1–2 fresh red chillies, seeded and finely sliced

2 small courgettes (zucchini), diagonally sliced

5ml/1 tsp grated fresh root ginger

60ml/4 tbsp rice vinegar

90ml/6 tbsp light soy sauce

about 475ml/16fl oz/2 cups beef stock

1 Beat the steak to about 2.5cm/1in thick. Place in a shallow dish, brush generously with the teriyaki sauce and set aside for 2–4 hours to marinate.

2 Separate the vermicelli into manageable loops. Pour the oil into a large wok to a depth of 5cm/2in, and heat until a strand of vermicelli cooks immediately. Carefully add a loop of vermicelli to the oil. Almost immediately, turn to cook on the other side. Remove and drain on kitchen paper. Repeat with the remaining loops. Transfer the cooked noodles to a deep serving bowl and keep warm.

3 Strain the oil into a heatproof bowl and set it aside. Return 15ml/1 tbsp oil to a clean wok. When it sizzles, fry the steak for about 30 seconds on each side, until browned on the outside but still pink inside. Cut into thick slices. Set aside.

4 Add a little extra oil to the wok, add the spring onions, garlic and carrots and stir-fry over a medium heat for 5–6 minutes, until the carrots are slightly soft and have a glazed appearance. Add the chillies, courgettes and ginger and stir-fry for 1–2 minutes. Stir in the rice vinegar, soy sauce and stock. Cook for 4 minutes, until the sauce has thickened slightly. Return the slices of steak and cook for 1–2 minutes.

5 Spoon the steak, vegetables and sauce over the noodles and toss carefully to mix. Serve immediately.

COOK'S TIP

The noodles will begin to soften as soon as you add the meat mixture. Leave a few on the surface to keep them crispy.

Nutritional information per portion: Energy 410Kcal/1712kJ; Protein 30.7g; Carbohydrate 41.4g, of which sugars 6.6g; Fat 13.5g, of which saturates 3g; Cholesterol 66mg; Calcium 49mg; Fibre 1.9g; Sodium 1687mg.

Beef and butternut squash with chilli

Stir-fried beef and squash flavoured with warm spices, oyster sauce and fresh herbs makes a robust meal when served with rice or noodles. Chilli and fresh root ginger give the dish a vigorous tang.

SERVES 4

30ml/2 tbsp sunflower oil

2 onions, cut into thick slices

500g/1¼lb butternut squash, peeled,
   seeded and cut into thin strips

675g/1½lb fillet steak (beef tenderloin)

60ml/4 tbsp soy sauce

90g/3½oz/½ cup golden caster
   (superfine) sugar

1 fresh bird's eye chilli, seeded and chopped

15ml/1 tbsp finely shredded fresh
   root ginger

30ml/2 tbsp Thai fish sauce

5ml/1 tsp ground star anise

5ml/1 tsp five-spice powder

15ml/1 tbsp oyster sauce

4 spring onions (scallions), shredded

a small handful of sweet basil leaves

a small handful of mint leaves

1 Heat a wok over a medium-high heat and add the oil, trickling it down below the rim to coat the surface. When hot, add the onions and squash. Stir-fry for 2–3 minutes, then reduce the heat, cover and cook gently for 5–6 minutes, or until just tender.

2 Place the beef between two sheets of clear film (plastic wrap) and beat, using a mallet or rolling pin, until thin. Using a sharp knife, cut into strips.

3 In a separate wok, mix the soy sauce, sugar, chilli, ginger, fish sauce, star anise, five-spice powder and oyster sauce. Stir-fry for 3–4 minutes.

4 Add the beef to the soy sauce mixture in the wok and cook over a high heat for 3–4 minutes. Remove from the heat. Add the onion and squash slices to the beef and toss well with the spring onions and herbs. Serve immediately.

Nutritional information per portion: Energy 500Kcal/2093kJ; Protein 41.3g; Carbohydrate 36.9g, of which sugars 33.8g; Fat 21.7g, of which saturates 7.2g; Cholesterol 98mg; Calcium 91mg; Fibre 2.9g; Sodium 1243mg.

Fried rice with beef

One of the joys of wok cooking is the ease and speed with which a really good meal can be prepared. This delectable beef and rice stir-fry can be on the table in 15 minutes.

SERVES 4

200g/7oz beef steak, chilled

15ml/1 tbsp vegetable oil

2 garlic cloves, finely chopped

1 egg

250g/9oz/2¼ cups cooked jasmine rice

½ medium head broccoli, coarsely chopped

30ml/2 tbsp dark soy sauce

15ml/1 tbsp light soy sauce

5ml/1 tsp palm sugar (jaggery) or
   light muscovado (brown) sugar

15ml/1 tbsp Thai fish sauce

ground black pepper

chilli sauce, to serve

1 Trim the steak and cut into very thin strips with a sharp knife.

2 Heat the oil in a wok and cook the garlic over a low to medium heat until golden. Do not let it burn. Increase the heat to high, add the steak and stir-fry for 2 minutes.

3 Move the beef to the edges of the wok. Break the egg into the centre.

4 When the egg starts to set, stir-fry it with the meat. Add the rice and toss all the contents of the wok together, scraping up any residue left on the base and mixing it in. Then add the broccoli, soy sauces, sugar and fish sauce and stir-fry for 2 minutes more.

5 Season to taste with pepper and serve immediately, in individual bowls, with chilli sauce.

Nutritional information per portion: Energy 385Kcal/1606kJ; Protein 20.7g; Carbohydrate 52.7g, of which sugars 2.5g; Fat 9.8g, of which saturates 2.8g; Cholesterol 81mg; Calcium 59mg; Fibre 1.6g; Sodium 590mg.

Warm lamb and noodle salad with mint

This Thai-inspired salad combines thin slices of wok-fried lamb with lightly cooked fresh vegetables and rice noodles, all tossed together with a deliciously fragrant, aromatic, Asian-style dressing.

SERVES 4

30ml/2 tbsp red Thai curry paste
60ml/4 tbsp sunflower oil
750g/1lb 11oz lamb neck fillets,
    thinly sliced
250g/9oz sugar snap peas
500g/1¼lb dried thick rice noodles
6–7 spring onions (scallions)
1 red (bell) pepper, seeded
    and very thinly sliced
1 cucumber, thinly sliced
a large handful of fresh mint leaves

FOR THE DRESSING

15ml/1 tbsp sunflower oil
juice of 2 limes
1 garlic clove, crushed
15ml/1 tbsp sugar
15ml/1 tbsp Thai fish sauce
30ml/2 tbsp soy sauce

1 In a non-metallic bowl, mix together the curry paste and half the oil. Add the lamb and coat well. Cover and leave in the refrigerator for up to 24 hours.

2 Blanch the sugar snap peas in lightly salted boiling water for 1–2 minutes. Drain, refresh under cold water, drain again and transfer to a large bowl.

3 Soak the noodles in boiling water for 5–10 minutes, until tender. Drain and separate with your fingers. Slice the spring onions diagonally. Add the noodles to the bowl containing the sugar snap peas, then add the sliced red pepper, cucumber and spring onions. Toss lightly to mix.

4 Heat a wok over a high heat and add the remaining sunflower oil. Stir-fry the lamb, in batches, for 3–4 minutes, until cooked, then add to the bowl of salad.

5 Place all the dressing ingredients in a screw top jar and shake well to combine. Pour the dressing over the warm salad, sprinkle over the mint and toss well.

Nutritional information per portion: Energy 820Kcal/3418kJ; Protein 46g; Carbohydrate 76.4g, of which sugars 9.4g; Fat 36g, of which saturates 11.7g; Cholesterol 143mg; Calcium 55mg; Fibre 4.1g; Sodium 709mg.

Coconut spiced lamb on poppadums

Crisp, melt-in-the-mouth mini poppadums make a great base for these divine little bites.
Top them with a drizzle of yogurt and a spoonful of mango chutney, then serve immediately.

MAKES 25

30ml/2 tbsp sunflower oil

4 shallots, finely chopped

30ml/2 tbsp medium curry paste

300g/11oz minced (ground) lamb

90ml/6 tbsp tomato purée (paste)

5ml/1 tsp caster (superfine) sugar

200ml/7fl oz/scant 1 cup coconut cream

juice of 1 lime

60ml/4 tbsp chopped fresh mint leaves

vegetable oil, for deep-frying

salt and ground black pepper

25 mini poppadums

natural (plain) yogurt and mango
    chutney, to drizzle

1 red chilli cut into slivers and mint
    leaves, to garnish

1 Heat the oil in a wok over a medium heat and stir-fry the shallots for 4–5 minutes, then add the curry paste. Stir-fry for 1 minute and then add the lamb. Stir-fry over a high heat for a further 4–5 minutes, then stir in the tomato purée, sugar and coconut cream.

2 Simmer the lamb for 25–30 minutes, until the liquid has been absorbed. Season and stir in the lime juice and mint. Turn off the heat and keep warm.

3 Fill a separate wok one-third full of oil and heat to 180°C/350°F or until a cube of bread browns in about 45 seconds. Deep-fry the poppadums for 30–40 seconds. Drain on kitchen paper.

4 Place the poppadums on a serving platter. Put a spoonful of spiced lamb on each one, then top with a little yogurt and mango chutney. Serve immediately, garnished with slivers of red chilli and mint leaves.

Nutritional information per portion: Energy 63Kcal/260kJ; Protein 2.7g; Carbohydrate 2.7g, of which sugars 1.3g; Fat 4.7g, of which saturates 1.4g; Cholesterol 9mg; Calcium 7mg; Fibre 0.3g; Sodium 45mg.

Vegetable Main Dishes

The recipes in this section are exciting and innovative without being overly intricate. Aromatic Okra and Coconut Stir-fry, for instance, tastes spectacular, but can be cooked in about 10 minutes. Other unusual offerings include Sweet Pumpkin and Peanut Curry and Jewelled Vegetable Rice with Crispy Fried Eggs. A few recipes in this chapter contain Thai fish sauce, but you can substitute it with mushroom ketchup for vegetarians.

Deep-fried beancurd rolls stuffed with spiced vegetables

Beancurd sheets are made from boiled soya milk; the skin that forms on the top is lifted off and dried in sheets. They are available in Asian supermarkets and need to be soaked in water before use.

SERVES 4

50g/2oz fresh enokitake mushrooms

30ml/2 tbsp groundnut (peanut) oil

1 garlic clove, crushed

5ml/1 tsp grated fresh root ginger

4 spring onions (scallions), finely shredded

1 small carrot, cut into thin matchsticks

115g/4oz bamboo shoots, cut into
   thin matchsticks

15ml/1 tbsp light soy sauce

5ml/1 tsp chilli sauce

5ml/1 tsp granulated (white) sugar

15ml/1 tbsp cornflour (cornstarch)

8 beancurd sheets (approximately
   18 x 23cm/7 x 9in each)

sunflower oil, for deep-frying

crisp salad leaves, to serve

1 Finely chop the mushrooms. Heat the oil in a wok over a high heat and add the mushrooms, garlic, ginger, spring onions, carrot and bamboo shoots. Stir-fry for 2–3 minutes, add the soy sauce, chilli sauce and sugar and toss to mix well.

2 Remove the vegetables from the heat and drain the juices. Set aside to cool.

3 In a small bowl, mix the cornflour with 60ml/4 tbsp of cold water to form a paste. Soak the beancurd sheets in a bowl of warm water for 10–15 seconds, then lay them out on a clean work surface and pat dry with kitchen paper.

4 Brush the edges of one of the beancurd sheets with the cornflour paste and place 30–45ml/2–3 tbsp of the vegetable mixture at one end of the sheet. Fold the edges over towards the centre and roll up tightly to form a neat roll. Repeat with the remaining beancurd sheets and filling.

5 Place the filled rolls on a baking parchment-lined baking sheet or tray, cover and chill for 3–4 hours.

6 To cook, fill a wok one-third full with sunflower oil and heat to 180°C/350°F or until a cube of bread, dropped into the oil, browns in about 45 seconds. Working in batches, deep-fry the rolls for 2–3 minutes, or until they are crisp and golden. Drain on kitchen paper and serve immediately with crisp salad leaves.

Nutritional information per portion: Energy 288Kcal/1190kJ; Protein 9.5g; Carbohydrate 3.2g, of which sugars 2.2g; Fat 26.5g, of which saturates 3.2g; Cholesterol 0mg; Calcium 524mg; Fibre 1g; Sodium 10mg.

Stir-fried crispy tofu

The asparagus grown in the part of Asia where this recipe originated tends to have slender stalks. Look for it in Thai markets or substitute the thin asparagus popularly known as sprue. If you use thicker asparagus, you may need to cook it for longer.

SERVES 2

250g/9oz fried tofu cubes
30ml/2 tbsp groundnut (peanut) oil
15ml/1 tbsp Thai green curry paste
30ml/2 tbsp light soy sauce
2 kaffir lime leaves, rolled into cylinders
    and thinly sliced
30ml/2 tbsp granulated (white) sugar
150ml/¼ pint/⅔ cup vegetable stock
250g/9oz Asian asparagus, trimmed and
    sliced into 5cm/2in lengths
30ml/2 tbsp roasted peanuts,
    finely chopped

1 Preheat the grill (broiler) to medium. Place the tofu cubes in a grill (broiling) pan and grill (broil) for 2–3 minutes, then turn them over and continue to cook until they are crisp and golden brown all over. Watch them carefully as they must not burn.

2 Heat the oil in a wok or heavy frying pan. Add the green curry paste and cook over a medium heat, stirring constantly, for 1–2 minutes, until fragrant.

3 Stir the soy sauce, lime leaves, sugar and vegetable stock into the wok or pan and mix well. Bring to the boil, then reduce the heat to low so that the mixture is just simmering.

4 Add the asparagus and simmer gently for 5 minutes. Chop each piece of tofu into four, then add to the pan with the peanuts.

5 Toss to coat all the ingredients in the sauce, then transfer into a warmed dish and serve immediately.

Nutritional information per portion: Energy 287Kcal/1195kJ; Protein 14.3g; Carbohydrate 20.3g, of which sugars 19.5g; Fat 17g, of which saturates 2.1g; Cholesterol 0mg; Calcium 682mg; Fibre 2.2g; Sodium 1075mg.

Sweet and sour vegetables with tofu

Big, bold and beautiful, this is a hearty stir-fry that will satisfy the hungriest guests. Stir-fries are always a good choice when entertaining, because you can prepare the ingredients ahead of time and then cook them incredibly quickly in the wok.

SERVES 4

4 shallots

3 garlic cloves

30ml/2 tbsp groundnut (peanut) oil

250g/9oz Chinese leaves (Chinese cabbage), shredded

8 baby corn cobs, sliced on the diagonal

2 red (bell) peppers, seeded and thinly sliced

200g/7oz/1³/₄ cups mangetouts (snow peas), trimmed and sliced

250g/9oz tofu, rinsed, drained and cut in 1cm/¹/₂in cubes

60ml/4 tbsp vegetable stock

30ml/2 tbsp light soy sauce

15ml/1 tbsp granulated (white) sugar

30ml/2 tbsp rice vinegar

2.5ml/¹/₂ tsp dried chilli flakes

small bunch coriander (cilantro), chopped

1 Slice the shallots thinly using a sharp knife. Finely chop the garlic.

2 Heat the oil in a wok or large frying pan and cook the shallots and garlic for 2–3 minutes over a medium heat, until golden. Do not let the garlic burn or it will taste bitter.

3 Add the shredded cabbage, toss over the heat for 30 seconds, then add the sliced baby corn cobs and repeat the process.

4 Add the red peppers, mangetouts and tofu in the same way, each time adding a single ingredient and tossing it over the heat for about 30 seconds before adding the next.

5 Pour in the stock and soy sauce. Mix together the sugar and vinegar in a small bowl, stirring until the sugar has dissolved, then add to the wok or pan. Sprinkle over the chilli flakes and coriander, toss to mix well and serve.

Nutritional information per portion: Energy 180Kcal/751kJ; Protein 9.1g; Carbohydrate 17g, of which sugars 15.6g; Fat 8.7g, of which saturates 1.1g; Cholesterol 0mg; Calcium 386mg; Fibre 4.1g; Sodium 575mg.

Tofu and green bean red curry

Red curry paste is one of the authentic flavourings of Thai cooking, and works just as well in vegetarian dishes as it does in meat-based recipes.

SERVES 4–6

175g/6oz firm tofu, rinsed and drained
600ml/1 pint/2$\frac{1}{2}$ cups coconut milk
15ml/1 tbsp Thai red curry paste
45ml/3 tbsp mushroom ketchup
10ml/2 tsp palm sugar (jaggery) or
   light muscovado (brown) sugar
225g/8oz/3$\frac{1}{4}$ cups button
   (white) mushrooms
115g/4oz/scant 1 cup green
   beans, trimmed
4 kaffir lime leaves
2 fresh red chillies
fresh coriander (cilantro) leaves,
   to garnish

1 Cut the firm tofu into 2cm/$\frac{3}{4}$in cubes and set aside.

2 Pour about one-third of the coconut milk into a wok. Cook until it starts to separate and an oily sheen appears on the surface.

3 Add the Thai red curry paste, mushroom ketchup and sugar to the wok. Mix thoroughly, then add the mushrooms. Stir and cook for 1 minute.

4 Stir in the remaining coconut milk. Bring back to the boil, then add the green beans and tofu cubes. Simmer gently for 4–5 minutes more.

5 Roughly tear the kaffir lime leaves and slice the red chillies. Stir them into the wok. Transfer the curry into a serving dish, garnish with the coriander leaves and serve immediately.

Nutritional information per portion: Energy 79Kcal/333kJ; Protein 3.9g; Carbohydrate 8.2g, of which sugars 7.8g; Fat 3.6g, of which saturates 0.6g; Cholesterol 0mg; Calcium 189mg; Fibre 0.8g; Sodium 647mg.

Marinated tofu and broccoli with crispy shallots

This meltingly tender tofu, flavoured with a fragrant blend of spices and served with tender young stems of broccoli, makes a perfect light supper or lunch.

SERVES 4

**10 Thai shallots, sliced into paper thin
    rings and separated**
vegetable oil for deep-frying
500g/1¼lb block of firm tofu, drained
45ml/3 tbsp kecap manis
30ml/2 tbsp sweet chilli sauce
45ml/3 tbsp soy sauce
5ml/1 tsp sesame oil
**5ml/1 tsp finely grated fresh
    root ginger**
**400g/14oz tenderstem broccoli,
    halved lengthways**
**45ml/3 tbsp roughly chopped
    coriander (cilantro)**
30ml/2 tbsp toasted sesame seeds
30ml/2 tbsp crispy fried shallots
**steamed white rice or noodles,
    to serve**

1 Add the shallot rings to a wok one-third full of hot oil, then lower the heat and stir constantly until crisp. Spread on kitchen paper to drain.

2 Cut the tofu into four triangular pieces and place in a heatproof dish.

3 Combine the kecap manis, chilli sauce, soy sauce, sesame oil and ginger, then pour over the tofu. Leave to marinate for 30 minutes, turning occasionally.

4 Place the broccoli on a heatproof plate on a trivet or steamer rack in the wok. Cover and steam for 4–5 minutes, until just tender. Remove and keep warm.

5 Put the dish of tofu on the trivet in the wok, cover and steam for 4–5 minutes. Divide the broccoli among four plates and top each with a piece of tofu. Spoon the remaining juices over the tofu and broccoli, then sprinkle over the coriander, sesame seeds and crispy shallots. Serve with steamed white rice or noodles.

Nutritional information per portion: Energy 202Kcal/840kJ; Protein 16.5g; Carbohydrate 6.9g, of which sugars 5.6g; Fat 12.1g, of which saturates 1.7g; Cholesterol 0mg; Calcium 750mg; Fibre 3.5g; Sodium 938mg.

Mee krob

The name of this popular Thai dish means 'deep-fried noodles'. The taste is a stunning combination of sweet and hot, salty and sour, while the texture contrives to be both crisp and chewy.

SERVES 2

vegetable oil, for deep-frying
130g/4¹/₂oz rice vermicelli noodles

FOR THE SAUCE

30ml/2 tbsp vegetable oil
130g/4¹/₂oz fried tofu, cut into thin strips
2 garlic cloves, finely chopped
2 small shallots, finely chopped
15ml/1 tbsp light soy sauce
30ml/2 tbsp palm sugar (jaggery) or
   light muscovado (brown) sugar
60ml/4 tbsp vegetable stock
juice of 1 lime
2.5ml/¹/₂ tsp dried chilli flakes

FOR THE GARNISH

15ml/1 tbsp vegetable oil
1 egg
25g/1oz/¹/₃ cup beansprouts
1 spring onion (scallion), thinly shredded
1 fresh red chilli, seeded and finely chopped
1 whole head pickled garlic

1 Heat the oil for deep-frying in a wok or large pan to 190°C/375°F or until a cube of bread, added to the oil, browns in about 40 seconds. Add the noodles and deep-fry until golden and crisp. Drain on kitchen paper and set aside.

2 To make the sauce, heat the oil in a wok, add the fried tofu and cook over a medium heat until crisp. Transfer to a plate. Add the garlic and shallots to the wok and cook until golden brown. Stir in the soy sauce, sugar, stock, lime juice and chilli flakes. Cook, stirring, until the mixture begins to caramelize. Add the reserved tofu and stir until it soaks up some of the liquid. Remove from the heat and set aside.

3 Prepare the egg garnish. Heat the oil in a wok or frying pan. Lightly beat the egg with 15ml/1 tbsp water. Pour into the wok in a thin stream to form trails. As soon as it sets, transfer it to a plate using a fish slice or metal spatula.

4 Slice across the bulb of the pickled garlic so that each slice looks like a flower. Crumble the noodles into the tofu sauce, mix well, then spoon into serving bowls. Sprinkle with the beansprouts, spring onion, fried egg strips, chilli and pickled garlic 'flowers' and serve immediately.

Nutritional information per portion: Energy 497Kcal/2075kJ; Protein 10.2g; Carbohydrate 70.2g, of which sugars 18.3g; Fat 20g, of which saturates 2.8g; Cholesterol 104.5mg; Calcium 51mg; Fibre .7g; Sodium 583.5mg.

Indian mee goreng

This is a truly international dish, combining Indian, Chinese and Western ingredients. Sold on the streets of Singapore and Malaysia, it is a delicious treat for lunch or evening meal.

SERVES 4–6

450g/1lb fresh yellow egg noodles

60–90ml/4–6 tbsp vegetable oil

115g/4oz fried tofu or 150g/5oz firm tofu

2 eggs

30ml/2 tbsp water

1 onion, sliced

1 garlic clove, crushed

15ml/1 tbsp light soy sauce

30–45ml/2–3 tbsp tomato ketchup

15ml/1 tbsp chilli sauce (or to taste)

1 large cooked potato, diced

4 spring onions (scallions), cut in half and shredded

1–2 fresh green chillies, seeded and finely sliced

1 Bring a large pan of water to the boil, add the fresh egg noodles and cook for just 2 minutes. Drain the noodles then rinse under cold water to halt cooking. Drain them again and set aside, spreading them out on a large platter to dry.

2 If using fried tofu, cut each cube in half, refresh it in a pan of boiling water, then drain well. Heat 30ml/2 tbsp of the oil in a wok or large frying pan. If using plain tofu, cut into cubes and fry until brown, then remove and set aside.

3 Beat the eggs with the water. Add to the wok and cook, without stirring, until set. Flip over, cook the other side, then remove, roll up and slice thinly.

4 Heat the remaining oil in the wok and fry the onion and garlic for 2–3 minutes. Add the drained noodles, soy sauce, ketchup and chilli sauce. Toss well over a medium heat for 2 minutes. Add the potato. Reserve a few shredded spring onions for the garnish and stir the rest into the wok with the chilli and tofu.

5 When hot, stir in the omelette. Serve garnished with the reserved spring onion.

Nutritional information per portion: Energy 478Kcal/2010kJ; Protein 16.8g; Carbohydrate 64.2g, of which sugars 5.1g; Fat 18.9g, of which saturates 3.2g; Cholesterol 86mg; Calcium 323mg; Fibre 2.9g; Sodium 466mg.

Sweet pumpkin and peanut curry

A hearty, soothing curry perfect for autumn or winter evenings. Its cheerful colour alone will raise the spirits – and the combination of pumpkin and peanuts tastes great.

SERVES 4

30ml/2 tbsp vegetable oil
4 garlic cloves, crushed
4 shallots, finely chopped
30ml/2 tbsp yellow curry paste
600ml/1 pint/2½ cups vegetable stock
2 kaffir lime leaves, torn
15ml/1 tbsp chopped fresh galangal
450g/1lb pumpkin, peeled, seeded
    and diced
225g/8oz sweet potatoes, diced
90g/3½oz/scant 1 cup unsalted,
    roasted peanuts, chopped
300ml/½ pint/1¼ cups coconut milk
90g/3½oz/1½ cups chestnut
    mushrooms, sliced
30ml/2 tbsp soy sauce
50g/2oz/⅓ cup pumpkin seeds,
    toasted, and fresh green chilli
    flowers, to garnish

1 Heat the oil in a wok. Add the garlic and shallots and cook over a medium heat, stirring occasionally, for 10 minutes, until softened and golden. Do not let them burn.

2 Add the yellow curry paste and stir-fry over medium heat for 30 seconds, until fragrant, then add the stock, lime leaves, galangal, pumpkin and sweet potatoes. Bring to the boil, stirring frequently, then reduce the heat to low and simmer gently for 15 minutes.

3 Add the chopped peanuts, coconut milk, mushrooms and soy sauce and simmer for 5 minutes more. Serve garnished with the toasted pumpkin seeds and chilli flowers and serve.

COOK'S TIP
The well-drained vegetables from any of these curries would make a tasty filling for a pastry or pie. This may not be a Thai tradition, but it is a good example of fusion food.

Nutritional information per portion: Energy 285Kcal/1189kJ; Protein 8.5g; Carbohydrate 24.8g, of which sugars 12.8g; Fat 17.5g, of which saturates 3g; Cholesterol 0mg; Calcium 94mg; Fibre 4.9g; Sodium 535mg.

Thai yellow vegetable curry

This hot and spicy curry made with coconut milk has a creamy richness that contrasts wonderfully with the heat of chilli and the bite of lightly cooked vegetables.

SERVES 4

30ml/2 tbsp sunflower oil
200ml/7fl oz/scant 1 cup coconut cream
200g/7oz snake beans
300ml/½ pint/1¼ cups coconut milk
150ml/¼ pint/⅔ cup vegetable stock
200g/7oz baby corn
4 baby courgettes (zucchini), sliced
1 small aubergine (eggplant), sliced
10ml/2 tsp palm sugar (jaggery)
fresh coriander (cilantro) leaves, to garnish
noodles or rice, to serve

FOR THE CURRY PASTE

10ml/2 tsp hot chilli powder
10ml/2 tsp ground coriander
10ml/2 tsp ground cumin
5ml/1 tsp ground turmeric
15ml/1 tbsp chopped fresh galangal
10ml/2 tsp finely grated garlic
30ml/2 tbsp finely chopped lemon grass
4 red Asian shallots, finely chopped
5ml/1 tsp finely chopped lime rind

1 Make the curry paste. Place the spices, galangal, garlic, lemon grass, shallots and lime rind in a food processor and blend with 30–45ml/2–3 tbsp cold water to make a smooth paste. Add a little more water if the paste seems too dry.

2 Heat a large wok over a medium heat and add the sunflower oil. When hot add 30–45ml/2–3 tbsp of the curry paste and stir-fry for 1–2 minutes. Add the coconut cream and cook gently for 8–10 minutes, until it starts to separate.

3 Cut the snake beans into 2cm/¾in lengths. Add the coconut milk, stock and vegetables to the wok and cook gently for 8–10 minutes, until the vegetables are just tender. Stir in the palm sugar, garnish with coriander leaves and serve with noodles or rice.

COOK'S TIP

To make your own curry paste you will need a good food processor or blender, preferably one with an attachment for processing smaller quantities. Alternatively, you can use a large mortar and pestle, but be warned – it will be hard work. Store any remaining curry paste in a screw-top jar in the refrigerator for up to a week.

Nutritional information per portion: Energy 126Kcal/528kJ; Protein 4.7g; Carbohydrate 12.7g, of which sugars 11.9g; Fat 6.7g, of which saturates 1.1g; Cholesterol 5mg; Calcium 90mg; Fibre 2.5g; Sodium 752mg.

Stuffed sweet peppers

These stuffed peppers are unusual in that they are steamed rather than baked, making them light and tender. The filling of lightly curried mushrooms looks attractive and tastes wonderful.

SERVES 4

3 garlic cloves, finely chopped

2 coriander (cilantro) roots, finely chopped

400g/14oz/3 cups mushrooms, quartered

5ml/1 tsp Thai red curry paste

1 egg, lightly beaten

15ml/1 tbsp Thai fish sauce or mushroom ketchup

15ml/1 tbsp light soy sauce

2.5ml/¹⁄₂ tsp granulated (white) sugar

3 kaffir lime leaves, finely chopped

4 yellow (bell) peppers, halved lengthways and seeded

1 In a mortar or spice grinder, pound or grind the garlic with the coriander roots. Scrape into a bowl.

2 Put the mushrooms in a food processor and pulse briefly until they are finely chopped. Add to the garlic mixture, then stir in the curry paste, beaten egg, sauces, sugar and chopped lime leaves.

3 Place the pepper halves in a single layer in a bamboo steamer. Spoon the mixture loosely into the pepper halves. Do not pack the mixture down tightly or the filling will dry out.

4 Bring the water in the wok to the boil, then lower the heat and steam the peppers for 15 minutes, or until the flesh is tender. Serve hot.

Nutritional information per portion: Energy 103Kcal/429kJ; Protein 6.1g; Carbohydrate 14.4g, of which sugars 12g; Fat 2.7g, of which saturates 0.7g; Cholesterol 48mg; Calcium 30mg; Fibre 4.4g; Sodium 297mg.

Noodles and vegetables in coconut sauce

When everyday vegetables are livened up with Thai spices and flavours, the result is a delectable dish that everyone will enjoy. Noodles add bulk and a welcome contrast in texture.

SERVES 4–6

30ml/2 tbsp sunflower oil
15ml/1 tbsp Thai red curry paste
1 lemon grass stalk, finely chopped
1 onion, thickly sliced
150g/5oz head of broccoli
3 courgettes (zucchini), thickly sliced
115g/4oz Savoy cabbage, thickly sliced
2 carrots, thickly sliced
2 x 400ml/14fl oz cans coconut milk
475ml/16fl oz/2 cups vegetable stock
150g/5oz dried egg noodles
30ml/2 tbsp soy sauce
60ml/4 tbsp chopped fresh coriander
   (cilantro), plus extra to garnish

1 Heat the oil in a wok. Add the curry paste and lemon grass and stir-fry for 2–3 seconds. Add the onion and cook over medium heat until softened.

2 Thickly slice the broccoli stem and separate the head into florets. Add the broccoli stem, courgettes, cabbage and carrots to the wok. Reduce the heat to low and cook gently, stirring occasionally, for 5 minutes.

3 Increase the heat to medium, stir in the coconut milk and vegetable stock and bring to the boil.

4 Add the broccoli florets and noodles, and simmer for 20 minutes.

5 Stir the soy sauce and chopped coriander into the wok. Transfer to bowls and serve, garnished with fresh coriander.

Nutritional information per portion: Energy 192Kcal/808kJ; Protein 5.6g; Carbohydrate 29.4g, of which sugars 11.5g; Fat 6.6g, of which saturates 1.4g; Cholesterol 8mg; Calcium 83mg; Fibre 2.4g; Sodium 554mg.

Thai noodles with Chinese chives

This recipe requires a little time for preparation, but the cooking time is very fast. Everything is cooked in a hot wok and should be eaten immediately. This is a filling and tasty vegetarian dish.

SERVES 4

350g/12oz dried thick rice noodles
1cm/½in piece fresh root ginger,
    peeled and grated
30ml/2 tbsp light soy sauce
45ml/3 tbsp vegetable oil
225g/8oz Quorn (mycoprotein),
    cut into small cubes
2 garlic cloves, crushed
1 large onion, cut into thin wedges
115g/4oz fried tofu, thinly sliced
1 fresh green chilli, seeded and thinly sliced
175g/6oz/3 cups beansprouts
2 large bunches garlic chives,
    total weight about 115g/4oz,
    cut into 5cm/2in lengths
50g/2oz/½ cup roasted peanuts, ground
30ml/2 tbsp dark soy sauce
30ml/2 tbsp chopped fresh coriander
    (cilantro), and 1 lemon,
    cut into wedges, to garnish

1 Soak the noodles in warm water for 30 minutes. Drain and set aside. Mix the ginger, light soy sauce and 15ml/1 tbsp of the oil in a bowl. Add the Quorn, then set aside for 10 minutes. Drain, reserving the marinade.

2 Heat 15ml/1 tbsp of the remaining oil in a wok and cook the garlic for a few seconds. Add the Quorn and stir-fry for 3–4 minutes. Using a slotted spoon, transfer to a plate and set aside.

3 Heat the remaining oil in the wok and stir-fry the onion for 3–4 minutes, until softened and tinged with brown. Add the tofu and chilli, stir-fry briefly and then add the noodles. Stir-fry over a medium heat for 4–5 minutes.

4 Stir in the beansprouts, garlic chives and most of the ground peanuts. Stir well, then add the Quorn, the dark soy sauce and the reserved marinade.

5 When hot, spoon on to serving plates and garnish with the remaining ground peanuts, the coriander and lemon.

Nutritional information per portion: Energy 584Kcal/2435kJ; Protein 19.7g; Carbohydrate 82.9g, of which sugars 7.5g; Fat 18.2g, of which saturates 2.6g; Cholesterol 0mg; Calcium 242mg; Fibre 5.8g; Sodium 984mg.

Sweet and hot vegetable noodles

Although it has 'hot' in the title, this dish has only the mildest suggestion of heat. Ginger and plum sauce give it a fruity flavour, while lime juice and tamarind paste add a tang to the aromatic stir-fry.

SERVES 4

2.5cm/1in piece fresh root ginger
130g/4½oz drained canned
   bamboo shoots
2 medium carrots
90g/3½oz mooli (daikon)
130g/4½oz dried thick rice noodles
30ml/2 tbsp groundnut (peanut) oil
1 garlic clove, crushed
1 small white cabbage, shredded
130g/4½oz/1½ cups beansprouts
10ml/2 tsp tamarind paste
30ml/2 tbsp soy sauce
30ml/2 tbsp plum sauce
10ml/2 tsp sesame oil
15ml/1 tbsp palm sugar (jaggery) or
   light muscovado (brown) sugar
juice of ½ lime
small bunch fresh coriander
   (cilantro), chopped
60ml/4 tbsp sesame seeds, toasted

1 Slice the fresh root ginger, bamboo shoots, carrots and mooli into thin batons. Cook the noodles in a pan of boiling water, following the packet instructions.

2 Meanwhile, heat the oil in a wok or large frying pan and stir-fry the ginger and garlic for 2–3 minutes over a medium heat, until golden. Drain the noodles and set aside.

3 Add the sliced bamboo shoots to the wok, increase the heat to high and stir-fry for 5 minutes. Add the carrot batons, shredded cabbage and beansprouts to the wok and stir-fry for a further 5 minutes, until they are beginning to char at the edges.

4 Stir in the tamarind paste, soy sauce, plum sauce, sesame oil, sugar and lime juice. Add the mooli, chopped coriander and drained noodles, then toss well to mix all the ingredients together and coat everything in the sauce.

5 Transfer into serving bowls, sprinkle with toasted sesame seeds and serve.

Nutritional information per portion: Energy 321Kcal/1333kJ; Protein 7.1g; Carbohydrate 37.8g, of which sugars 9.8g; Fat 15.4g, of which saturates 2.1g; Cholesterol 0mg; Calcium 142mg; Fibre 4.3g; Sodium 413mg.

Vegetable noodles with bean sauce

Yellow bean sauce adds a distinctive Chinese flavour to this wonderfully simple dish of spicy vegetables and noodles. The sauce is made from fermented yellow beans and has a marvellous texture and spicy, aromatic flavour, if used in the right proportion.

SERVES 4

150g/5oz thin egg noodles

200g/7oz baby leeks, sliced lengthways

200g/7oz baby courgettes (zucchini),
   halved lengthways

200g/7oz sugarsnap peas, trimmed

200g/7oz peas

15ml/1 tbsp sunflower oil

5 garlic cloves, sliced

45ml/3 tbsp yellow bean sauce

45ml/3 tbsp sweet chilli sauce

30ml/2 tbsp sweet soy sauce

roasted cashew nuts, to garnish

1 Cook the noodles according to the packet instructions, drain and set aside.

2 Line a large bamboo steamer with perforated baking parchment and place the leeks, courgettes and both types of peas in it.

3 Cover the steamer and suspend it over a wok of simmering water. Steam the vegetables for about 5 minutes, then remove and set aside.

4 Pour the water from the wok and wipe dry with kitchen paper. Pour the sunflower oil into the wok and place over a medium heat. Add the sliced garlic and stir-fry for 1–2 minutes.

5 In a separate bowl, mix together the yellow bean, sweet chilli and soy sauces, then pour into the wok. Stir to mix with the garlic, then add the steamed vegetables and the noodles and toss to combine.

6 Cook the vegetables and noodles for 2–3 minutes, stirring frequently, until heated through.

7 To serve, divide the noodles among four serving bowls and scatter over the cashew nuts to garnish.

Nutritional information per portion: Energy 296Kcal/1241kJ; Protein 14.2g; Carbohydrate 44.9g, of which sugars 7.4g; Fat 7.8g, of which saturates 1.6g; Cholesterol 11mg; Calcium 61mg; Fibre 8.2g; Sodium 209mg.

Corn and cashew nut curry

A substantial curry, due to the potatoes and corn, this dish combines all the essential flavours of southern Thailand. It is deliciously aromatic, but the flavour is fairly mild.

SERVES 4

400g/14oz potatoes
30ml/2 tbsp vegetable oil
4 shallots, chopped
90g/3¹/₂oz/scant 1 cup cashew nuts
5ml/1 tsp Thai red curry paste
1 lemon grass stalk, finely chopped
200g/7oz can chopped tomatoes
600ml/1 pint/2¹/₂ cups boiling water
200g/7oz/generous 1 cup drained
    canned whole kernel corn
4 celery sticks, sliced
2 kaffir lime leaves, rolled into
    cylinders and thinly sliced
15ml/1 tbsp tomato ketchup
15ml/1 tbsp light soy sauce
5ml/1 tsp palm sugar (jaggery) or
    light muscovado (brown) sugar
4 spring onions (scallions), thinly sliced
small bunch fresh basil, chopped,
    to garnish

1 Peel the potatoes and cut them into chunks.

2 Heat the vegetable oil in a wok. Add the chopped shallots and stir-fry over a medium heat for 2–3 minutes, until softened.

3 Add the cashew nuts to the wok and stir-fry for a few minutes until they are golden.

4 Stir in the Thai red curry paste. Stir-fry for 1 minute, then add the potatoes, chopped lemon grass, canned chopped tomatoes and boiling water.

5 Bring back to the boil, then reduce the heat to low, cover and simmer gently for 15–20 minutes, or until the potatoes are tender.

6 Stir in the canned corn, sliced celery, lime leaves, tomato ketchup, soy sauce, sugar and spring onions, reserving a few slices for garnish.

7 Simmer for a further 5 minutes, until heated through.

8 Spoon the curry into warmed serving bowls. Sprinkle with the reserved sliced spring onions and chopped basil and serve.

Nutritional information per portion: Energy 401Kcal/1681kJ; Protein 9.9g; Carbohydrate 51.7g, of which sugars 16.3g; Fat 18.6g, of which saturates 3.2g; Cholesterol 0mg; Calcium 41mg; Fibre 3.9g; Sodium 698mg.

Stir-fried seeds and vegetables

The contrast between crunchy seeds, tender vegetables and a rich, savoury sauce is what makes this dish so delicious. Super-speedy to cook in the wok, it can be served on its own, or with rice or noodles.

SERVES 4

2 garlic cloves
2.5cm/1in piece fresh root ginger, peeled
2 large carrots
2 large courgettes (zucchini)
90g/3½oz/1½ cups oyster mushrooms
30ml/2 tbsp vegetable oil
30ml/2 tbsp sesame seeds
30ml/2 tbsp sunflower seeds
30ml/2 tbsp pumpkin seeds
150g/5oz watercress or spinach leaves,
   coarsely chopped
small bunch fresh mint or coriander
   (cilantro), leaves and stems chopped
60ml/4 tbsp black bean sauce
30ml/2 tbsp light soy sauce
15ml/1 tbsp palm sugar (jaggery) or
   light muscovado (brown) sugar
30ml/2 tbsp rice vinegar

1 Finely chop the garlic and ginger. Cut the carrots and courgettes into batons and tear the mushrooms into pieces.

2 Heat the oil in a wok and add the seeds. Toss over a medium heat for 1 minute, then add the garlic and ginger and continue to stir-fry until the ginger is fragrant and the garlic is golden. Do not let the spices or garlic burn or they will taste bitter.

3 Add the carrots, courgettes and mushrooms to the wok and stir-fry over a medium heat for a further 5 minutes, until all the vegetables are tender and golden at the edges.

4 Add the watercress or spinach with the fresh herbs. Toss over the heat for 1 minute, then stir in the black bean sauce, soy sauce, sugar and vinegar. Stir-fry for 1–2 minutes, until hot and combined. Serve immediately.

Nutritional information per portion: Energy 205Kcal/849kJ; Protein 6.9g; Carbohydrate 9.7g, of which sugars 7.7g; Fat 15.6g, of which saturates 2g; Cholesterol 0mg; Calcium 159mg; Fibre 3.4g; Sodium 294mg.

Aromatic okra and coconut stir-fry

Stir-fried okra spiced with mustard, cumin and red chillies and sprinkled with freshly grated coconut makes a great quick supper. It is the perfect way to enjoy these succulent pods, with the sweetness of the coconut complementing the warm spices.

SERVES 4

600g/1lb 6oz okra
60ml/4 tbsp sunflower oil
1 onion, finely chopped
15ml/1 tbsp mustard seeds
15ml/1 tbsp cumin seeds
2–3 dried red chillies
10–12 curry leaves
2.5ml/½ tsp ground turmeric
90g/3½oz freshly grated coconut
salt and ground black pepper
poppadums, rice or naan, to serve

1 Cut each of the okra diagonally into 1cm/½in lengths. Set aside.

2 Heat the wok and add the sunflower oil. When the oil is hot add the chopped onion and stir-fry over a medium heat for about 5 minutes until softened.

3 Add the mustard seeds, cumin seeds, red chillies and curry leaves to the onions and stir-fry over a high heat for about 2 minutes. Add the okra and turmeric to the wok and continue to stir-fry over a high heat for 3–4 minutes.

4 Remove from the heat, sprinkle over the coconut and season with salt and ground black pepper. Serve with poppadums, steamed rice or naan bread.

COOK'S TIP
Fresh okra is widely available from most supermarkets and Asian stores. Choose fresh, firm, green specimens and avoid any that are limp or turning brown.

Nutritional information per portion: Energy 211Kcal/873kJ; Protein 5g; Carbohydrate 6.3g, of which sugars 5.2g; Fat 18.7g, of which saturates 7.1g; Cholesterol 0mg; Calcium 246mg; Fibre 7.6g; Sodium 15mg.

Jewelled vegetable rice with crispy fried eggs

Inspired by the traditional Indonesian dish nasi goreng, this vibrant, colourful stir-fry makes a tasty light meal. Alternatively, serve it as an accompaniment to simply grilled meat or fish. To make an extra-healthy option, use brown basmati rice in place of the white rice.

SERVES 4

2 fresh corn on the cob
60ml/4 tbsp sunflower oil
2 garlic cloves, finely chopped
4 red Asian shallots, thinly sliced
1 small fresh red chilli, finely sliced
90g/3½oz carrots, cut into
    thin matchsticks
90g/3½oz fine green beans,
    cut into 2cm/¾in lengths
1 red (bell) pepper, seeded and
    cut into 1cm/½in dice
90g/3½oz baby button
    (white) mushrooms
500g/1¼lb cooked long grain rice,
    completely cooled
45ml/3 tbsp light soy sauce
10ml/2 tsp green Thai curry paste
4 eggs
crisp green salad leaves and
    lime wedges, to serve

1 First shuck the corn cobs. Remove all the papery leaves, and the silky threads. With a sharp knife cut at the base of the kernels down the length of the cob.

2 Heat 30ml/2 tbsp of the sunflower oil in a wok over a high heat. When hot, add the garlic, shallots and chilli. Stir-fry for about 2 minutes. Add the carrots, green beans, corn, red pepper and mushrooms and stir-fry for 3–4 minutes. Add the cooked, cooled rice and stir-fry for a further 4–5 minutes.

3 Mix together the light soy sauce and curry paste and add to the wok. Toss to mix well and stir-fry for 2–3 minutes until piping hot.

4 Meanwhile, fry the eggs one at a time in a clean wok. Make sure that the oil is sizzling hot before you pour the egg in, to give the white a crispy edge. When each egg is cooked, remove it from the wok and keep warm.

5 Ladle the rice into four bowls and top each portion with a crispy fried egg. Serve with the green salad leaves and wedges of lime to squeeze over.

Nutritional information per portion: Energy 392Kcal/1648kJ; Protein 13.6g; Carbohydrate 51.4g, of which sugars 8.2g; Fat 16.1g, of which saturates 3.6g; Cholesterol 261mg; Calcium 79mg; Fibre 2.1g; Sodium 968mg.

Savoury fried rice

The title makes this sound like rather an ordinary dish, but it is nothing of the kind. Chilli, nuts and toasted coconut give the mixture of rice and beans and wilted greens plenty of flavour, and the egg that is stirred in provides the protein content.

SERVES 2

30ml/2 tbsp vegetable oil

2 garlic cloves, finely chopped

1 small fresh red chilli, seeded and
    finely chopped

50g/2oz/1/2 cup cashew nuts, toasted

50g/2oz/2/3 cup desiccated
    (dry unsweetened shredded)
    coconut, toasted

2.5ml/1/2 tsp palm sugar (jaggery) or
    light muscovado (brown) sugar

30ml/2 tbsp light soy sauce

15ml/1 tbsp rice vinegar

1 egg

115g/4oz/1 cup green beans, sliced

1/2 spring cabbage or 115g/4oz spring
    greens (collards) or pak choi
    (bok choy), shredded

90g/31/2oz jasmine rice, cooked

lime wedges, to serve

1 Heat the oil in a wok or large, heavy frying pan. Add the garlic and cook over a medium to high heat until golden. Do not let it burn or it will taste bitter.

2 Add the red chilli, cashew nuts and toasted coconut and stir-fry briefly, taking care to prevent the coconut from scorching. Stir in the sugar, soy sauce and rice vinegar. Toss over the heat for 1–2 minutes.

3 Push the stir-fry to one side of the wok and break the egg into the other side. When the egg is almost set, stir it into the garlic and chilli mixture with a wooden spatula or spoon.

4 Add the green beans, greens and cooked rice. Stir over the heat until the greens have just wilted, then spoon into a dish to serve. Offer the lime wedges separately, for squeezing over the rice.

Nutritional information per portion: Energy 570Kcal/2366kJ; Protein 16.1g; Carbohydrate 30.5g, of which sugars 8.7g; Fat 43.6g, of which saturates 18.2g; Cholesterol 95mg; Calcium 187mg; Fibre 8.5g; Sodium 1196mg.

Rice congee

Originating in China, this dish has now spread throughout the whole of South-east Asia and is loved for its comforting simplicity. It is invariably teamed with a few strongly flavoured accompaniments to provide contrasting tastes and textures.

SERVES 2

900ml/1½ pints/3¾ cups
   vegetable stock
200g/7oz cooked rice
15ml/1 tbsp Thai fish sauce,
   or mushroom ketchup
2 heads pickled garlic, finely chopped
1 celery stick, finely diced
ground black pepper

TO GARNISH
4 garlic cloves
4 small red shallots
30ml/2 tbsp groundnut (peanut) oil

1 To make the garnishes, thinly slice the garlic cloves and the shallots. Heat the groundnut oil in a wok and cook the garlic and shallots over a low heat until brown. Drain on kitchen paper and reserve for the soup.

2 Pour the vegetable stock into a wok or large pan. Bring to the boil and add the rice.

3 Stir in the Thai fish sauce or mushroom ketchup and pickled garlic and simmer for 10 minutes to let the flavours develop.

4 Stir in the finely diced celery.

5 Serve the rice congee in individual warmed bowls. Sprinkle the prepared garlic and shallots on top and season with plenty of ground pepper.

Nutritional information per portion: Energy 509Kcal/2126kJ; Protein 27.3g; Carbohydrate 37.2g, of which sugars 0.8g; Fat 29g, of which saturates 6.3g; Cholesterol 74mg; Calcium 39mg; Fibre 1.8g; Sodium 86mg.

Vegetables and Side Dishes

Although it is perfectly possible to cook an

entire meal in a wok – and many of the recipes

in this book let you do just that – it can also

be useful for making side dishes. Try serving

a vegetable stir-fry with the Sunday roast

– the crisp, clean flavours and stunning

colours make an ideal contrast to the classic

meat. A wok is also great for making a warm

salad, for example Bamboo Shoot Salad,

where it is used for dry-roasting rice.

Bamboo shoot salad

Grains of glutinous rice are dry-roasted in the wok, then ground to fine crumbs, to give an interesting crunchy addition to this colourful and unusual salad.

SERVES 4

400g/14oz canned bamboo shoots
25g/1oz/about 3 tbsp Thai sticky
   rice, cooked
30ml/2 tbsp chopped shallots
15ml/1 tbsp chopped garlic
45ml/3 tbsp chopped spring
   onions (scallions)
30ml/2 tbsp Thai fish sauce
30ml/2 tbsp fresh lime juice
5ml/1 tsp granulated (white) sugar
2.5ml/$\frac{1}{2}$ tsp dried chilli flakes
20–25 small fresh mint leaves
15ml/1 tbsp toasted sesame seeds

1 Cut the bamboo shoots into large pieces, rinse under cold running water, then drain and pat them thoroughly dry with kitchen paper. Set aside.

2 Dry-roast the cooked Thai sticky rice in a wok until it is golden brown. Leave to cool slightly, then grind to fine crumbs using a pestle and mortar.

3 Transfer the rice to a bowl and add the chopped shallots, garlic and spring onions, as well as the fish sauce, lime juice, sugar, dried chilli flakes and half the mint leaves. Mix well.

4 Add the bamboo shoots to the bowl and toss to mix. Serve sprinkled with the sesame seeds and remaining mint leaves.

Nutritional information per portion: Energy 85Kcal/357kJ; Protein 4.2g; Carbohydrate 11.3g, of which sugars 4.1g; Fat 2.7g, of which saturates 0.4g; Cholesterol 0mg; Calcium 51mg; Fibre 2g; Sodium 6mg.

Cabbage salad

This is a simple and delicious way of serving a somewhat mundane vegetable. The wok comes in handy for stir-frying the aromatic vegetables that flavour the cabbage.

SERVES 4–6

30ml/2 tbsp vegetable oil

2 large fresh red chillies, seeded
   and cut into thin strips

6 garlic cloves, thinly sliced

6 shallots, thinly sliced

1 small cabbage, shredded

30ml/2 tbsp coarsely chopped
   roasted peanuts, to garnish

FOR THE DRESSING

30ml/2 tbsp Thai fish sauce

grated rind of 1 lime

30ml/2 tbsp fresh lime juice

120ml/4fl oz/½ cup coconut milk

1 Make the dressing by mixing the fish sauce, lime rind and juice and coconut milk in a bowl. Whisk until thoroughly combined. Set aside.

2 Heat the oil in a wok. Stir-fry the chillies, garlic and shallots over a medium heat for 3–4 minutes, until the shallots are brown and crisp. Remove and set aside.

3 Bring a large pan of lightly salted water to the boil. Add the cabbage and blanch for 2–3 minutes. Tip into a colander, drain and put into a bowl.

4 Whisk the dressing again, add it to the warm cabbage and toss to mix. Transfer the salad to a serving dish. Sprinkle with the fried shallot mixture and the peanuts. Serve immediately.

Nutritional information per portion: Energy 96Kcal/400kJ; Protein 2.7g; Carbohydrate 7.7g, of which sugars 6.6g; Fat 6.2g, of which saturates 0.9g; Cholesterol 0mg; Calcium 50mg; Fibre 2.2g; Sodium 147mg.

Noodle, tofu and sprouted bean salad

Bean thread noodles look like spun glass on this stunning salad, which owes its goodness to fresh beansprouts and diced tomato and cucumber. It takes only minutes to toss together.

SERVES 4

25g/1oz bean thread noodles

500g/1¼lb mixed sprouted beans
   and pulses (aduki, chickpea,
   mung, red lentil)

4 spring onions (scallions), finely shredded

115g/4oz firm tofu, diced

1 ripe plum tomato, seeded and diced

½ cucumber, peeled, seeded and diced

60ml/4 tbsp chopped fresh
   coriander (cilantro)

45ml/3 tbsp chopped fresh mint

60ml/4 tbsp rice vinegar

10ml/2 tsp caster (superfine) sugar

10ml/2 tsp sesame oil

5ml/1 tsp chilli oil

salt and ground black pepper

1 Place the bean thread noodles in a bowl and pour over enough boiling water to cover. Leave to soak for 12–15 minutes.

2 Drain the noodles and then refresh them under cold, running water and drain again. Using a pair of scissors, cut the noodles into lengths of roughly 13cm/5in and transfer to a bowl.

3 Fill a wok one-third full of boiling water and place over a high heat. Add the sprouted beans and pulses and blanch for 1 minute. Drain, transfer to the bowl of noodles and add the spring onions, tofu, tomato, cucumber and herbs.

4 Combine the rice vinegar, sugar, sesame oil and chilli oil and toss into the noodle mixture. Transfer to a serving dish and chill for 30 minutes before serving.

COOK'S TIP
If you leave the salad to stand for half an hour to an hour before serving, the flavours will improve as they develop and fuse together.

Nutritional information per portion: Energy 113Kcal/475kJ; Protein 6.8g; Carbohydrate 14.1g, of which sugars 6.6g; Fat 3.5g, of which saturates 0.5g; Cholesterol 0mg; Calcium 184mg; Fibre 2.4g; Sodium 11mg.

Fried vegetables with chilli sauce

A wok makes the ideal pan for frying slices of aubergine, butternut squash and courgette because they become beautifully tender and succulent, and the beaten egg in this recipe provides a satisfyingly substantial batter. Serve with a sweet chilli sauce dip.

SERVES 4

3 large (US extra large) eggs
1 aubergine (eggplant), halved
   lengthways and cut into long,
   thin slices
½ small butternut squash, peeled,
   seeded and cut into long, thin slices
2 courgettes (zucchini), trimmed and cut
   into long, thin slices
105ml/7 tbsp vegetable or sunflower oil
salt and ground black pepper
sweet chilli sauce, to serve

1 Beat the eggs in a large bowl. Season the egg mixture with salt and pepper. Add the slices of aubergine, butternut squash and courgette. Toss the vegetable slices until they are coated all over in the egg.

2 Have a warmed dish ready lined with kitchen paper. Heat the oil in a wok. When it is hot, add the vegetables, one strip at a time, making sure that each strip has plenty of egg clinging to it.

3 Do not cook more than eight strips of vegetable at a time or the oil will cool down too much.

4 As each strip turns golden and is cooked, lift it out, using a wire basket or slotted spoon, and transfer to the plate. Keep hot while cooking the remaining vegetables. Serve with the sweet chilli sauce as a dip.

Nutritional information per portion: Energy 281Kcal/1162kJ; Protein 8.8g; Carbohydrate 5.7g, of which sugars 4.8g; Fat 25.1g, of which saturates 3.9g; Cholesterol 171mg; Calcium 92mg; Fibre 3.2g; Sodium 65mg.

Asian-style courgette fritters

This is a twist on Japanese tempura, using Indian spices and gram flour in the batter. Also known as besan, gram flour is more commonly used in Indian cooking and gives a wonderfully crisp texture, while the courgette baton inside becomes meltingly tender.

SERVES 4

90g/3¹/₂oz/³/₄ cup gram flour
5ml/1 tsp baking powder
2.5ml/¹/₂ tsp ground turmeric
10ml/2 tsp ground coriander
5ml/1 tsp ground cumin
5ml/1 tsp chilli powder
250ml/8fl oz/1 cup beer
600g/1lb 6oz courgettes (zucchini),
    cut into batons
sunflower oil, for deep-frying
salt
steamed basmati rice, natural (plain)
    yogurt and pickles, to serve

1 Sift the gram flour, baking powder, turmeric, coriander, cumin and chilli powder into a large bowl. Stir lightly to mix through.

2 Season the mixture with salt and then gradually add the beer, mixing gently as you pour it in, to make a thick batter – be careful not to overmix.

3 Fill a large wok, one-third full with sunflower oil and heat to 180°C/350°F or until a cube of bread, dropped into the oil, browns in 45 seconds.

4 Working in batches, dip the courgette batons in the spiced batter and then deep-fry for 1–2 minutes, or until crisp and golden. Lift out of the wok using a slotted spoon. Drain on kitchen paper and keep warm. Serve the courgettes immediately with steamed basmati rice, yogurt and pickles.

Nutritional information per portion: Energy 241Kcal/999kJ; Protein 7.3g; Carbohydrate 15.3g, of which sugars 4.6g; Fat 15.6g, of which saturates 1.9g; Cholesterol 0mg; Calcium 83mg; Fibre 3.8g; Sodium 15mg.

Light and crispy seven-spice aubergines

Thai seven-spice powder is a commercial blend of spices, including coriander, cumin, cinnamon, star anise, chilli, cloves and lemon peel. It gives these aubergines a lovely warm flavour that goes very well with the light, curry batter. Serve with a hot chilli sauce for dipping.

SERVES 4

2 egg whites

90ml/6 tbsp cornflour (cornstarch)

15ml/1 tbsp Thai or Chinese
    seven-spice powder

5ml/1 tsp salt

15ml/1 tbsp mild chilli powder

500g/1¼lb aubergines (eggplants),
    thinly sliced

sunflower oil, for deep-frying

fresh mint leaves, to garnish

steamed rice or noodles and
    hot chilli sauce, to serve

1 Whisk the egg whites in a bowl until light and foamy, but not dry.

2 Combine the cornflour, seven-spice powder, salt and chilli powder and spread evenly on to a large plate.

3 Fill a wok one-third full of oil and heat to 180°C/350°F or until a cube of bread browns in about 45 seconds.

4 Dip the aubergine slices in the egg white and then into the spiced flour mixture to coat. Deep-fry in batches for 3–4 minutes, or until crisp and golden. Drain on kitchen paper and keep warm.

5 Serve the aubergines garnished with mint leaves and with hot chilli sauce on the side for dipping.

Nutritional information per portion: Energy 203Kcal/850kJ; Protein 2.7g; Carbohydrate 23.5g, of which sugars 2.5g; Fat 11.7g, of which saturates 1.4g; Cholesterol 0mg; Calcium 17mg; Fibre 2.5g; Sodium 45mg.

Herb and chilli aubergines

Plump and juicy aubergines are delicious steamed in the wok until tender and then tossed in a fragrant minty dressing with coriander, crunchy peanuts and water chestnuts. The combination of textures and flavours is absolutely sensational.

SERVES 4

500g/1¼lb firm, baby
   aubergines (eggplants)
30ml/2 tbsp sunflower oil
6 garlic cloves, very finely chopped
15ml/1 tbsp very finely chopped
   fresh root ginger
8 spring onions (scallions), cut diagonally
   into 2.5cm/1in lengths
2 fresh red chillies, seeded and thinly sliced
45ml/3 tbsp light soy sauce
15ml/1 tbsp Chinese rice wine
15ml/1 tbsp golden caster (superfine)
   sugar or palm sugar (jaggery)
a handful of fresh mint leaves
30–45ml/2–3 tbsp roughly chopped fresh
   coriander (cilantro) leaves
115g/4oz water chestnuts
50g/2oz/½ cup roasted peanuts,
   roughly chopped
steamed egg noodles or rice, to serve

1 Halve the aubergines lengthways and place on a heatproof plate.

2 Place a steamer rack in a wok and add 5cm/2in of water. Bring the water to the boil, lower the plate on to the rack and reduce the heat to low.

3 Cover and steam the aubergines for 25–30 minutes, until they are cooked through. (Check the water level regularly, adding more if necessary.) Set the aubergines aside to cool.

4 Place the oil in a clean, dry wok and place over a medium heat.

5 When the oil is hot, add the finely chopped garlic and ginger, spring onions and chillies and stir-fry for 2–3 minutes.

6 Remove from the heat and stir in the soy sauce, rice wine and sugar.

7 Add the mint leaves, chopped coriander, water chestnuts and chopped peanuts to the aubergines and toss well.

8 Pour the garlic-ginger mixture evenly over the vegetables, toss gently and serve with steamed egg noodles or rice.

Nutritional information per portion: Energy 177Kcal/739kJ; Protein 6.2g; Carbohydrate 12.1g, of which sugars 9g; Fat 12g, of which saturates 1.9g; Cholesterol 0mg; Calcium 46mg; Fibre 4.4g; Sodium 823mg.

Pak choi with lime dressing

The lime dressing for this Thai speciality is traditionally made using fish sauce, but vegetarians could use mushroom ketchup instead. This is a wok dish that packs a fiery punch; use fewer chillies if you prefer, or remove the seeds before stir-frying.

SERVES 4

30ml/2 tbsp oil

3 fresh red chillies, cut into thin strips

4 garlic cloves, thinly sliced

6 spring onions (scallions),
  sliced diagonally

2 pak choi (bok choy), shredded

15ml/1 tbsp crushed peanuts

FOR THE DRESSING

30ml/2 tbsp fresh lime juice

15–30ml/1–2 tbsp Thai fish sauce

250ml/8fl oz/1 cup coconut milk

1 Make the dressing. Put the lime juice and Thai fish sauce in a bowl and mix well together, then gradually whisk in the coconut milk until combined.

2 Heat the oil in a wok and stir-fry the chillies for 2–3 minutes, until crisp. Transfer to a plate using a slotted spoon.

3 Add the garlic to the wok and stir-fry for 30–60 seconds, until golden brown. Transfer to the plate.

4 Stir-fry the white parts of the spring onions for about 2–3 minutes, then add the green parts and stir-fry for 1 minute more. Transfer to the plate.

5 Bring a large pan of lightly salted water to the boil. Add the pak choi, stir twice, then drain immediately.

6 Place the pak choi in a large bowl, add the dressing and toss to mix. Transfer to a large serving bowl and sprinkle with the peanuts and stir-fried ingredients. Serve warm or cold.

Nutritional information per portion: Energy 93Kcal/384kJ; Protein 2.9g; Carbohydrate 6.2g, of which sugars 5.7g; Fat 6.4g, of which saturates 0.9g; Cholesterol 0mg; Calcium 157mg; Fibre 2.1g; Sodium 354mg.

Stir-fried pineapple with ginger

This dish makes an interesting accompaniment to grilled meat or strongly flavoured fish such as tuna or swordfish. If the idea seems strange, think of it as resembling a fresh mango chutney, but with pineapple as the principal ingredient.

SERVES 4

1 pineapple
15ml/1 tbsp vegetable oil
2 garlic cloves, finely chopped
2 shallots, finely chopped
5cm/2in piece fresh root ginger,
    peeled and finely shredded
30ml/2 tbsp light soy sauce
juice of ½ lime
1 large fresh red chilli, seeded
    and finely shredded

1 Trim and peel the pineapple. Cut out the core and dice the flesh.

2 Heat the oil in a wok or frying pan. Stir-fry the garlic and shallots over a medium heat for 2–3 minutes, until golden. Do not let the garlic burn or the dish will taste bitter.

3 Add the pineapple. Stir-fry for about 2 minutes, or until the pineapple starts to brown at the edges.

4 Add the ginger, soy sauce, lime juice and shredded chilli. Toss until well mixed. Cook over a low heat for a further 2 minutes, then serve.

Nutritional information per portion: Energy 115Kcal/490kJ; Protein 1.2g; Carbohydrate 22g, of which sugars 21.6g; Fat 3.2g, of which saturates 0.3g; Cholesterol 0mg; Calcium 41mg; Fibre 2.6g; Sodium 539mg.

Thai asparagus

If you've never had asparagus cooked in the wok, do yourself a favour and try this delicious recipe. The zingy flavours of galangal and chilli, coupled with the sweet and spicy sauce, transform what can be a subtle taste into something of a sensation.

SERVES 4

350g/12oz asparagus stalks
30ml/2 tbsp vegetable oil
1 garlic clove, crushed
15ml/1 tbsp sesame seeds, toasted
2.5cm/1in piece fresh galangal,
    finely shredded
1 fresh red chilli, seeded
    and finely chopped
15ml/1 tbsp Thai fish sauce
15ml/1 tbsp light soy sauce
45ml/3 tbsp water
5ml/1 tsp palm sugar (jaggery) or
    light muscovado (brown) sugar

1 Snap the asparagus stalks. They will break naturally at the junction between the woody base and the more tender part of the stalk. Discard the woody ends.

2 Heat a wok and add the oil. Stir-fry the garlic, sesame seeds and galangal for 3–4 seconds, until the garlic is just beginning to turn golden. Add the asparagus stalks and chilli, toss to mix, then add the fish sauce, soy sauce, water and sugar.

3 Using two spoons, toss over the heat for a further 2 minutes, or until the asparagus is just beginning to soften and the liquid is reduced by about half. Serve the asparagus immediately, with the sauce spooned over it.

Nutritional information per portion: Energy 99Kcal/410kJ; Protein 3.4g; Carbohydrate 3.1g, of which sugars 3g; Fat 8.2g, of which saturates 1.1g; Cholesterol 0mg; Calcium 50mg; Fibre 1.8g; Sodium 269mg.

Baby asparagus with crispy noodles

Tender asparagus spears tossed with sesame seeds and served on a bed of crispy, deep-fried noodles makes a lovely dish for casual entertaining. The lightly cooked asparagus retains all its fresh flavour and bite and contrasts wonderfully with the noodles.

SERVES 4

15ml/1 tbsp sunflower oil
350g/12oz thin asparagus spears
5ml/1 tsp salt
5ml/1 tsp ground black pepper
5ml/1 tsp golden caster (superfine) sugar
30ml/2 tbsp Chinese cooking wine
45ml/3 tbsp light soy sauce
60ml/4 tbsp oyster sauce
10ml/2 tsp sesame oil
60ml/4 tbsp toasted sesame seeds

FOR THE NOODLES

sunflower oil, for deep-frying
50g/2oz dried bean thread noodles
   or thin rice noodles

1 First make the crispy noodles. Fill a wok one-third full of oil and heat to 180°C/350°F, or until a cube of bread browns in about 45 seconds. Add a small bunch of noodles to the oil; they will crisp and puff up in seconds. Remove from the wok and drain on kitchen paper. Set aside and cook the remaining noodles.

2 Heat a clean wok over a high heat and add the sunflower oil. Add the asparagus and stir-fry for 3 minutes. Add the salt, pepper, sugar, wine, soy sauce and oyster sauce to the wok and stir-fry for 2–3 minutes. Add the sesame oil, toss to combine and remove from the heat.

3 Divide the crispy noodles between four warmed plates and top with the asparagus and juices. Scatter over the sesame seeds and serve immediately.

Nutritional information per portion: Energy 210Kcal/872kJ; Protein 3.8g; Carbohydrate 18.2g, of which sugars 7.7g; Fat 13g, of which saturates 1.6g; Cholesterol 0mg; Calcium 30mg; Fibre 1.6g; Sodium 1540mg.

Steamed aubergines with sesame sauce

This Japanese recipe represents a typical Zen temple cooking style. Fresh seasonal vegetables are chosen and simply cooked with care. Then a sauce made of carefully balanced flavours is added.

SERVES 4

2 large aubergines (eggplants)
400ml/14fl oz/1²/₃ cups second dashi
   stock made using water and instant
   dashi powder
25ml/1¹/₂ tbsp caster (superfine) sugar
15ml/1 tbsp shoyu
15ml/1 tbsp sesame seeds, finely ground
15ml/1 tbsp sake
15ml/1 tbsp cornflour (cornstarch)
salt

FOR THE ACCOMPANYING VEGETABLES

130g/4¹/₂oz shimeji mushrooms
115g/4oz/³/₄ cup fine green beans
100ml/3fl oz/scant ¹/₂ cup second dashi
   stock, made using water and instant
   dashi powder
25ml/1¹/₂ tbsp caster (superfine) sugar
15ml/1 tbsp sake
1.5ml/¹/₄ tsp salt
dash of shoyu

1 Peel the aubergines and cut them in quarters lengthways. Prick all over with a skewer, then plunge into a bowl of salted water for 30 minutes. Drain the aubergines and lay them side by side in a bamboo steamer basket. Place the basket on a trivet, on top of a wok of boiling water. Cover and steam for 20 minutes. Do not let the water touch the bottom of the steamer basket.

2 Mix the dashi stock, sugar, shoyu and 1.5ml/¹/₄ tsp salt in a large pan. Add the aubergines to this pan. Cover and cook over a low heat for 15 minutes. Take a few tablespoonfuls of stock from the pan and mix with the ground sesame seeds. Add this mixture to the pan. Thoroughly mix the sake with the cornflour, add to the pan with the aubergines and stock and shake the pan gently, but quickly. When the sauce becomes quite thick, remove the pan from the heat.

3 Cook the accompanying vegetables. Cut off the hard base of the mushrooms and separate the large block into smaller chunks with your fingers. Trim and halve the green beans. Mix the stock with the sugar, sake, salt and shoyu in a shallow pan. Add the green beans and mushrooms and cook for 7 minutes until just tender. Serve the aubergines and their sauce in individual bowls with the accompanying vegetables over the top.

Nutritional information per portion: Energy 127Kcal/536kJ; Protein 3.3g; Carbohydrate 20.9g, of which sugars 16.8g; Fat 3.1g, of which saturates 0.5g; Cholesterol 0mg; Calcium 60mg; Fibre 4.3g; Sodium 8mg.

Indian-style spiced red lentil dhal

A karahi is the Indian equivalent of the wok. Here it is used to great effect to create classic comfort food. A bowl of dhal spiced with mustard seeds, cumin and coriander is sure to clear away the blues.

SERVES 4

30ml/2 tbsp sunflower oil
1 fresh green chilli, halved
2 red onions, halved and thinly sliced
10ml/2 tsp crushed garlic
10ml/2 tsp finely grated fresh root ginger
10ml/2 tsp black mustard seeds
15ml/1 tbsp cumin seeds
10ml/2 tsp crushed coriander seeds
10 curry leaves
250g/9oz/generous 1 cup red lentils
700ml/1 pint 2fl oz/scant 3 cups
    cold water
2.5ml/¹⁄₂ tsp ground turmeric
2 plum tomatoes, chopped
salt
coriander (cilantro) leaves and crispy
    fried onion, to garnish (optional)
yogurt, poppadums and griddled
    flatbread or naans, to serve

1 Heat a karahi or wok and add the sunflower oil. When it is hot add the green chilli and onions, stir to combine, lower the heat and cook gently for 10–12 minutes, until softened.

2 Increase the heat slightly and add the garlic, ginger, mustard seeds, cumin seeds, coriander seeds and curry leaves and stir-fry for 2–3 minutes.

3 Rinse the lentils in cold water, drain, then add to the wok with the water. Stir in the turmeric and season with salt. Bring to the boil. Add the tomatoes. Reduce the heat and cook gently for 25–30 minutes, stirring occasionally.

4 Check the seasoning, then garnish with coriander leaves and crispy fried onion, if liked, and serve with yogurt, poppadums and flatbread or naans.

VARIATION
If you prefer, you can use yellow split peas in place of the lentils. Like red lentils, these only need to be rinsed, not soaked, before cooking.

Nutritional information per portion: Energy 284Kcal/1198kJ; Protein 16.1g; Carbohydrate 42.7g, of which sugars 7.3g; Fat 6.6g, of which saturates 0.8g; Cholesterol 0mg; Calcium 54mg; Fibre 4.6g; Sodium 29mg.

Fragrant mushrooms in lettuce leaves

This quick and easy vegetable dish is served on lettuce leaf 'saucers' so can be eaten with the fingers – a great treat for children and fun for adults too.

SERVES 2

30ml/2 tbsp vegetable oil

2 garlic cloves, finely chopped

2 baby cos or romaine lettuces,
    or 2 Little Gem (Bibb) lettuces

1 lemon grass stalk, finely chopped

2 kaffir lime leaves, rolled in cylinders
    and thinly sliced

200g/7oz/3 cups oyster or chestnut
    mushrooms, sliced

1 small fresh red chilli, seeded
    and finely chopped

juice of ½ lemon

30ml/2 tbsp light soy sauce

5ml/1 tsp palm sugar (jaggery) or
    light muscovado (brown) sugar

small bunch fresh mint leaves

1 Heat the oil in a wok or frying pan. Add the chopped garlic and cook over a medium heat, stirring occasionally, until golden. Do not let it burn or it will taste bitter.

2 Meanwhile, separate the individual lettuce leaves. Wash and dry them, then set them aside in a bowl.

3 Increase the heat under the wok or pan and add the lemon grass, lime leaves and sliced mushrooms. Stir-fry for about 2 minutes. Add the chilli, lemon juice, soy sauce and sugar to the wok or pan. Toss the mixture over the heat to combine the ingredients together, then stir-fry for a further 2 minutes.

4 Arrange the lettuce on a plate. Spoon a small amount of mushroom mixture on to each leaf and top with a mint leaf.

Nutritional information per portion: Energy 154Kcal/641kJ; Protein 3.9g; Carbohydrate 7.1g, of which sugars 6.8g; Fat 12.5g, of which saturates 1.6g; Cholesterol 0mg; Calcium 66mg; Fibre 2.9g; Sodium 1079mg.

Steamed vegetables with chilli dip

A bamboo steamer is a great wok accessory, allowing you to cook vegetables quickly and easily, retaining maximum nutrients and colour. Add a spicy dip and you have a healthy and tasty dish.

SERVES 4

1 head broccoli, divided into florets
130g/4¹/₂oz/1 cup green beans, trimmed
130g/4¹/₂oz asparagus, trimmed
¹/₂ head cauliflower, divided into florets
8 baby corn cobs
130g/4¹/₂oz mangetouts (snow peas)
   or sugar snap peas
salt

FOR THE DIP

1 fresh green chilli, seeded
4 garlic cloves, peeled
4 shallots, peeled
2 tomatoes, halved
5 pea aubergines (eggplants)
30ml/2 tbsp lemon juice
30ml/2 tbsp soy sauce
2.5ml/¹/₂ tsp salt
5ml/1 tsp granulated (white) sugar

1 Place the broccoli, green beans, asparagus and cauliflower in a bamboo steamer and steam over boiling water in a wok for about 4 minutes, until just tender but still with a 'bite'.

2 Transfer to a bowl and add the corn cobs and mangetouts or sugar snap peas. Season to taste with a little salt. Toss to mix.

3 Make the dip. Preheat the grill (broiler). Wrap the chilli, garlic cloves, shallots, tomatoes and aubergines in a foil package. Grill (broil) for 10 minutes, until the vegetables have softened, turning the package over once or twice.

4 Unwrap the foil and tip its contents into a mortar or food processor. Add the lemon juice, soy sauce, salt and sugar. Pound with a pestle or process to a fairly liquid paste. Transfer the dip into a serving bowl or four individual bowls.

5 Serve, surrounded by the steamed and raw vegetables.

Nutritional information per portion: Energy 129Kcal/541kJ; Protein 13.3g; Carbohydrate 13.3g, of which sugars 11.3g; Fat 2.8g, of which saturates 0.6g; Cholesterol 0mg; Calcium 138mg; Fibre 8.5g; Sodium 772mg.

Carrot in sweet vinegar

For this Japanese side dish carrot strips are marinated in rice vinegar, shoyu and mirin. It is a good accompaniment for rich dishes.

SERVES 4

2 large carrots, peeled
5ml/1 tsp salt
30ml/2 tbsp sesame seeds

FOR THE SWEET VINEGAR MARINADE
75ml/5 tbsp rice vinegar
30ml/2 tbsp shoyu (use the pale awakuchi soy sauce if available)
45ml/3 tbsp mirin

1 Cut the carrots into thin matchsticks, 5cm/2in long. Put the carrots and salt into a mixing bowl, and mix well with your hands.

2 After 25 minutes, rinse the wilted carrot in cold water, then drain.

3 In another bowl, mix together the marinade ingredients. Add the carrots, and leave to marinate for 3 hours.

4 Put a wok on a high heat, add the sesame seeds and toss constantly until the seeds start to pop. Remove from the heat and cool.

5 Chop the sesame seeds with a sharp knife on a chopping board.

6 Place the carrots in a bowl, sprinkle with the sesame seeds and serve cold.

Nutritional information per portion: Energy 66Kcal/272kJ; Protein 1.9g; Carbohydrate 4.6g, of which sugars 4.3g; Fat 4.5g, of which saturates 0.7g; Cholesterol 0mg; Calcium 64mg; Fibre 1.8g; Sodium 1039mg.

Spicy chickpeas with spinach

This richly flavoured dish is a great accompaniment to a dry curry, or rice-based stir-fry.
Serve drizzled with plain yogurt – the sharp, creamy flavour complements the spices perfectly.

SERVES 4

200g/7oz dried chickpeas
30ml/2 tbsp sunflower oil
2 onions, halved and thinly sliced
10ml/2 tsp ground coriander
10ml/2 tsp ground cumin
5ml/1 tsp hot chilli powder
2.5ml/¹/₂ tsp ground turmeric
15ml/1 tbsp medium curry powder
400g/14oz can chopped tomatoes
5ml/1 tsp caster (superfine) sugar
105ml/7 tbsp water
salt and ground black pepper
30ml/2 tbsp chopped mint leaves
115g/4oz baby leaf spinach
steamed rice or bread, to serve

1 Soak the chickpeas in cold water overnight. Drain, rinse and place in a large pan. Cover with water and bring to the boil. Reduce the heat and simmer for 45 minutes, or until just tender. Drain and set aside.

2 Heat the oil in a wok, add the onions and cook over a low heat for 15 minutes, until lightly golden. Add the ground coriander and cumin, chilli powder, turmeric and curry powder and stir-fry for 1–2 minutes.

3 Add the tomatoes, sugar and water to the wok and bring to the boil. Cover, reduce the heat and simmer gently for 15 minutes.

4 Add the chickpeas, season well and cook gently for 8–10 minutes. Stir in the chopped mint.

5 Divide the spinach leaves between shallow bowls, top with the chickpea mixture and serve with some steamed rice or bread.

Nutritional information per portion: Energy 267Kcal/1122kJ; Protein 13.3g; Carbohydrate 35.5g, of which sugars 10.2g; Fat 9g, of which saturates 1.1g; Cholesterol 0mg; Calcium 170mg; Fibre 8.2g; Sodium 83mg.

Hot and spicy yam

In this recipe, yam isn't the sweet potato-like vegetable, but a spicy sauce based on coconut milk and mushrooms. It's easy to make in the wok and perks up steamed vegetables perfectly.

SERVES 4

90g/3½oz/scant 1 cup green beans
90g/3½oz Chinese leaves
   (Chinese cabbage), shredded
90g/3½oz/scant 2 cups beansprouts
90g/3½oz broccoli, preferably the purple
   sprouting variety, divided into florets
15ml/1 tbsp sesame seeds, toasted

FOR THE YAM

60ml/4 tbsp coconut cream
5ml/1 tsp Thai red curry paste
90g/3½oz/1¼ cups oyster mushrooms
   or field (portabello) mushrooms, sliced
60ml/4 tbsp coconut milk
5ml/1 tsp ground turmeric
5ml/1 tsp thick tamarind juice, made by
   mixing tamarind paste with warm water
juice of ½ lemon
60ml/4 tbsp light soy sauce
5ml/1 tsp palm sugar (jaggery) or
   light muscovado (brown) sugar

1 Trim the green beans. Steam the shredded Chinese leaves, beansprouts, green beans and broccoli separately or blanch them in boiling water for 1 minute per batch. Drain, transfer to a serving bowl and leave to cool.

2 To make the yam, pour the coconut cream into a wok and heat gently for 2–3 minutes, until it separates. Stir in the red curry paste. Cook over a low heat for 30 seconds. Increase the heat to high and add the mushrooms. Cook for a further 2–3 minutes. Pour in the coconut milk and add the ground turmeric, tamarind juice, lemon juice, soy sauce and sugar. Mix thoroughly.

3 Pour the yam over the prepared vegetables in the serving bowl and toss so they are all coated with the sauce. Sprinkle with the sesame seeds and serve.

COOK'S TIP

There's no need to buy coconut cream especially for this dish. Use a carton or can of coconut milk. Skim the cream off the top and cook 60ml/4 tbsp of it before adding the curry paste. Add the measured coconut milk later, as described in the recipe.

Nutritional information per portion: Energy 66Kcal/277kJ; Protein 3.9g; Carbohydrate 6.6g, of which sugars 5.8g; Fat 2.9g, of which saturates 0.5g; Cholesterol 0mg; Calcium 74mg; Fibre 2.4g; Sodium 752mg.

New potatoes cooked in dashi stock

This scrumptious Japanese dish involves little more than new season's potatoes and onion cooked in dashi stock. The onion is meltingly soft and caramelized, creating a wonderful sauce.

SERVES 4

15ml/1 tbsp toasted sesame oil
1 small onion, thinly sliced
1kg/2¼lb baby new potatoes, unpeeled
200ml/7fl oz/scant 1 cup second
   dashi stock, made using water
   and instant dashi powder
45ml/3 tbsp shoyu

1 Heat the sesame oil in a wok or large pan. Add the onion slices and stir-fry for 30 seconds, then add the potatoes. Stir constantly to coat all the potatoes.

2 Pour on the dashi stock and shoyu and reduce the heat to the lowest setting. Cook, covered, for 15 minutes, turning the potatoes often to ensure even cooking.

3 Uncover the wok or pan for a further 5 minutes to reduce the liquid. If there is already very little liquid remaining, remove the wok or pan from the heat, cover and leave to stand for 5 minutes. Check that the potatoes are cooked, then remove from the heat.

4 Transfer the potatoes and onions to a deep serving bowl. Pour the sauce over the top and serve immediately.

COOK'S TIP

Japanese chefs use toasted sesame oil for its distinctive strong aroma. If the smell is too strong, use a mixture of half sesame and half vegetable oil instead.

Nutritional information per portion: Energy 207Kcal/876kJ; Protein 4.6g; Carbohydrate 41.8g, of which sugars 4.4g; Fat 3.5g, of which saturates 0.7g; Cholesterol 0mg; Calcium 20mg; Fibre 2.7g; Sodium 295mg.

Morning glory with fried shallots

Other names for morning glory include water spinach, water convolvulus and swamp cabbage. It is a green leafy vegetable with long jointed stems and arrow-shaped leaves. The stems remain crunchy while the leaves wilt like spinach when cooked.

SERVES 4

2 bunches morning glory, total weight about 250g/9oz, trimmed
30ml/2 tbsp vegetable oil
4 shallots
6 large garlic cloves
sea salt
1.5ml/¼ tsp dried chilli flakes

1 Coarsely chop the morning glory into 2.5cm/1in lengths. Thinly slice the shallots and garlic.

2 Place the morning glory in a steamer and steam over a pan of boiling water for 30 seconds, until just wilted. If necessary, cook it in batches. Place the leaves in a bowl or spread them out on a large serving plate.

3 Heat the oil in a wok and stir-fry the shallots and garlic over a medium to high heat until golden. Spoon the mixture over the morning glory, sprinkle with a little sea salt and the chilli flakes and serve immediately.

VARIATIONS
Use spinach instead of morning glory, or substitute young spring greens (collards), sprouting broccoli or Swiss chard.

Nutritional information per portion: Energy 77Kcal/316kJ; Protein 2.4g; Carbohydrate 3.2g, of which sugars 1.9g; Fat 6.1g, of which saturates 0.7g; Cholesterol 0mg; Calcium 111mg; Fibre 1.8g; Sodium 88mg.

Slow-cooked shiitake with shoyu

Shiitake cooked slowly are so rich and filling, that some people call them 'vegetarian steak'. Mushrooms cooked in this manner will keep for several days in the refrigerator, and can be eaten as they are or used to flavour other dishes.

SERVES 4

20 dried shiitake mushrooms
45ml/3 tbsp vegetable oil
30ml/2 tbsp shoyu
25ml/1½ tbsp caster (superfine) sugar
15ml/1 tbsp toasted sesame oil

1 Start soaking the dried shiitake the day before. Put them in a large bowl almost full of water. Cover the shiitake with a plate or lid to stop them floating to the surface of the water. Leave to soak overnight.

2 Measure 120ml/4fl oz/½ cup liquid from the bowl. Drain the shiitake into a sieve (strainer). Remove and discard the stalks.

3 Heat the oil in a wok or a large pan. Stir-fry the shiitake over a high heat for 5 minutes, stirring constantly.

4 Reduce the heat to the lowest setting, then add the measured liquid, the shoyu and sugar. Cook until there is almost no moisture left, stirring frequently. Add the sesame oil and remove from the heat.

5 Leave to cool, then slice and arrange the shiitake on a large plate.

Nutritional information per portion: Energy 133Kcal/553kJ; Protein 1.2g; Carbohydrate 7.4g, of which sugars 7.2g; Fat 11.2g, of which saturates 1.4g; Cholesterol 0mg; Calcium 8mg; Fibre 0.6g; Sodium 537mg.

Sweet Dishes
and Desserts

It may surprise you to discover how many

sweet dishes can be cooked in the wok. It is

a practical pan for deep-fried treats, such as

fritters and crispy wontons, and can also be

used for poaching fruit, like Vanilla, Honey

and Saffron Pears, or cooking desserts, such

as Caramelized Pineapple with Lemon Grass.

If you use a wok for poaching fruit, make

sure it is non-stick, or the acidity may react

with the metal, causing discoloration.

Steamed custard in nectarines

Steaming nectarines in the wok brings out their natural colour and sweetness, so this is a good way of making the most of fruit that isn't quite as ripe as it could be, or which needs a flavour boost.

SERVES 4–6

6 nectarines
1 large (US extra large) egg
45ml/3 tbsp palm sugar (jaggery) or
**   light muscovado (brown) sugar**
30ml/2 tbsp coconut milk

1 Cut the nectarines in half. Using a teaspoon, scoop out the stones (pits) and a little of the surrounding flesh.

2 Lightly beat the egg, then add the sugar and the coconut milk. Beat until the sugar has dissolved.

3 Transfer the nectarines to steamer tiers and carefully fill the cavities three-quarters full with the custard mixture. Steam over a pan of simmering water for 5–10 minutes. Remove from the heat and leave to cool completely before serving.

COOK'S TIP
Palm sugar, also known as jaggery, is made from the sap of certain Asian palm trees, such as coconut and palmyrah. It is available from Asian food stores. If you buy it as a cake or large lump, you need to grate it before use. Muscovado sugar makes a good substitute as it has a similar, toffee-like flavour.

Nutritional information per portion: Energy 213Kcal/897kJ; Protein 12.6g; Carbohydrate 21.6g, of which sugars 21.6g; Fat 9.4g, of which saturates 2.6g; Cholesterol 317mg; Calcium 64mg; Fibre 1.8g; Sodium 124mg.

Chinese-style toffee apples

This classic dessert will make a great end to any meal. Wedges of crisp apple are encased in a light batter, then dipped in crispy caramel to make a sweet, sticky dessert.

SERVES 4

115g/4oz/1 cup plain (all-purpose) flour
10ml/2 tsp baking powder
60ml/4 tbsp cornflour (cornstarch)
sunflower oil, for deep-frying
4 firm apples, peeled and cored
    and cut into 8 thick wedges
200g/7oz/1 cup caster (superfine) sugar

1 In a large mixing bowl, combine the flour, baking powder, cornflour and 175ml/6fl oz/³/₄ cup water. Mix to make a smooth batter and set aside.

2 Fill a wok one-third full of the oil and heat to 180°C/350°F or until a cube of bread browns in about 45 seconds.

3 Working quickly, in batches, dip the apple wedges in the batter, drain any excess and deep-fry for 2 minutes, or until golden brown. Remove and drain on kitchen paper.

4 Reheat the oil to 180°C/350°F and fry the wedges for a second time, for about 2 minutes. Drain and set aside.

5 Carefully pour off all but 30ml/ 2 tbsp of the oil from the wok and stir in the sugar. Heat gently until the sugar starts to caramelize. When the mixture is light brown, add the apple, in batches, and toss to coat evenly.

6 Fill a large bowl with ice cubes and chilled water. Plunge the apple pieces briefly into the iced water to harden the caramel. Serve immediately.

Nutritional information per portion: Energy 457Kcal/1940kJ; Protein 3.4g; Carbohydrate 97.3g, of which sugars 61.6g; Fat 8.8g, of which saturates 1.1g; Cholesterol 0mg; Calcium 73mg; Fibre 2.5g; Sodium 14mg.

Coconut and mandarin custards

These scented custards with a fabulous melt-in-the-mouth texture are best served warm. However, they are also delicious served chilled, making them perfect for hassle-free entertaining. You can make the praline a few days in advance.

SERVES 4

200ml/7fl oz/scant 1 cup coconut cream
200ml/7fl oz/scant 1 cup double
   (heavy) cream
2.5ml/¹/₂ tsp finely ground star anise
75ml/5 tbsp golden caster (superfine) sugar
15ml/1 tbsp very finely grated mandarin
   or orange rind
4 egg yolks

FOR THE PRALINE

175g/6oz/scant 1 cup caster
   (superfine) sugar
50g/2oz/¹/₂ cup roughly chopped
   mixed nuts (cashews, almonds
   and peanuts)

1 To make the praline, place the sugar in a non-stick wok with 15–30ml/1–2 tbsp water. Cook over a medium heat until the sugar dissolves and turns light gold.

2 Remove the syrup from the heat and pour on to a baking sheet lined with baking parchment. Spread out using the back of a spoon, then sprinkle the chopped nuts evenly over the top and leave to harden.

3 Meanwhile, place the coconut cream, double cream, star anise, sugar, mandarin or orange rind and egg yolks in a large bowl. Whisk to combine and pour the mixture into four lightly greased ramekins or small, heatproof bowls.

4 Place the ramekins or cups in a large steamer, cover and place in a wok and steam over gently simmering water for 12–15 minutes, or until the custards are just set.

5 Carefully lift the custards from the steamer and leave to cool slightly for about 10 minutes.

6 To serve, break up the praline into rough pieces and serve on top of, or alongside, the custards.

Nutritional information per portion: Energy 643Kcal/2688kJ; Protein 6.7g; Carbohydrate 71g, of which sugars 69.3g; Fat 38.9g, of which saturates 19.6g; Cholesterol 270mg; Calcium 100mg; Fibre 0.4g; Sodium 115mg.

Mango wontons with raspberry sauce

These crisp, golden parcels filled with meltingly sweet, hot mango are perfect for a casual supper or a sophisticated dinner. The sweet raspberry sauce looks stunning drizzled over the wontons and tastes even better. Serve any extra sauce in a bowl.

SERVES 4

2 firm, ripe mangoes
24 fresh wonton wrappers
    (approximately 7.5cm/3in square)
oil, for deep-frying
icing (confectioners') sugar, to dust

FOR THE SAUCE
400g/14oz/3¹/₂ cups raspberries
45ml/3 tbsp icing (confectioners') sugar
a squeeze of lemon juice

1 First make the sauce. Place the raspberries and icing sugar in a food processor and blend until smooth. Press the raspberry purée mixture through a sieve (strainer) to remove the seeds, then stir a squeeze of lemon juice into the sauce. Cover and place in the refrigerator until ready to serve.

2 Peel the mangoes, then carefully slice the flesh away from one side of the flat stone (pit). Repeat on the second side, then trim off any remaining flesh from around the stone. Cut the mango flesh into 1cm/¹/₂in dice.

3 Lay 12 wonton wrappers on a clean work surface and place two or three pieces of mango in the centre of each one. Brush the edges with water and top with the remaining wrappers. Press the edges to seal. Heat the oil in a wok to 180°C/350°F or until a cube of bread browns in 45 seconds. Deep-fry the wontons, two or three at a time, for about 2 minutes, or until crisp and golden.

4 Remove the cooked wontons from the oil and drain on kitchen paper. Dust with icing sugar and serve on individual plates drizzled with the raspberry sauce.

Nutritional information per portion: Energy 314Kcal/1331kJ; Protein 5.5g; Carbohydrate 56.1g, of which sugars 27.3g; Fat 9.2g, of which saturates 1.2g; Cholesterol 0mg; Calcium 93mg; Fibre 5.6g; Sodium 6mg.

Sweet and spicy rice fritters

These delicious little golden balls of rice are scented with sweet, warm spices and will fill the kitchen with a wonderful aroma while you're cooking. To enjoy them at their best, serve piping hot, as soon as you've dusted them with sugar.

SERVES 4

175g/6oz cooked basmati rice
2 eggs, lightly beaten
60ml/4 tbsp caster (superfine) sugar
a pinch of nutmeg
2.5ml/1/2 tsp ground cinnamon
a pinch of ground cloves
10ml/2 tsp vanilla extract
50g/2oz/1/2 cup plain (all-purpose) flour
10ml/2 tsp baking powder
a pinch of salt
25g/1oz desiccated (dry unsweetened shredded) coconut
sunflower oil, for deep-frying
icing (confectioners') sugar, to dust

1 Place the cooked basmati rice, beaten eggs, sugar, nutmeg, ground cinnamon, ground cloves and vanilla extract in a large bowl and whisk together to combine.

2 Sift in the flour, baking powder and salt and add the coconut. Mix well until thoroughly combined.

3 Fill a wok one-third full of the oil and heat to 180°C/350°F or until a cube of bread, dropped into the oil, browns in 45 seconds.

4 Very gently, drop tablespoonfuls of the mixture into the oil, one at a time, and fry for 2–3 minutes, or until golden. Carefully remove the fritters from the wok using a slotted spoon and drain well on kitchen paper.

5 Divide the fritters into four portions, or simply pile them up on a single large platter. Dust them with icing sugar and serve immediately.

Nutritional information per portion: Energy 316Kcal/1321kJ; Protein 6.6g; Carbohydrate 45.8g, of which sugars 16.3g; Fat 12.4g, of which saturates 4.8g; Cholesterol 95mg; Calcium 46mg; Fibre 1.3g; Sodium 38mg.

Vanilla, honey and saffron pears

These sweet juicy pears, poached in a honey syrup infused with vanilla, saffron and lime, make a truly elegant dessert. For a low-fat version you can eat them on their own, but for a really luxurious, indulgent treat, serve with cream or ice cream.

SERVES 4

150g/5oz/³/₄ cup caster (superfine) sugar
105ml/7 tbsp clear honey
5ml/1 tsp finely grated lime rind
a large pinch of saffron

2 vanilla pods (beans)
500ml/17fl oz/scant 2³/₄ cups water
4 large, firm ripe dessert pears
single (light) cream or ice cream, to serve

1 Place the sugar and honey in a medium, non-stick wok, then add the lime rind and the saffron.

2 Using a small, sharp knife, split the vanilla pods in half and scrape the seeds into the wok, then add the vanilla pods, too.

3 Pour the water into the wok and bring the mixture to the boil. Reduce the heat to low and simmer, stirring occasionally.

4 Peel the pears, then add to the wok and gently coat them in the syrup. Cover and simmer for 12–15 minutes, turning the pears halfway through cooking, until just tender.

5 Lift the pears from the syrup using a slotted spoon and transfer to four serving bowls. Set aside.

6 Bring the syrup back to the boil and cook gently for about 10 minutes, or until reduced and thickened. Spoon the syrup over the pears and serve either warm or chilled with single cream or ice cream.

VARIATIONS
You can try using a variety of different flavourings in the syrup. Use 10ml/2 tsp chopped fresh root ginger and 1 or 2 star anise in place of the saffron and vanilla, or 1 cinnamon stick, 3 cloves and 105ml/7 tbsp maple syrup in place of the spices and honey. If the syrup seems too sweet for your taste, you can sharpen it with a little lemon or lime juice.

Nutritional information per portion: Energy 283Kcal/1207kJ; Protein 0.8g; Carbohydrate 74.3g, of which sugars 74.3g; Fat 0.2g, of which saturates 0g; Cholesterol 0mg; Calcium 38mg; Fibre 3.3g; Sodium 10mg.

Caramelized pineapple with lemon grass

This stunning dessert, garnished with jewel-like pomegranate seeds, is superb for entertaining. The tangy, zesty flavours of lemon grass and mint bring out the exquisite sweetness of the pineapple to create a truly luscious combination.

SERVES 4

30ml/2 tbsp very finely chopped
    lemon grass, and 2 lemon grass
    stalks, halved lengthways
350g/12oz/1³/₄ cups caster
    (superfine) sugar
10ml/2 tsp chopped fresh mint leaves
2 small, ripe pineapples, about
    600g/1lb 5oz each
15ml/1 tbsp sunflower oil
60ml/4 tbsp pomegranate seeds
crème fraîche, to serve

1 Place the chopped lemon grass, 250g/9oz of the sugar and the mint leaves in a non-stick wok. Pour over 150ml/¹/₄ pint/²/₃ cup of water and bring to the boil. Reduce the heat and simmer for 10–15 minutes, until thickened. Strain into a glass bowl, reserving the halved lemon grass stalks. Set aside.

2 Using a sharp knife, peel and core the pineapples and then cut them into 1cm/¹/₂in-thick slices. Sprinkle the slices with the remaining sugar.

3 Brush a large non-stick wok with the oil and place over a medium heat. Working in batches, cook the sugared pineapple slices for 2–3 minutes until lightly caramelized, then turn over and cook the other side for 2–3 minutes.

4 Transfer the pineapple slices to a flat serving dish and scatter over the pomegranate seeds. Pour the lemon grass syrup over the fruit and garnish with the reserved stalks. Serve hot or at room temperature with crème fraîche.

Nutritional information per portion: Energy 493Kcal/2101kJ; Protein 1.6g; Carbohydrate 121.7g, of which sugars 121.7g; Fat 3.4g, of which saturates 0.3g; Cholesterol 0mg; Calcium 101mg; Fibre 3.6g; Sodium 11mg.

Orange and date buttermilk pancakes

Serve these sweet, sticky, golden pancakes for breakfast, brunch or dessert. They're bursting with the flavour of zesty orange and sweet juicy dates and are utterly moreish. Medjool dates have an intensely sweet flesh and will give the best results.

SERVES 4

150g/5oz/1¼ cups self-raising
   (self-rising) flour
2.5ml/½ tsp baking powder
a pinch of salt
250ml/8fl oz/1 cup buttermilk
3 eggs
15ml/1 tbsp caster (superfine) sugar
200g/7oz/1¼ cup Medjool dates, stoned
finely grated rind and juice from
   1 small orange
50g/2oz/¼ cup unsalted (sweet)
   butter, melted
sunflower oil, for greasing
clear honey, to drizzle
natural (plain) yogurt, to serve

1 Sift the flour and baking soda into a large bowl with a pinch of salt. Whisk in the buttermilk, eggs, sugar, dates, orange rind and juice and melted butter. Leave to stand for 15 minutes.

2 Brush a wok with a little oil and heat over a medium heat. When hot, pour a small ladleful of the pancake mixture into the wok. Cook for 2–3 minutes until just set.

3 Cook the second side for 35–45 seconds. Transfer to a plate and keep warm while you cook the remaining batter in the same way. (You should make about 16 pancakes in total.)

4 To serve, divide the pancakes among four warmed plates, piling them up in a stack. Drizzle honey over each stack, top with a dollop of yogurt and serve immediately.

Nutritional information per portion: Energy 373Kcal/1569kJ; Protein 11.2g; Carbohydrate 51.5g, of which sugars 23g; Fat 15.2g, of which saturates 7.8g; Cholesterol 172mg; Calcium 166mg; Fibre 2.1g; Sodium 161mg.

Calas

These sweet rice fritters are an American/Creole speciality, sold by 'Calas' women on the streets of the French quarter of New Orleans as a popular and tasty breakfast.

MAKES OVER 40

115g/4oz/generous ¹/₂ cup short grain
   pudding rice
900ml/1¹/₂ pints/3³/₄ cups mixed milk
   and water
30ml/2 tbsp caster (superfine) sugar
50g/2oz/¹/₂ cup plain (all-purpose) flour
7.5ml/1¹/₂ tsp baking powder
5ml/1 tsp grated lemon rind
2.5ml/¹/₂ tsp ground cinnamon
1.5ml/¹/₄ tsp ground ginger
generous pinch of grated nutmeg
2 eggs
sunflower oil, for deep-frying
salt
icing (confectioners') sugar, for dusting
cherry or strawberry jam and thick
   cream, to serve

1 Put the rice in a pan and pour in the milk and water. Add a pinch of salt and bring to the boil. Stir, then cover and simmer over a very gentle heat for 15–20 minutes until the rice is tender. Switch off the heat under the pan, then add the sugar. Stir well, cover and leave until completely cool, by which time the rice should have absorbed all the liquid and become very soft.

2 Put the rice in a food processor or blender and add the flour, baking powder, lemon rind, spices and eggs. Process for about 20–30 seconds so that the mixture is like a thick batter.

3 Heat the oil in a wok to 160°C/325°F. Scoop up a generous teaspoon of batter and, using a second spoon, push into the hot oil. Add four or five more and fry for 3–4 minutes, turning them occasionally, until the calas are golden brown. Drain on kitchen paper and keep warm while cooking in batches.

4 Dust the calas generously with icing sugar and serve warm with fruit jam and thick cream.

Nutritional information per portion: Energy 50Kcal/206kJ; Protein 0.9g; Carbohydrate 3.5g, of which sugars 1.3g; Fat 3.6g, of which saturates 0.6g; Cholesterol 10mg; Calcium 16mg; Fibre 0g; Sodium 8mg.

Rich spiced carrot and raisin halwa

Halwa is a classic Indian sweet, with many variations. In this one, grated carrots are cooked in milk with sugar, spices and raisins until meltingly tender and sweet.

SERVES 4

300g/11oz carrots
90g/3¹/₂oz ghee
250ml/8fl oz/1 cup milk
150g/5oz/³/₄ cup golden caster
   (superfine) sugar
5–6 lightly crushed cardamom pods
1 clove
1 cinnamon stick
50g/2oz/scant ¹/₂ cup raisins

1 Peel and grate the carrots. Place a non-stick wok over a low heat and add half the ghee. When the ghee has melted, add the grated carrot and stir-fry for 6–8 minutes, until the carrot has softened and taken on more colour.

2 Pour the milk into the wok and bring to the boil, reduce the heat to low and simmer gently for 10–12 minutes.

3 Stir the remaining ghee into the carrot mixture, then stir in the sugar, crushed cardamom pods, clove, cinnamon stick and raisins.

4 Gently simmer the carrot mixture for 6–7 minutes, stirring occasionally, until thickened and glossy. Serve immediately in small serving bowls.

COOK'S TIP
Ghee is clarified butter and is widely used in Indian cooking. It is an essential ingredient in halwa and is available in cans from Asian stores.

Nutritional information per portion: Energy 439Kcal/1838kJ; Protein 3g; Carbohydrate 56.7g, of which sugars 56.3g; Fat 23.8g, of which saturates 15.6g; Cholesterol 67mg; Calcium 120mg; Fibre 2.1g; Sodium 56mg.

Caramelized plums with coconut rice

Red, juicy plums are quickly seared in a wok with sugar to make a rich caramel coating, then served with sticky coconut-flavoured rice for a satisfying dessert. The glutinous rice is available from Asian stores, but remember that you have to soak it overnight.

SERVES 4

6 or 8 firm, ripe plums
90g/3¹/₂oz/¹/₂ cup caster
 (superfine) sugar

FOR THE RICE
115g/4oz sticky glutinous rice
150ml/¹/₄ pint/²/₃ cup coconut cream
45ml/3 tbsp caster (superfine) sugar
a pinch of salt

1 First prepare the rice. Rinse it in several changes of water, then leave to soak overnight in a bowl of cold water.

2 Line a large bamboo steamer with muslin (cheesecloth). Drain the rice and transfer it to the lined steamer. Cover the rice and steam over simmering water for 25–30 minutes, until the rice is tender. (Check the water level and add more if necessary.)

3 Transfer the steamed rice to a wide bowl and set aside for a moment.

4 Combine the coconut cream with the sugar and salt and pour into a clean wok. Heat gently and bring to the boil, then remove from the heat and pour over the rice. Stir to mix well.

5 Using a sharp knife, cut the plums in half and remove the stones (pits). Sprinkle caster sugar over the cut sides.

6 Heat a non-stick wok over a medium-high flame. Working in batches, place the plums in the wok, cut side down, and cook for 1–2 minutes, or until the sugar caramelizes. You may need to wipe out the wok with kitchen paper in between batches.

7 Mould the rice into rounds and place on warmed plates, then spoon over the caramelized plums. Alternatively, simply spoon the rice into four warmed bowls and top with the plums. Drizzle any syrup remaining in the wok over and around the fruit.

Nutritional information per portion: Energy 298Kcal/1265kJ; Protein 3.6g; Carbohydrate 71.7g, of which sugars 50.2g; Fat 0.7g, of which saturates 0.1g; Cholesterol 0mg; Calcium 53mg; Fibre 2.4g; Sodium 47mg.

Wok Basics

This section gives you all the information you need to use your wok to its full potential. It demonstrates the range of woks and tools available, and gives detailed instructions on taking care of your wok. You will discover the range of cooking methods suited to the wok, and how to prepare ingredients, from rice and noodles to meat, poultry, fish and shellfish, vegetables and aromatics.

Woks, tools and accessories

Choosing a wok isn't difficult. There are dozens of versions on the market, from conventional carbon steel and stainless steel models to modern non-stick woks that often come complete with a variety of tools.

If you're a serious cook who likes the classical approach, begin your search at a large Asian food store, where you can examine traditional carbon steel woks in a range of shapes and sizes, hefting them in your hands to find the weight and size that suits. If you buy a good quality pan and season it properly, it will give you years of excellent service, and will actually improve with age. A cheaper wok may well have to be replaced after a year or so.

Non-stick woks

If you prefer a non-stick wok, look for one made from reinforced titanium, which is guaranteed against scratching and can safely be washed in the dishwasher. You won't get the patina and flavour build-up that comes with using a steel wok over time, but you will gain by having an easy-care utensil that will give you satisfactory results. It is essential to use a non-stick pan if you are cooking acidic foods such as fruits, which would discolour in a steel wok.

Size and shape

An average 36cm/14in wok is ideal for most kitchens, and will sit comfortably on the average burner. If you have a large family, or intend to cook whole fish on a regular basis, choose a 40cm/16in model. Whether you buy a round-based wok or a flat-based one depends on your type of stove, as well as your personal preference. Purists plump for round-based woks, claiming the shape gives perfect results, as the area of intense heat is very small and the upward slope uninterrupted. However, a round-based wok will wobble if placed on an electric stove. To stabilize it, you would have to use a wok stand or ring, but the round base could still reflect heat back and damage the electric element. So, for electric stoves, or any stove with a

level cooking surface, flat-based woks are best. With a gas stove, you can use either style of wok. You probably won't need a wok ring, but if you do, make sure that the wok sits down snugly, so that it is close to the heat source.

Both single-handled woks and twin-handled Cantonese woks are available. The single-handed wok is reckoned to be best for stir-frying, while the twin is more stable and is recommended for deep-frying, steaming and braising. Some woks offer you both features by giving you a 30cm/12in long handle matched with a short, round 'helper' handle on the opposite side so that the wok can easily be moved from stove to table. Whichever type you buy, get a domed lid, so that you can use your wok for steaming or braising.

LEFT: *A double handled wok is ideal for using as a serving dish as well as a cooking vessel.*

ABOVE: *An electric wok is ideal for braising and slow cooking.*

Cleavers and knives

Cutting meat and vegetables for stir-frying, exposing maximum surface area to the heat, is quite an art, and Chinese cooks swear that the best tool for this is a cleaver. This short-handled implement has a large, flat blade that can be used to cut everything from paper-thin vegetable slices to meat on the bone. When the blade is held flat, it can be used like a spatula, to move prepared food to the wok. Cleavers come in several sizes and weights. The heaviest, number one, is more like a chopper than a knife. Its blade is 23cm/9in long and 10cm/4in wide, and is mainly used for slicing. Number two, the medium weight cleaver, is popular for general kitchen use. It is used for both slicing and chopping. The back of the blade is ideal for pounding meat to tenderize it, and the flat surface can be used to crush garlic or ginger. Good quality kitchen knives can be used instead.

A 10cm/4in paring knife and a 20cm/8in cook's knife will be the most useful. It is vital to keep blades sharp.

Electric wok

The electric wok doesn't get quite as hot as a carbon steel wok over high heat, but is efficient, convenient and good for cooking braised dishes and risotto. It can make a meal in moments and busy cooks like it because it leaves the stove free for cooking other items. Others value its stability and the fact that the heat is thermostatically controlled. Electric woks come in various sizes but all are similar in design, with a heat element recessed in the stay-cool base. The wok that sits securely on the base will inevitably have a non-stick coating, but may need to be given a token seasoning before being used for the first time. The electric wok's handbook will give instructions on how this is to be done.

BELOW: *A Chinese cleaver is finely balanced.*

TOOLS AND ACCESSORIES

It isn't necessary to buy special tools for wok cooking, but there are a few items that will prove useful.

Mortar and pestle

South-east Asian cooks like to use their woks for making quick curries. These depend for their flavour on freshly made curry pastes. A granite mortar is best for this purpose, since the rough surface amplifies the pounding action of the pestle and helps to grip the ingredients and keep them in the bowl. Buy a mortar that is at least 18cm/7in across. This is sufficient for mixtures of up to 450ml/^{3}/$_4$ pint/scant 2 cups.

BELOW: *A granite mortar and pestle is useful for making traditional spice pastes.*

Ladle

A ladle is necessary for spooning soups or other liquids out of the wok. Choose one with a deep bowl. Black nylon ladles are recommended for non-stick woks, but they do scorch easily, so stainless steel is a better bet. Some ladles have graduated markings inside that indicate how much liquid they hold. This is useful when you need to spoon out a specific quantity of stock. If your ladle is not marked in this way, measure the liquid it holds by spooning a ladleful of water into a measuring jug (cup). Make a note of the amount to help when you are following a recipe that specifies an amount of liquid to be removed from the wok.

BELOW: Essential tools include a dome-shaped lid, wooden or bamboo chopsticks, a long-handled spatula and a large ladle.

RIGHT: A perforated metal scoop and a traditional wire skimmer.

Spatulas and scoops

It is useful to have at least two wooden spatulas for stir-frying, preferably with a rounded side that follows the contours of the wok. Another useful implement is the charn, a long-handled spatula shaped like a shovel, which makes it easy to scoop and toss foods that are being stir-fried. If you use a charn in a non-stick pan, take care not to scratch the surface.

Chopsticks

If you wander through an Asian street market you might sometimes see large amounts of food being stirred in giant woks by cooks using extra-long chopsticks. These can be ideal for the dextrous, but tongs or two spatulas can be used instead.

Draining or steaming rack

Most woks, standard or electric, come with a rainbow-shaped metal rack that clips on to the rim. Sometimes called a tempura rack, this item is useful when deep-frying. As items cook, they can be set to drain on the rack. Surplus oil will drip back into the pan, and the drained foods can be moved to kitchen paper when the rack is full. The rack can also be used for steaming, and is especially useful in an electric wok.

Skimmers

These are long handled utensils with wire or bamboo scoops at one end. These can be cup- or saucer-shaped and are used to scoop food out of hot oil or stock. Saucer-shaped skimmers are also called spiders, as they resemble circular webs.

Wok ring

This circular metal stand gives stability to a round-based wok when used on an electric or gas stove. The rings come in several sizes and designs. The most common ones look like crumpet rings or cookie cutters, and consist of solid metal that may be punched with ventilation holes. Thick wire stands are also available, and are recommended for gas stoves. It is important to buy a ring that supports your wok securely while allowing it to be as close to the heat source as possible without putting out the flame. If your wok has a flat base you won't need a ring. If you intend using a wok ring on an electric stove, check with the manufacturer, as this can damage the element.

ABOVE: *Racks can be clipped to the side of a wok to drain deep-fried food.*

Steamers

Steaming is one of the healthiest ways of cooking, since no fat is required and the natural flavour of the food is preserved. A wok is ideal for this purpose, since its shape gives you a large surface area of water to turn into steam. There are several ways you can steam food in a wok. For steaming just a few items, you can use the semicircular steaming rack that clips on to the side of the pan.

Alternatively, you can place items to be steamed on a heatproof plate, provided you raise the plate above the surface of the water or stock by means of a trivet or upturned cup. You can also use the Chinese method of stackable bamboo baskets. An expanding metal steamer will also work well, but take care that the feet do not scratch the surface of the wok if it has a non-stick coating. Whichever means you use, you will need to trap the steam somehow, either by fitting a domed lid over the wok, or making sure the steamer itself is tightly covered.

Bamboo steamers

Although stainless-steel steamers are regarded as being more hygienic, natural bamboo steamers do an excellent job, since the material allows steam to circulate freely around the food with only minimal condensation. The steamer baskets can be bought either singly or in sets and come in various sizes. Standard steamers have a diameter of 25cm/10in and are about 15cm/6in tall. This is the ideal size for a 36cm/14in wok. When the basket is in use, there should be at least 5cm/2in space between it and the side of the wok. Steamers can be stacked above eachother.

LEFT: *A stack of bamboo steamers increases the amount of food you can cook at one time.*

Seasoning a wok

Wash the wok in warm, soapy water to remove any preservative coating. Rinse well, shake off the excess water, then place the wok over low heat to dry. Add a little cooking oil (not olive oil) and, using kitchen paper, coat it evenly. Take care not to burn yourself. Heat gently for 10–12 minutes, then wipe off the oil with clean kitchen paper. Don't be alarmed when it blackens – this is natural. Repeat the process until the paper comes away clean, by which time the wok itself will have darkened. The more it is used, the better the wok's natural non-stick coating will be and the easier it will be to clean. If a wok should rust, rub it down with wire wool or fine sandpaper and then season it again. A cast iron or carbon steel wok is less likely to rust if it is oiled lightly before being stored.

Cleaning a wok

A properly seasoned wok should not be washed with soap. Remove any food sticking to the surface, then wash the wok in hot water. Dry thoroughly by placing the wok over the heat for a few minutes. Leave to cool, then rub a little oil into the surface.

Fish and shellfish

Given the versatility of the wok, there's literally no end to the ingredients that can be cooked in it. However, there are some items that lend themselves particularly well to stir-frying, steaming and braising. Inevitably, these are ingredients that cook quickly, prime examples of which are fish and shellfish.

Fish and shellfish can be cooked in a wok in a variety of ways. The more robust types of fish, such as cod, haddock and halibut, can be cut into bitesize portions and stir-fried. Stir-frying is also an excellent way of cooking prawns (shrimp) and scallops. Salmon and sea bass lend themselves more ideally to steaming.

BELOW: *Firm-fleshed, white fish, such as cod and haddock, are ideal for cooking as steaks or in bitesize pieces.*

Cod and haddock
White fish such as cod is a great choice for soups and fish curries. Add the pearly white cubes to the wok towards the end of cooking so that they keep their shape. They will be ready to eat in a couple of minutes. Cod and haddock can also be steamed. Haddock has a more delicate flavour and softer texture. This fish is a good choice for deep-frying. Dip pieces in batter before adding them to hot oil.

Halibut
A delicious flatfish, halibut has a fine, meaty texture. For steaming whole, choose the small variety, often called chicken halibut, or opt for steaks cut from the middle. Halibut is robust enough to be used with spicy flavours.

Scallops
These tender molluscs are delectable but very delicate, so take care not to overcook them. Scallops are delicious steamed with ginger and spring onions (scallions), or try them seared and served on wilted pak choi (bok choy).

ABOVE: *Scallops should be flash fried or steamed to retain their soft texture.*

Sea bass
Fish such as sea bass can be steamed whole in the wok. Choose a fish that weighs about 450g/1lb for two people. Strong flavours such as ginger, garlic, soy sauce and lemon grass work well.

Prawns
The most common shellfish ingredient in Asian cooking, prawns (shrimp) are a wonderful ingredient for stir-frying, steaming or deep-frying, as they need so little time to cook. Larger varieties, such as tiger prawns, are particularly good. When buying prawns in the shell, allow about 300g/11oz per serving.

Salmon
Although salmon can be cooked in a variety of ways, it is particularly good steamed in a bamboo basket. Flaked salmon makes great fish cakes.

Squid
For stir-frying, slit the body from top to bottom and turn it inside out. Flatten it, then score the flesh with a knife in a criss-cross pattern. Cut lengthwise into ribbons. These will curl when stir-fried.

Meat and poultry

Only the tenderest cuts of meat are suitable for wok cookery, especially if they are to be stir-fried. Traditional Asian recipes favour chicken, duck and pork, but there is no reason to limit yourself to these choices. Beef, lamb and even ostrich taste great when cooked in the wok.

Pork

Fillet (tenderloin) is the most tender cut and is relatively inexpensive, given that it consists of solid meat with very little wastage. Choose fillets that are pale pink all over, with no areas of discoloration. The flesh should be fairly firm, never flaccid, and slightly moist.

To prepare pork fillet, first pull away the membrane surrounding the meat and remove any fat. Cut away the tendon and sinew, which looks like a tougher strip of membrane. To stir-fry, slice in neat, even strips; for braising, opt for medallions, cut on the diagonal.

BELOW: Pork is a great favourite in Chinese and Asian dishes.

ABOVE: *Duck is tender and full of flavour, and ideal for fast wok cooking.*

Duck

In China and Thailand, duck is sometimes cooked whole, but is more often thinly sliced and stir-fried, or cubed and used to make a spicy curry. Most of the meat on a duck is concentrated in the breast, so, despite the cost, it can be more practical to buy breast portions instead of whole birds. Duck breasts can be steamed in a wok, then sliced, moistened with a little of the stock from the steamer and served in a salad.

Beef

Steak is ideal for stir-frying, whether you choose fillet (tenderloin), rump (round) or sirloin. Look for deep red meat with a light marbling of fat. If a recipe requires beef to be very thinly sliced, place it in the freezer for at least half an hour beforehand. For stir-fries, strips of beef are often marinated in a mixture that includes soy sauce and oil. When cooking, have the wok very hot, add a few strips at a time, and move them to the sides of the wok before adding more.

ABOVE: *Chicken, when flattened and cut into thin strips, is ideal for stir fries.*

Chicken

Tender breast portions or fillets are perfect for stir-frying. If thin strips of chicken are required, flatten the fillets by placing them between two sheets of clear film (plastic wrap) and beating lightly but firmly with a rolling pin.

Lamb

Choose lean leg of lamb for stir-frying, or lamb fillet (tenderloin), which is cut from the middle of the neck. The meat should be firm and pink. The paler the meat, the younger the lamb. To make medallions, cut the fillet into thin, even slices. These can be stir-fried or braised in the wok. Alternatively, cut into strips.

BELOW: The best cuts of beef are superb for fast frying, while cheaper cuts can be slow-cooked to tenderize.

Vegetables and aromatics

When you cook vegetables and aromatics in a wok, the aim is to retain maximum taste and texture. The flavour must be there in the first place, so shopping carefully is the first step towards good cooking.

Buy vegetables at the peak of condition, preferably from a farmer's market or greengrocer that sources produce locally, rather than buying shrink-wrapped items that have travelled great distances between soil and superstore. The best vegetables for wok cookery are those that stay crisp after stir-frying.

Beansprouts

Highly nutritious, beansprouts are delicious in stir-fries. They are highly perishable, so make sure they are absolutely fresh and use them as soon as possible after you purchase them.

BELOW: *Beansprouts.*

Pak choi

Known by various names, including 'bok choy' and 'Chinese chard', this member of the cabbage family is distinguished by its fat white stems. Many people think the stalks taste even better than the glossy green leaves, but both are great steamed or in a stir-fry. The stems take slightly longer to cook than the leaves, so start them first.

Baby corn

These miniature corn cobs are good for stir-frying, either whole or sliced in half lengthways. Their shape and colour create interest and they stay crunchy when cooked.

ABOVE: *Baby corn.*

Chinese leaves

This sweet-tasting green vegetable is often mistaken for a type of lettuce but is actually a brassica, which accounts for its American name, 'Chinese cabbage'. An excellent salad ingredient, when stir-fried, the white stalk stays crisp and contrasts with the softer texture of the leaves. To prepare, remove any discoloured or damaged leaves, trim the root, then slice the head across into thin shreds. Chinese leaves are sometimes used to make a bed in a bamboo steamer for cooking pieces of fish or meat.

ABOVE: *Pak choi.*

RIGHT: *Chinese leaves.*

Mangetout peas

Americans call these 'snow peas' but the French word, which literally translates to 'eat all', describes them better, since the entire pod is consumed. They need no preparation.

Mooli

A long white root also known as 'daikon' used as a crisp, sharp, cool addition to a salad – or cooked. Whether steamed or fried, it retains its crisp texture, but develops a sweeter flavour.

BELOW: *Mooli.*

ABOVE: *Mushrooms.*

Mushrooms

All mushrooms cook quickly and are great for the wok. Fresh shiitake and oyster mushrooms are readily available and are good in stir-fries, but button (white) mushrooms can also be used . Dried mushrooms give intense flavour. Soak in warm water for 30 minutes, discard the stems and slice the caps. The soaking water is good for stocks.

Peppers

Sweet 'bell' peppers are ideal for the wok, adding colour as well as flavour. When cooked quickly they retain some crunch and are delightfully juicy. Make an incision all the way around the stem-end. Pull off the lid and core and the seeds should come away too. Halve the pepper, remove any remaining seeds and hard ribs, then dice or slice it. Cut the flesh off the lid too.

Seaweed

There are several types of edible seaweed, like kombu, nori, wakame and hijiki. Their main use is flavouring stocks, soups and simmered dishes.

Chillies

These fiery peppers are used in curries and spicy stir-fries. There are many varieties in different strengths, so treat them with caution. Protect yourself from the capsaicin they contain by wearing gloves, or wash your hands afterwards to prevent chilli-burn. Slit them and scrape out the seeds and pith. Most of the heat is in the seeds, so add them only for a very spicy result. If grinding chillies, don't stand with your face directly over the mortar.

Spring onions

Many wok recipes call for spring onions (scallions) to be stir-fried at the start of cooking. Regular onions or shallots can be used instead. Using these aromatic vegetables gives depth of flavour, so they should be finely sliced so they blend with other ingredients and do not dominate the dish.

Garlic

The universal aromatic, garlic is great for stir-frying but burns easily at the high temperatures achieved in the wok. Cook it briefly or add with other vegetables. It can be crushed easily with a cleaver.

ABOVE: *Seaweed.*

BELOW: *Ginger.*

Ginger

A favourite ingredient in Eastern cooking, ginger adds a wonderful warmth and flavour to savoury and sweet foods. Peel off the skin and either chop or grate the flesh.

Galangal

This looks like ginger but can be distinguished by its finger-like sprouts. When young, these are pale pink in colour and taste almost lemony. As it matures, the skin thickens and turns pale gold. The flavour is then quite peppery. It is used like ginger and often incorporated in pastes.

LEFT: *Lemon grass.*

Lemon grass

The distinctive citrus flavour makes this a popular ingredient in stir-fries or curry pastes. Lemon grass stalks are sold in bundles. Peel away and discard the fibrous layers around each stalk. Only the tenderest part of the stalk – the bottom 10–15cm/4–6in – is suitable for stir-frying. Slice it, or pound into a paste. Add offcuts to water for steaming fish or chicken. Lemon grass can be bought dried in jars, but this is a poor substitute.

Rice

Many savoury dishes cooked in a wok either incorporate rice or are served with rice. Fried rice is a wok standard, but the pan can also be used to make a pilaff or a risotto.

Thai jasmine rice

This delicately scented long grain rice is an ideal accompaniment for stir-fries and similar dishes, and is also a good choice for making fried rice. Uncooked grains are translucent and become fluffy and white, with a slightly nutty flavour, when boiled. Fried rice often includes vegetables, like pak choi (bok choy) or spring greens (collards), along with aromatic flavourings, such as garlic and chilli. In vegetarian versions, coconut or cashew nuts are favourite additions. Add omelette, chicken, beef, pork or prawns (shrimp) for protein.

Basmati rice

For Indian cooking and fusion food, basmati is the obvious choice. This long grain rice lives up to its Hindi name, which translates as 'the fragrant one'.

BELOW: *Thai jasmine rice.*

The grains are long and slender with a very good texture. Basmati is the best type of rice for a pilaff, and a wok with a tight-fitting lid is ideal for the task.

Risotto rice

Italians recommend using a heavy pan for making risotto, but maybe that's because they didn't invent the wok. The latter works extremely well, the only drawback being that the large surface area makes for more rapid evaporation of the liquid, so it is really important to stir constantly and check the rice frequently to prevent it from becoming overcooked. You may also need to add slightly more liquid than listed in a recipe, so make sure you have some spare. The risotto is ready when the rice is creamy, but the grains retain a hint of firmness at the centre.

Long grain rice isn't suitable for risotto. You need a comparatively large, plump short grain with a high proportion of starch. As the rice cooks, it dissolves in the stock that is constantly added, to give a creamy texture. There are several varieties of risotto rice. Carnaroli and Vialone Nano give excellent results. The starchy outer

BELOW: *Basmati rice.*

ABOVE: *Risotto rice.*

layer of the grain dissolves, but the centre retains enough 'bite' to provide the perfect contrast. Arborio also works well but contains more amylopectin, so has a tendency to become pappy if overcooked. Removing the risotto from the heat before it is fully cooked, and leaving it to stand, covered, for 4–5 minutes, overcomes this drawback.

Serving rice safely
Serve rice as soon as it is cooked, if possible. Never keep it warm for long periods or food poisoning might result. The danger comes from bacillus cereus, which is often present in uncooked rice. If the rice is boiled and served straight away there is little risk, but if cooked rice is left to stand at room temperature, or kept warm for a long period, any toxic spores may multiply. If you intend using cooked rice in a salad, it is important to cool it quickly and keep it covered in the refrigerator. If you reheat rice, don't just warm it; it must be piping hot right through.

Noodles and wrappers

In Asia, where the wok originated, noodles are an integral part of the diet, served in soups, salads, stir-fries and sweet dishes. They are a symbol of longevity in China and are often on the menu at birthday parties, weddings and wakes.

Although noodles are traditionally used with wok dishes, there's nothing to stop you using pasta if you prefer.

Noodles are usually made from rice or wheat flour, but can also be based on other ingredients, such as mung beans, buckwheat or seaweed. They come in bundles or nests, and can be fresh, semi-cooked or dried. Noodles taste fairly bland, which makes them a good vehicle for spicy food. They can be served alone, with a sauce, or as part of an elaborate dish. Noodle paste is also used to make wrappers for spring rolls and other deep-fried treats.

BELOW: *Egg noodles are available in both fresh and dried form and come packed in bundles or nests.*

Egg noodles

Like pasta, wheat noodles can be plain or enriched with egg. Egg noodles (usually labelled as such) are those most familiar to people in the West. Japanese egg noodles are called ramen.

Wheat flour noodles

Plain wheat noodles go by various names. In Japan they are called udon. They come in several widths; somen is slim, similar to the Korean somyen. They need to be boiled briefly before use. Fresh ones will often take less than 1 minute; dried take 3–5 minutes. Exact timing will vary – some can be added straight to the wok.

Buckwheat and cellophane noodles

Soba are Japanese noodles made from buckwheat with wheat flour to give elasticity. They have an earthy flavour. Soba are often served cold, with enough sauce to coat the strands but not swamp the taste. Cook in boiling water until tender. Made from mung beans, cellophane noodles (also sold as glass, jelly or bean thread noodles) are transparent when cooked and look pretty in a salad or stir-fry.

Rice flour noodles

Pre-cooking is part of the process of making rice noodles, so they need even less preparation than wheat noodles. Before use, just soak in hot water for 5–10 minutes, or until they become soft. If you intend to fry them, you can skip this step, but use the thin noodles rather than the thicker rice sticks.

ABOVE: *Japanese somen noodles are wheat-based.*

Wrappers

Simple snacks such as spring rolls, wontons, tung tong and rice paper parcels are easy to deep-fry in the wok, and because of the shape of the pan, you need less oil than in a deep-fat fryer. Square, rectangular and round wrappers are available in packets from Asian food stores. Like noodles, they are made from either rice or from wheat, or wheat mixed with egg.

BELOW: *Square wonton wrappers.*

Oils and fats

Although the design of a wok means that oil is the ingredient you need least of – unless you are deep-frying – the type you use is important because of the high temperatures involved.

Groundnut oil

Also known as peanut oil, this type of oil is ideal for use in the wok, as it reaches a high temperature without smoking and has a neutral flavour that won't mask the taste of the food. Like olive oil, groundnut oil is monounsaturated, although it does contain a slightly higher percentage of saturated fat than corn oil or sunflower oil. Some people can be allergic to groundnut oil, so make sure you inform guests if you have used it for cooking.

Corn oil

Extracted from the germ of the corn kernel, this polyunsaturated oil is almost tasteless, although it can have a discernible odour. It is very good for both stir-frying and deep-fat frying since it can withstand high heat without reaching smoking point.

Lard

Although this animal fat is no longer widely used for frying in the West, due to health implications, it remains a common cooking medium in parts of China. The disadvantage of using lard, other than it being a saturated fat, is that it is often strongly flavoured.

Olive oil

This oil is never used for Asian cooking. The flavour simply doesn't go with the ingredients. You can still use it in a wok, however, for Mediterranean-type dishes with tomato-based sauces, olives, and herbs such as oregano.

Rapeseed (canola) oil

This monounsaturated oil is particularly popular in North America. It is pale gold in colour and has a mild flavour and aroma. The smoking point is slightly lower than corn oil, but it is regarded as a good choice for stir-frying and deep-frying.

LEFT: sunflower oil (left); groundnut oil (middle); olive oil (right).

ABOVE: *Sesame oil (top); chilli oil (bottom). These oils are used to flavour dishes rather than as a frying medium.*

Sesame oil

Light sesame oil can be used for frying, but the dark type made from roasted sesame seeds is largely used for flavouring. It has a nutty taste, which becomes more pronounced if the oil is warmed. It mustn't be allowed to get too hot, though, or it will burn. A few drops of sesame oil are often added to soup, noodles or a stir-fry before serving.

Sunflower oil

Another much-used polyunsaturated oil, this has a mild flavour. With a smoking point that rivals that of corn oil and groundnut oil, it is a very good choice for wok cookery.

Wok oil

This product, specially developed for the wok, combines soya and sesame oils and is flavoured with ginger, garlic and pepper. It's an expensive way to start a stir-fry, but gives good results and is convenient if you have little time.

Tofu and soya products

This inexpensive protein food is made from soya beans, and was invented by the Chinese. It is now widely used throughout the world as an alternative to fish and meat.

When it comes to wok cookery, tofu and similar soya products score on several fronts. They are nutritious, easy to use and need little or no cooking. Although most forms are virtually tasteless, they take on surrounding flavours, so are useful for adding bulk while boosting food values. Tofu is low in fat and cholesterol-free.

Silken tofu
This white product is the most delicate form of tofu. A creamy version comes in tubs and can be used for dips or desserts, including a

RIGHT*: Deep-fried tofu.*

BELOW*: Fresh firm tofu.*

FAR RIGHT*: Silken tofu.*

ABOVE*: Pressed fried tofu.*

non-dairy ice cream. The slightly firmer type of silken tofu comes in cubes, which break down easily, so must be handled gently. If you use silken tofu cubes in a stir-fry, add them right at the end and don't toss the mixture too vigorously.

Firm tofu
This lightly pressed product is sold in cakes or blocks, either submerged in water or vacuum-packed, and can be cubed or sliced. It makes a good addition to a stir-fry, especially when marinated in soy sauce with strong flavours such as ginger, garlic or fermented black beans.

Fried tofu
At first glance, this doesn't look much like tofu. Slice the nut-brown block, however, and the white interior is exposed. The outer colour is the result of deep-frying in vegetable oil, a

process than not only adds flavour, but also makes the beancurd more robust. Fried tofu won't break down when cooked.

Tempeh
To make this Indonesian speciality, whole soya beans are fermented with a cultured starter, which gives the product a nutty, savoury flavour and causes it to solidify so that it can be cut into blocks. The beans remain visible under a velvety coating that resembles the rind you find on Brie. Their presence makes for a product that is firmer and more chewy than most other forms of tofu. In the wok, tempeh can be steamed, stir-fried, deep-fried or braised.

LEFT*: Tempeh.*

TVP/Textured vegetable protein
This meat substitute is made from soya flour from which the fat has been removed. It can be flavoured and shaped to mimic minced (ground) beef and is also sold in cubes or slices. The very low fat content of TVP means that it keeps well even without refrigeration.

Sauces and flavourings

When you own a wok, being a spontaneous cook becomes second nature. As long as you start with oil and aromatics, you can add almost any variety of vegetable, plus meat, poultry, tofu or whatever else takes your fancy. A good sauce, or a stock made from a paste, will bring all the flavours together.

Curry paste blocks

If you can find the imported curry paste blocks in specialist food stores, then do use them, as they impart a wonderful authentic flavour. Bottled curry sauces can be used instead. Shrimp paste has a strong flavour. It is made from salted, dried and pulverized shrimp, which is compressed and sold in blocks or small cans or tubs. It must always be cooked, and used sparingly.

Chilli sauce

Mainly used as a dipping sauce, it comes in various strengths and sweetnesses and is great with fried prawns (shrimp).

RIGHT: *There are several kinds of soy sauce available.*

ABOVE: *Sweet chilli sauce.*

RIGHT: *Dark hoisin sauce.*

Fish sauce

Read the ingredients for this Thai sauce, and you might be disinclined to try it. It has a very pungent odour, but add it to a soup, stir-fry or braised dish and you will be amazed at the depth of flavour it gives.

Hoisin sauce

Thick and sweet, this Chinese sauce is made from fermented beans, sugar, vinegar, salt, chillies, garlic and sesame oil, combined in varying proportions. It makes a good marinade, but you may need to thin it.

Oyster sauce

Based on soy sauce and oyster extract, it has a distinctive taste and is great in soups and stir-fries.

Plum sauce

Fruity, sweet and spicy, this is made from plums, ginger, garlic and chilli. It makes a good dip.

Miso paste

This Japanese fermented soya bean and grain paste is produced in various strengths. White miso is the lightest and sweetest. The most widely used form is the medium strength mugi miso, and there is also a very strong dark brown variety, hacho miso. Miso's principal use is for making different kinds of soup, but it can also be used in sauces, marinades and dressings.

Soy sauce

Made from fermented soya beans, soy sauce is an essential ingredient throughout the Far East. There are three basic types, the colour governed by the stage at which the sauce is bottled, and the presence of other ingredients. The lightest soy sauce is Japanese. Then comes the Chinese light soy sauce. China also has a dark soy sauce that is good with red meats. Tamari is a Japanese dark sauce that is full of flavour but isn't too salty. Thailand has a sweet soy sauce.

Teriyaki sauce

This Japanese sauce is sold commercially but you can make your own by mixing equal proportions of shoyu and mirin in a pan. Add a little sugar to sweeten the mixture. Stir over gentle heat until the sugar has dissolved, then cool. If not using immediately, store in the refrigerator.

Herbs and spices

In view of the speed of wok cookery, any added flavourings need to deliver pretty smartly. Most herbs do the job well, but spices need to be chosen with care, as many of them have an impact only after lengthy cooking.

Basil
Thai basil is popular in South-east Asian cooking. It has a typical sweet basil aroma, overlaid with hints of aniseed. The leaves can be added whole to stir-fries and curries.

Coriander
You can use a wide range of herbs in wok cookery, but coriander (cilantro) is probably the most useful. Its fresh leaves have a distinctive, spicy flavour. The roots and stems are often used in curry pastes. Add chopped coriander to stir-fries at the last minute to retain its flavour. Dried coriander is used in curry.

BELOW: *Kaffir lime leaves.*

Five-spice powder
A classic spice mix, particularly good in braised dishes. It contains star anise, Szechuan peppercorns, fennel seeds, cloves and cinnamon and has a pungent, slightly sweet flavour.

Kaffir lime leaves
Although difficult to find fresh, lime leaves are easily obtained dried. They give a lovely warm, spicy citrus flavour.

Mint
Often used with fresh coriander in spring rolls and similar deep-fried snacks, it is also good in a noodle salad.

Pandanus leaves
These fragrant leaves are principally used as a wrapper, or as a liner for ramekins. They look attractive wrapped around deep-fried skewered chicken.

BELOW: *Pandanus leaves.*

LEFT: *Star anise.*

BELOW: *Shiso.*

Shiso
A herb with a distinctive aroma, this is an important ingredient in Japanese cooking. Despite being a form of mint, the flavour is redolent of basil.

Star anise
This distinctive-looking spice has a warm flavour that puts it in the same category as cinnamon and nutmeg. It is used in savoury and sweet dishes.

Tamarind
Imagine a very intense lemon taste with no bitterness. That's tamarind, a popular product in South-east Asia. It is sold in blocks that need soaking, but can be bought pre-prepared in jars.

Wasabi
This is often referred to as Japanese horseradish, but it is no relation. Like watercress, it grows wild in mountain streams, but is also cultivated. Like mustard, it is mainly sold either as a paste or as a powder which must be mixed with warm water. Treat it with caution – the pale green colour may look pretty but it packs a terrific punch, and too much could ruin a dish.

Preparation techniques

Successful wok cooking is all about preparation, especially when you are stir-frying. That means slicing vegetables, meat or fish to the size required, having sauces handy and making sure that implements needed are within reach.

Cutting and slicing vegetables

Asian cooks take great care over the preparation of ingredients. There's an aesthetic reason for this – food must look as well as taste good – but cutting all the pieces to a similar size means they cook quickly and evenly.

Root vegetables

Firm root vegetables, such as carrots, parsnips and mooli (daikon) can be diced, sliced or cut into matchsticks. Use a cook's knife or a cleaver. Trim the vegetable, then take a thin slice off each side to square it up. Slice lengthways, then cut into sticks.

BELOW: *Aubergine, sliced for tempura.*

ABOVE: *Use a mixture of peppers for maximum colour impact.*

Onions

Used for their flavour, all members of the onion family are used in stir-fries and other dishes. Shallots have a mild flavour but are fiddly to prepare. Spring onions (scallions) are often used cooked, raw and as a garnish in many Asian and Eastern cooking traditions. They make a perfect stir-fry ingredient, as their flavour is retained. If shreds are called for, cut off the dark green top, then slice the portions of stem lengthways in half, then into strips.

Other vegetables

Aubergines (eggplants), courgettes (zucchini), sweet (bell) peppers, green beans, mushrooms and corn are common stir-fry ingredients. Less robust than root vegetables, courgettes shouldn't be cut too small. Sliced at an angle, giving ovals, works best. Aubergines are thinly sliced for tempura, cubed for slow-cooked dishes, or cut into strips for frying. If peppers are called for in a dish, cut them in thin slices, as they can take longer to cook than other ingredients.

Mushrooms of all kinds are favourite ingredients. Shiitake mushrooms are a

ABOVE: *Cut meat into small pieces or strips so that it cooks quickly.*

particular favourite of Chinese and Thai cooks, and are often used dried for a more intense flavour.

If fresh corn is in season, and a recipe calls for it, use this instead of tinned or frozen. To free the corn from the cob, hold the top with one hand, and slice the kernels away.

Preparing meat, fish and poultry

How you prepare meat and fish depends on the type and dish, but for stir-fries you should always use the best and freshest cuts. The cheaper cuts, such as stewing beef or belly pork, are ideal for slow cooked dishes that have time to tenderize. When you are using chicken or pork in a stir-fry, make sure it is cooked right through, and shows no sign of pinkness.

For stir-fries, cut meat and fish across the grain. This not only helps the food to cook evenly, but also prevents it from disintegrating. Prawns (shrimp) and scallops can be left whole, and need only minutes to cook. They are usually the last ingredient to be added to a stir-fry, to prevent them going rubbery.

Stir-frying techniques

Most of the cooking you are likely to do in your wok will be stir-frying, so it makes sense to get to grips with the technique from the start.

Preheating the wok
The most important thing to do is to preheat the wok. If the wok is hot when you add the oil, it will coat the surface with a thin film, stopping food from sticking. The best way to do this is to add a trickle of oil around the inner rim so that it runs down evenly. About 15–30ml/1–2 tbsp will be ample. Tilt the pan, to spread it evenly.

Have the heat as high as possible if you are stir-frying meat, so that it sears the moment it touches the wok. For fish or vegetables, have it slightly lower. To check the wok is hot enough, flick a few drops of water on to the surface after oiling. If there is a loud sizzling sound, and it immediately boils off, add your meat. If the water sizzles but remains visible for a few seconds, the heat is right for fish or vegetables. Use oil with a high smoking point, such as groundnut (peanut) or corn oil.

Cooking aromatics
Individual recipes vary, but it is usual to start by adding aromatics such as garlic, ginger, chillies and spring onion (scallions) to the oil, then to fry meat, and finish with the vegetables. This flavours the oil. Sometimes they are removed before anything else is added.

Stir-frying meat
When stir-frying meat, don't overload the wok or you will bring down the temperature. Add a few pieces at a time, sear them for a few seconds on each side, then push away from the centre, where the heat is concentrated, and add more meat to the well. Once sealed, either push the pieces on to the sloping sides of the wok, so they will stay warm without continuing to fry, or transfer them to a dish.

Stir-frying vegetables
Add the vegetables to the wok, starting with varieties that take the longest to cook, such as carrots, broccoli and sweet (bell) peppers. Vegetables that

ABOVE: *Make sure the oil in the wok is hot before adding any ingredients.*

BELOW: *The wok is ideal for frying meat because of its high and even heat.*

need very little cooking, such as mooli (daikon) and mushrooms are added next, with leafy vegetables tossed in right at the end. Keep the food on the move all the time. Although it is called stir-frying, use a tossing and turning action, rather than stirring.

Adding a sauce
When the vegetables are lightly cooked but still crisp, mix in the meat or other ingredients and then add any sauces. A cornflour (cornstarch) mixture will thicken as well as flavour the mixture. If using a cornflour-based sauce, make a well in the stir-fry so you can stir it on its own for a minute or so before mixing it in.

ABOVE: *When cooking aromatics, be careful not to let them burn.*

BELOW: *Sauces are added at the end of the cooking process.*

Deep-frying techniques

Provided a few safety precautions are taken, a wok is a useful pan for shallow and deep-frying. The shape means that you need less oil than in a conventional deep-fryer, yet still have a large surface area for cooking the food.

ABOVE: *Coating food before frying helps retain its moisture and flavour.*

ABOVE: *Wrappers create a delicious crispy coating and keep food moist.*

Heating the oil

First make sure that the wok is stable. A flat-based wok is safest. If you use a round-based wok, make sure it will not wobble. Use a stand if necessary. The wok must be cold when the oil is added. This is opposite to stir-frying, when oil is added to a hot wok. Use an oil with a low smoking point and never fill the wok more than one-third full. This is usually more than enough, and there is less risk of being splashed with hot fat or of it catching fire. If it does catch fire, turn off the heat if you can and cover the wok with a heavy cloth or mat. Never throw water on an oil fire and don't try to move the wok.

The right temperature

For deep-frying, oil needs to be at just the right temperature, so that the outside of the food is beautifully crisp while the centre cooks to tender perfection. The precise temperature required will depend upon the density of what is being cooked and whether it has a coating of some kind, but around 180–190°C/350–375°F is suitable for most foods. A deep-fat thermometer, which can be clipped safely to the side of the wok before the oil is heated, is the safest and surest way of checking the temperature, but you can also test it by adding a cube of bread to the hot oil. It should brown in 45 seconds, if it sinks or fries more slowly any food

cooked in the wok would be greasy; if it burns, the food will burn; if it sizzles on contact and bobs up to float on the surface, the temperature is just right.

Coating

Food can be coated in batter or a simple egg-and-breadcrumb mixture before being deep-fried. This protects, adds a contrasting texture and locks in the flavour. Dip the item into the batter and gently shake off any excess before adding it to the hot oil. Flour or cornflour (cornstarch), breadcrumbs and egg can also be used for coating. Delicate food can also be protected by being enclosed in a dough wrapper. This method is used for wontons and spring rolls, and the result is delicious.

BELOW: *Make sure there is enough oil.*

BELOW: *Use a long-handled tool for safety.*

Deep-frying tips

Don't overcrowd the wok. Add a few pieces at a time, lowering them gently into the oil to avoid splashing. Lift out carefully and drain on a rack which is clipped on to the wok, or drain on kitchen paper and keep hot. Wait a few minutes between batches, for the oil to return to its optimum temperature.

Steaming techniques

This is a supremely healthy method, since the food is cooked without added fat and most of the nutrients are preserved. It is also simple, fast and efficient.

Suitable for steaming

All sorts of foods can be steamed, from fish to vegetables, poultry and even pancakes, custards and breads. Tender cuts of chicken cook well in the steamer but this is not the ideal cooking method for red meat. Check your chosen recipe for any advance preparation required. If you are cooking fish, is it whole or cut in to portions? If whole, you may be advised to slit the skin and insert flavourings, such as fresh herbs, citrus slices or even a spicy rub. Delicate foods may need to be wrapped before being steamed. Banana leaves and lettuce leaves are popular for this purpose, either to wrap the food in, or to line the steamer.

BELOW: *Whole chickens can be steamed.*

Selecting a steamer

A steamer is simply a device for cooking foods by means of moist heat. The food should never touch the water that generates the steam, and the moisture must be trapped. You can steam food by simply placing it on a raised plate inside your wok, but it is simpler in a utensil designed for the purpose. Bamboo steamers are efficient and easy to use. So are stainless-steel steamers, but they are more expensive.

Assembling the steamer

Food can be placed directly in the steamer basket, but this method tends to be reserved for dim sum or breads. It is more usual for a recipe to recommend lining the steamer with baking parchment or leaves before adding the food. This stops the food sticking and prevents small pieces from slipping through the slats. If you use this technique, make sure steam can still circulate. Using leaves for lining won't pose problems as steam will find its way around them, but parchment should be pierced. Alternatively, the food can be put on a plate or bowl in the steamer so long as the steam

BELOW: *Steaming retains taste and texture.*

ABOVE: *A bamboo steamer is best when steaming in a wok, as it fits perfectly.*

holes are not blocked. Custards and some fish dishes are cooked this way.

Before you use a steamer in your wok for the first time, check the fit. You may need a trivet or upturned cup to keep the base of the steamer above the water. If a steamer is large, the sloping sides of the wok may prevent it from descending to the water level.

Steamer baskets are stackable, so you can cook several items at once, with the most delicate foods on top. If the steamer doesn't have a cover, you will need to cover the wok itself. A domed lid is best – condensed water runs down the sides and into the base, rather than on to the food.

Getting up steam

The liquid to generate the steam can be water or stock. Aromatic flavourings such as lemon grass, ginger or seaweed can be used to scent the steam. Fill the wok to a depth of around 5cm/2in, bring to the boil, carefully insert the steamer and cover with the lid. During steaming, keep checking the water level and top up if necessary. Tip the lid away from you to avoid being scalded.

Simmering and smoking

Although the wok is most closely associated with stir-fries and steamed food, it is also great for soups and sauced dishes such as Thai curries or Beef Rendang. The frying stage that is the starting point for many of these dishes is easy to accomplish in a wok, and after more ingredients are added, simmering is a cinch.

Rapid reduction

The shape of the wok, with a wide surface area tapering to a narrow heat base, makes for rapid reduction of sauces. This is ideal when the aim is to concentrate the liquid, but you need to keep an eye on it, and top up the stock or sauce if necessary. A wok is not the best pan for a stew or dish that needs to be cooked for a long time. A heavy pan is better for this, but if you do use a wok, use a stainless steel or non-stick one. Slow cooking in a carbon steel wok may erode the seasoned surface.

BELOW: *Reduce a sauce for intense flavour.*

ABOVE: *The wok is perfect for boiling or blanching green leafy vegetables.*

Blanching and boiling

For stir-frying, vegetables are usually cooked in relays, as some are much denser than others. Blanching toughies such as carrots and broccoli in boiling water gives them a head start so they can be stir-fried alongside more tender vegetables. Bring a wok of water to the boil, add the vegetables and cook for the required length of time (usually about 2–3 minutes). Lift the vegetables out of the wok with a skimmer or spider, plunge them into cold water so that they stop cooking, then drain and pat dry.

A wok can also be used for poaching fruit and cooking rice or noodles.

BELOW: *The wok is ideal for slow simmering.*

Wok smoking

You don't need elaborate equipment to smoke poultry or seafood. A carbon steel wok works well, especially if you follow the Chinese tradition and use a tea leaf mixture as the smoking medium. The only drawback to smoking is the obvious one – use an extractor fan.

1 Line a carbon steel wok (not any other type) with foil, allowing a generous overlap. Sprinkle in 30ml/2 tbsp each of raw long grain rice, sugar and tea leaves.

2 Fit a wire rack on top of the wok and place the food to be smoked in a single layer on top. Mackerel fillets, salmon and duck or chicken breast portions work well. Cover the wok with a lid or inverted pan and cook over a very high heat until you see smoke.

3 Lower the heat so that the smoke reduces to wisps that seep from under the lid, and cook until the food is done. A mackerel fillet takes around 8–10 minutes; large fresh prawns (shrimp) 5–7 minutes; duck or chicken breast portions 18–20 minutes.

Cooking rice and noodles

Many of the Chinese and Thai recipes in this book are based on rice or noodles, which may be used as an accompaniment rather than part of the main dish. If you are using your wok for the meat or vegetable accompaniment, you will probably be cooking your rice or noodles in a separate pan.

Cooking rice

There are several ways of cooking rice, but the absorption method is best for jasmine, basmati, short grain and glutinous rice. The proportion of rice to water will depend on the type of rice, but as a guide, you will need about 600ml/1 pint/2 1/2 cups water for every 225g/8oz/generous 1 cup rice.

1 Rinse the rice thoroughly and put it in a pan. Pour in the water. Do not add salt. Bring to the boil, then reduce the heat to the lowest possible setting.

2 Cover and cook for 20–25 minutes, or until the liquid is absorbed. Without lifting the lid, remove the pan from the heat. Leave to stand for 5 minutes to finish cooking. If cooked rice is required for a fried rice dish, cool it quickly, then chill it before frying.

Making risotto in the wok

The wok is not only suitable for Asian dishes, it also makes great risotto. Have the hot stock ready in a pan.

1 Melt butter, oil or a mixture in a wok and fry an onion. Add risotto rice and stir to coat the grains.

2 Add a dash of white wine, then when absorbed begin adding hot stock, a ladleful at a time. Stir constantly until the stock is absorbed, then add more. It will take about 20 minutes for the rice to become tender. Stir in a little butter. Remove the pan from the heat and cover. Leave for 2 minutes. Serve.

Steamed sticky rice

Thais like their accompanying rice to be sticky. To get the authentic texture steam it in a bamboo steamer. Make sure you buy the right type of rice — usually called sticky or glutinous rice.

1 Rinse the rice several times, then soak overnight in cold water. Line a bamboo steamer with muslin (cheesecloth).

2 Drain the rice and spread out evenly on the muslin. Cover and steam for 25–30 minutes, until tender. (Check the water level, adding more if necessary.)

Cooking noodles

When cooking noodles, do not rely entirely on the recipe — check the packet, too. Par-cooked noodles only need to be soaked in hot water; others must be boiled. Ready-to-use noodles are simply added to a stir-fry and tossed over the heat until hot.

Preparing rice noodles

Rice noodles are par-cooked when you buy them, so they only need to be soaked in hot water before use. Add the noodles to a large bowl of just-boiled water and leave for 5–10 minutes or until softened, stirring occasionally to separate.

Preparing wheat noodles

Wheat noodles have to be cooked in boiling water, but take very little time. Add the noodles to a pan of boiling water and cook for 2–4 minutes, until tender. Drain well. If they are going to be cooked further in a stir-fry, give the noodles just 2 minutes initially.

Dips and garnishes

With a wok, it takes next to no time to rustle up treats such as spring rolls, potato puffs and crisp-fried crab claws. Try them with these delicious dips.

Wasabi and soy dip

Try this with crab cakes or fish cakes. The combination works extremely well, especially if you add a squeeze of lime just before dipping.

SERVES 4

175ml/6fl oz/³⁄₄ cup soy sauce or shoyu
10ml/2 tsp wasabi paste
2 spring onions (scallions), diagonally sliced
1 fresh red chilli, seeded and thinly sliced
 in rings (optional)

Mix the soy sauce or shoyu with the wasabi paste in a bowl. Float the spring onion slices on top. The chilli slices can be added or left out, depending on how spicy you want the dip to be. Top with just one or two rings for colour.

BELOW: *Wasabi and soy dip.*

Thai red curry dip

This tastes good with mini spring rolls, or can be tossed with rice noodles for a simple accompaniment.

SERVES 4

200ml/7fl oz/scant 1 cup coconut cream
10–15ml/2–3 tsp Thai red curry paste
4 spring onions (scallions), plus extra,
 thinly sliced, to garnish
1 fresh red chilli, seeded and thinly
 sliced in rings
30ml/2 tbsp chopped fresh
 coriander (cilantro)
5ml/1 tsp soy sauce
juice of 1 lime
sugar, to taste
25g/1oz/3 tbsp dry-roasted peanuts,
 finely chopped
salt and ground black pepper

Pour the coconut cream into a bowl and stir in the curry paste. Trim the spring onions, slice diagonally, then stir into the coconut cream with the chilli, coriander, soy sauce and lime juice. Add enough sugar to give a sweet-sour flavour and season. Spoon into a serving bowl and top with the peanuts and thinly sliced spring onion.

BELOW: *Thai red curry dip.*

ABOVE: *Sweet chilli sauce.*

Sweet chilli sauce

This sweet, spicy sauce has an aromatic flavour and translucent red colour. It can be used for flavouring and as a dipping sauce. Store any remaining sauce in the refrigerator for 1–2 weeks.

SERVES 4

6 large red chillies
60ml/4 tbsp white vinegar
250g/9oz caster (superfine) sugar
5ml/1tsp salt
4 garlic cloves, chopped

Put all the ingredients in a food processor. Blend until smooth, transfer to a pan and cook over a medium heat until thickened. Allow to cool.

BELOW: *Tamarind sauce.*

Tamarind sauce

This sweet, tangy dipping sauce has a fruity flavour and is perfect with spicy deep-fried snacks. This quantity makes one serving, but any leftovers can be stored in the refrigerator for 1–2 weeks.

MAKES 1 SMALL JAR

90ml/6 tbsp tamarind paste
90ml/6 tbsp water
45ml/3 tbsp caster (superfine) sugar

Place all the ingredients in a small pan and bring the mixture to the boil. Reduce the heat and cook gently for 3–4 minutes, stirring occasionally. Remove from the heat and transfer to a small bowl. Leave to cool then serve.

Ginger and hoisin dip

Chunky and bursting with flavour, this dip is delicious with prawn (shrimp) crackers. Any remaining dip can be stored in the refrigerator in an airtight container for up to 1 week.

SERVES 4

60ml/4 tbsp hoisin sauce
120ml/4fl oz/1/2 cup passata
    (bottled strained tomatoes)
4 spring onions (scallions), thinly sliced
4cm/11/2 in piece fresh root ginger,
    peeled and finely chopped
2 fresh red chillies, seeded and cut
    into fine strips
2 garlic cloves, crushed
few drops of roasted sesame oil

Mix the hoisin and passata in a bowl. Stir in the spring onions, ginger, chillies and crushed garlic. Add the sesame oil, mix well and serve.

ABOVE: *Ginger and hoisin dip.*

Cucumber garnish

A cucumber frill is a lovely garnish for duck, steamed salmon or a salad.

1 Cut a cucumber in half lengthways. Scoop out the seeds from one half and place it cut side down. Using a knife held at an angle, thinly slice the cucumber, cutting almost through so the slices remain attached at the base.

2 Fan the slices out. Tuck in alternate slices to form loops. Bend it into a semi-circle with the loops on the outside, to look like petals.

Chilli garnish

Fresh red chillies can be made into delicate curly flowers, which look stunning on a stir-fry.

1 Using scissors, slit a chilli lengthways from the tip to within 1cm/1/2 in of the stem end. Repeat at regular intervals, keeping the stem end intact, to look like a tassel. Repeat with more chillies.

2 Rinse in cold water. Place in a bowl of iced water and chill for at least 4 hours.

Wasabi paste

This bright green paste packs a whopping punch. It tastes like a cross between mustard and horseradish. A little goes a long way to flavour dips and sauces. Mix it with mayonnaise for a dip to serve with asparagus. The most convenient way to buy wasabi is in a tube. If you use powdered wasabi, mix it in an egg cup with the same volume of tepid water, then stand the egg cup upside down for 10 minutes.

Index

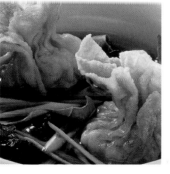